Schneider
on
Schneider

Schneider on Schneider

The Conversion of the Jews and

Other Anthropological Stories

David M. Schneider as told to Richard Handler

Edited, Transcribed, and with an Introduction

by Richard Handler

DUKE UNIVERSITY PRESS   *Durham and London 1995*

© 1995 Duke University Press
All rights reserved
Printed in the United States of America on acid-free paper ∞
Typeset in Berkeley Medium by Tseng Information Systems, Inc.
Library of Congress Cataloging-in-Publication Data
appear on the last printed page of this book.

The field work tradition seems to have created a disciplinary bias toward oral history—as a group, anthropologists have a large stock of anecdotes about the elders of the tribe.—George W. Stocking, "The History of Anthropology: Where, Whence, Whither?"

Contents

Editor's Acknowledgments

Many people have taken an interest in the interviews with David Schneider that led to this book. James Boon, Claire Farrer, Lynne Goldstein, Mary Handler, Charles Kaut, Adria LaViolette, Susan McKinnon, David Sapir, Jonathan Schneider, Michael Schneider, Daniel Segal, Elizabeth Stassinos, George Stocking, Pauline Turner Strong, Bonnie Urciuoli, Roy Wagner, and Marlie Wasserman have provided encouragement and advice. At Duke University Press, Ken Wissoker guided the book through the review process and was always available to me as a sympathetic critic. Thanks are also due to the three reviewers, anonymous to me, whose advice I have followed in preparing the final version of the manuscript. George Stocking and Bonnie Urciuoli went out of their way to help with photographs, as did David Schneider. Finally, as David has assigned responsibility to the interviewer for any shortcomings this work may contain, so I must gratefully thank the interviewee for its many virtues.

Introduction

The Origin of the Dog

Richard Handler

In the spring of 1991, Adam Kuper asked me to interview Clifford Geertz for *Current Anthropology,* of which Kuper was then editor. I agreed. I felt honored to have been chosen for the task of interviewing such an eminent anthropologist and scholar as Geertz. Moreover, I was at that time conducting extensive interviews as part of an ongoing research program at a large American history museum, Colonial Williamsburg. Thus Kuper's telephone call caught me at a time when I was becoming increasingly intrigued with the interview—as a research tool, a social encounter, a political resource, a creative practice, and a literary genre.

The Geertz interview took place on 27 June 1991 and was duly published in December 1991.[1] While it was in press, I wrote Kuper asking him if he would be interested in an interview with David Schneider. I could not remember ever having seen an interview with Schneider, yet it seemed to me that, like Geertz, Schneider had been a key figure in defining the direction American anthropology had taken in the 1960s and 1970s. Kuper replied that he had been after Schneider for years, but that Schneider had repeatedly refused to be interviewed. He expressed an editor's interest in such an interview, and wished me well in the endeavor.

In the fall of 1991, I wrote Schneider, who responded not with a letter but with a statement expressing his ambivalence about being interviewed:

> Not long ago I was asked to do an interview for The American Ethnologist and recently the possibility of doing an interview for another Anthropological journal arose. Feeling strongly that so

many interviews prove to be turgid, dull, and trivial, I resolved that if I were actually to do an interview I would insist that it deal with serious methodological and theoretical issues, the intellectually central concerns of anthropology and do so in a way that was not simply the eructation of ex cathedra pomposities. Rather, I would seize on the major issues of the disciplines and discuss them in a forthright manner, pulling no punches, saying exactly what I think and letting the chips fall where they may, but staying close to the major issues and avoiding the trivialities that beset so many of the interviews I have read.

There followed, without further introduction, a witty and provocative eight-page text which purported to be an interview between "RH" and "DMS." Schneider had, in effect, gone ahead and created his own interview, writing both voices, that of the interviewer and that of the interviewee. This allowed him, perhaps, to try out the genre, to parody it, and to exercise a certain critique of anthropology—about which he remains ambivalent—by placing it in the mouth of "RH." The complete text of Schneider's fantasy interview follows.

RH: How did you first become interested in anthropology?

DMS: Actually, I was born in Brooklyn. I have usually claimed New York City as my birthplace, but in point of fact it was Brooklyn. But I spent the first nine years of my life in the Bronx.

RH: Was your interest in anthropology first aroused at Cornell?

DMS: Well, no, not exactly. I was in the New York State College of Agriculture. I really wanted to be a bacteriologist.

RH: I see. That's very interesting. Why did you leave bacteriology?

DMS: I found organic chemistry too difficult and so took rural sociology where everyone said that anyone could get an A average. They were right.

RH: Moving along now to your years at Harvard, what was the Department of Social Relations like? I have heard many stories about that new, experimental, interdisciplinary department.

DMS: Actually, my formative years were heavily influenced by Elbert Hubbard. I am sure that I need not spend any time recounting Elbert Hubbard's message. He was committed, you know, to the higher and more spiritual aspects of commerce but he was a profound materialist in that he felt very strongly that spiritual qualities grew out of and rested upon the material ones, so that a good salesman, and only a good salesman (you notice he used the term "man"), could appreciate the finer, higher things of life. He was definitely not an elitist, arguing, with Ralph Waldo Emerson (you remember Ralph, don't you?) that self-reliance, individual initiative, aggressive retailing were the essential qualities of this life. He was, therefore, an inspiration to us all in the social sciences. George Herbert Mead, too, seized my imagination and his formulation of The Self and The Other have informed my work throughout my career. As you know, George Herbert Mead's concept of The Other remains central to the work of contemporary Anthropology and the discipline of Cultural Studies as well as much literary criticism. Some people think that Nietzsche invented the notion of The Other, but in fact it was George Herbert Mead.

RH: You did your first fieldwork on the Island of Yap. What made you decide to go there?

DMS: Money. That's where the money was. You can't do fieldwork without money, you know, and if someone says there's money to go to Yap and you need to do fieldwork, you go to Yap. At that point in my life I either had to get a doctorate or go to work. It only took a moment's thought for me to decide to go for the doctorate.

RH: I see. Tell me something about your fieldwork on Yap.

DMS: What's to tell? It was hot, the mosquitoes were impossible, I had to use a mangrove swamp near my tent as a bathroom and every time I exposed myself the mosquitoes attacked. I found this discouraging to serious intellectual effort.

RH: And the natives?

DMS: The natives were quite nice. You see, I got there just a short time after the Japanese were evacuated, shortly after the American Navy had taken over. The Yapese could not speak English and had been told that the Americans would kill them and beat them and enslave them and they were terrified of Americans. I had no trouble establishing rapport. Everyone was most kind. They brought me chickens, bananas, taro, fish and girls galore. I never did learn to like taro, and the chickens were pretty tough and stringy. I reciprocated by giving them gifts.

RH: Oh, you didn't pay your informants then?

DMS: Good lord no! At that time it was thought to be imperative to establish good rapport and be on close egalitarian terms with the natives you were studying. Margaret Mead made this point very emphatically. And nothing destroyed that relationship so effectively as money. It became a crass commercial relationship. So it was generally felt that it was important to establish a relationship based on reciprocity and warm human relations. I followed that important precept as closely as I could.

RH: So you reciprocated the gifts that the natives offered. How did you do that? With mirrors and trinkets?

DMS: No, not at all! That is the sort of thing that field-workers did in the very early years of anthropology when they believed they were dealing with savages. I found out what the natives really wanted and tried to give them what they wanted.

RH: And what was it that they really wanted?

DMS: Beer and whiskey. They liked gin, too, when it was available. And sugar, which they added to their coconut toddy, raising the alcohol content to maybe 11 percent. And they really went for American Girlie Magazines.

RH: What would you say were the main theoretical problems you pursued during your fieldwork on Yap?

DMS: I was in something of a bind, really. You see, [Clyde] Kluckhohn was my principal advisor, and he was all for studying culture. But I had Talcott Parsons as a second member of the committee, and he was pretty heavily into structural functionalism. As if that weren't enough, I had gone out under the auspices of the Peabody Museum, and so Douglas Oliver had to be on my committee as well. There was very little love lost between Kluckhohn and Oliver. Oliver was a homophobe and Kluckhohn was gay, and Oliver a very empiricist old-line ethnographer and Kluckhohn very much avant-garde, interested in culture and personality, a humanist and close to [Edward] Sapir and [Alfred] Kroeber. Meanwhile, Parsons was pushing his own grand synthesis. You can imagine that pleasing that trio was not easy. So I sent home field notes which had a little something for everyone, and that took some careful attention to the writing of field notes. As James Clifford has pointed out, written field notes *are* the text and the data, the real stuff of which ethnography is made. Those notes are preserved to this day in the Special Collections Department of the Regenstein Library at the University of Chicago, and they are open for inspection by any serious, reputable scholar. The ethnography I wrote was based on those notes, of course, not on subjective impressions and intuitions.

RH: Was your thesis turned into your first book, then?

DMS: No way. It was the usual mishmash, which quoted liberally from all my senior mentors and those juniors whom I expected to amount to something in the coming years. Your identity and the identity of your work is established by the scholars you quote and cite while your list of acknowledgments is closely scrutinized, as I am sure you know. Who you list in the acknowledgments is vital in establishing your scholarly image, and so that must be put together with great care. Each reader is pleased to see how much the thesis supported their intellectual view, but each was aware of the fact that I had to be respectful of the other members of the committee, and so the trick was to convince each that what I had written for them was the true, authentic stuff while the other material was just the obligatory genuflection to a powerful member of the committee. To pull that off, a good deal of personal, one-on-one discussion with each member of the committee was required as the thesis was being written. There was always the risk that they might talk to each other, but given academic jealousies, the narcissism of academics, and a little skill at keeping a straight face on my part, that risk was fairly low. Anyway, they approved the thesis, I got my degree and lived happily ever after.

RH: That's most interesting. Writing a Ph.D. thesis is difficult, then, isn't it?

DMS: Yes indeed; it is the most difficult problem of one's whole career, and that's why I have always insisted that the Ph.D. thesis is, and must remain, the single most important demonstration of the student's ability to successfully complete a piece of independent research. But there is one very serious problem which occasionally arises that makes the thesis less than convincing evidence of the ability to do independent research. I well remember a thesis defense I once attended at one of our most highly respected institutions. The candidate had appeared, been questioned at judicious length, and been asked to leave the room while the committee deliberated. I leaned across the table and said to my slightly senior colleague (I had tenure by that time, of course), "That was terrific, Willy. By my count that was the eighth superb thesis you have written. Was the candidate a serious impediment?" I knew that Willy was no jock and I was still quite agile then, and when he tried to climb across the table after me, I was able to move behind the third member of the committee quickly enough so that I was in no real danger. Of course the candidate passed. But he could never get a job in a department where I worked. I just don't think that there is any merit in the stuff Willy writes.

RH: That's interesting. What would you say your major theoretical contributions have been to our discipline?

DMS: I have always felt that a judicious balance between theory and fact is what has made anthropology one of the leading disciplines of the social sciences. We can't get away from facts. But facts don't speak for themselves. What is needed now is serious, systematic attention to process and history. Without history we are bound to repeat history. But history has a structure. It's not just an aimless flow of meaningless episodes. The study of that process may not yield eternal cultural laws, but should yield some feeling for, and understanding of, the nature of social life. I am, I should add, a committed materialist and condemn idealism in all its forms.

It is important to remember that culture emerges from practice, and so practice is of the very essence of what the anthropologist studies. And practice is always the site of contestation. Culture is contested, not shared. Human beings are intentional agents, they are not just robots following some cultural script written by an anthropologist. And what motivates people is some transformation of the material conditions of their existence. These material conditions, in turn, determine their position in society. Gender, class, race, and the state are all fundamental in defining the identity and social position of each subject, so that by simply knowing the gender, class, race, and relationship to the state of the subject, predictions with a very high probability can be made about what their action is likely to be. This does not mean, for example, that all white middle-class Jews are materialistic and will always act in the same way. But the probability is high that they will. What we must be most careful to avoid, of course, is the kind of stereotyping that says, for example, that lower-class male blacks harassed by the police will all act in the same way. They won't, because each is a different individual with a unique lived experience and hence a different self and identity.

RH: What of the future? What do you see in the future for anthropology?

DMS: If history teaches us any lesson, it is that the future is built on the past and extends and continues the past. At one point anthropology was interested in human evolution. That went away, and now we have sociobiology. At one point anthropology was interested in functionalism. Functionalism became part of structuralism (if it wasn't all along), but now we are in a period of poststructural theory where process and practice are at the center of our analytic constructs. During the 1930s the rallying cry was "dynamic" as opposed to the prevailing "static" analysis. Fortunately, we have come a long way from those days. Today we understand that practice is where it's at and that structure is an outmoded concept. Of course, there has always been a fundamental opposition between materialist and idealist approaches, but today I don't think that any reputable scholar defends idealist theories. It is perfectly clear that there has been significant progress in our analytic tools, and I am sure that that progress will continue as our ideas develop and are refined.

But I would insist on one more point which is of the essence in any discussion of where anthropology is going. Anthropology is, after all, what anthropologists do. As I said, culture emerges from practice. If the practice of anthropology is to be maintained at its present high level of scholarship, then it is of the essence that we continue to maintain the very highest standards in training the next generation of anthropologists. Training for independent research is the very essence of the problem. We must be ever vigilant to be sure that senior anthropologists do not simply reproduce themselves by demanding that their students conform closely to their ideas. New ideas, new methods, and innovation are vital to the development and expansion of the trade. But at the same time we must be alert to be sure that the people who will be replacing us are competent! They must know how to pose a problem and how to go about solving the problem. It is our responsibility to teach them how to do that and to be sure that they have learned their lessons well. And so the thesis remains the single most important test of competence now, as it was when I was a student. If students can't write a good thesis, they should not be allowed to continue. But even that is not enough. Research is the name of the game. They have to be able to write and publish, for writing and publishing are the ways in which science is communicated. For one person to know something is no help; that knowledge has to be disseminated, for knowledge, as we all know, is not merely cultural capital, it is seminal! It is for this reason that a productive scholar, a scholar who publishes, is the best scholar. In this game, if you don't have something to offer, you won't be around very long. You go belly-up. You won't get tenure, you won't get promoted. You will be out of business.

RH: It's been very good talking to you.

(At this point in the interview a short break occurred.)

RH: I know that although you are retired, you keep up with what is going on, so tell me what you think of the so-called postmoderns or poststructuralists.

DMS: Who did you have in mind?

RH: Oh, you know, [James] Clifford, [George] Marcus and [Michael] Fischer, [Stephen] Tyler, [Vincent] Crapanzano, [Paul] Rabinow, [Bernard] Cohn—that crowd.

DMS: Well, that's an easy question. They are all, to a man, idiots.

RH: Why do you say that?

DMS: Because they are idiots. They are all in an irreversible vegetative state.

RH: Perhaps you have some more precise criticism you could share with us.

DMS: They are idiots. What more can you say?

RH: Well, for one thing, they are deeply concerned with some of the serious social and political problems, some of the injustices, which make life very hard for some people now. Other anthropologists tend to ignore these problems.

DMS: Not at all. Anthropology has always been concerned with social and political problems. The Ford Foundation, the Rockefeller Foundation, the Social Science Research Council, for example, have always given money to fund research which is directly or indirectly supportive of American foreign and domestic policy. The whole movement in medical anthropology, for example, is directly concerned with major social problems, and political anthropology, too, addresses itself to political problems.

RH: Well, one might argue that there is a difference between the postmoderns and those you mention in that the orthodox address their efforts to the maintenance of the status quo while the PMs feel that the status quo has some serious defects.

DMS: Nonsense. Those "PMs," as you call them, are simply out to destroy the very basis on which true scholarship and real research are founded. They deny the very meaning of words, for example, arguing that words don't mean what they say. They deny that reason and intelligence are the ultimate criteria in terms of which truth can be established. They insist that social life is just contestation, when anthropology has devoted its life to showing the nature of social order.

RH: A pretty fragile social order, don't you think? Wars, colonialism, apartheid, racism, sexism, and so on. Do you call that social order?

DMS: Nobody said that life was a bed of roses.

RH: But it's been the PMs who pointed to the thorns.

DMS: What do you want anthropology to do? Change its spots?

RH: Yes indeed. Anthropology must face the fact that a social order built on special privilege, the unjust distribution of the good things of life, legal systems that fortify injustice, and the inhumanity of man to man should perish from this earth and that it is anthropology's moral responsibility to help get rid of that kind of society and culture.

DMS: That's certainly an interesting position. Tell me, do you have any other thoughts on the PMs you would like to share with us?

RH: Yes indeed. It has always been my opinion that moral questions and political questions motivate research even when people deny this. Even apparently morally and politically unmotivated research has moral and political implications, if none other than by virtue of their pretense to ignore them. It is time now to move moral and political questions to stage center and openly acknowledge their centrality to our intellectual, scholarly, and research interests—stage center, where they can be plainly seen and evaluated, instead of lurking in the background, in the dark, and who knows what insidious role they play.

DMS: I disagree with you completely. The best research is morally and politically neutral research, pure research, value-neutral research, as Max Weber said.

RH: Let's leave Max Weber out of this. If you think that [Bronislaw] Malinowski's work was value-neutral, or that [E. E.] Evans-Pritchard was value-neutral, or even Margaret Mead's work was morally and politically neutral, you just don't know what you are talking about.

DMS: That's very interesting. As you know, I am always interested in hearing your views, and I know that our readers will be, too.

(Another short break while the interviewer and interviewee resumed their normal positions.)

To this remarkable text, I responded by sending Schneider a typescript copy of the final draft of the Geertz interview. By return mail, Schneider queried: "The Geertz interview was very good. Do you really think you can get anything as coherent as that from me???" A week later, he wrote again:

> My ambivalence is . . . clear. I think that if it [an interview] were to be done, it would be well if it were well done. There are two formats that seem possible; one is Straight, one is Funny. I admit to a somewhat crude, Mel Brooks type of humor, a brief sample of which [e.g., the fictional interview] you have seen. And I can be as pompous, asinine, and absurd as anyone when I play it straight.
>
> Hence, it seems to me that if we do it, it should be carefully constructed—carefully crafted is the better way to put it—and not one of these Spontaneous Unrehearsed Off the Kuff types of things. I do not mean that you should submit your questions in writing 30 days in advance, though that might be a good idea. And if you were to help craft my answers, that would also be a good idea (do more than fix the spelling, that is).

The outcome of this ongoing correspondence was that we decided to try an interview during the 1991 annual meeting of the American Anthropological Association, in Chicago. We agreed on the specifics of the first meeting, confirmed in a postcard from Schneider to me: "1:30 Thursday Nov. 21 at Marriott Hotel desk and we start from conception minus two generations as in your letter 10/21. It's a deal, but no sex or violence please!" That Schneider remained ambivalent about the interviews seemed to me to be confirmed by his failure to meet me at the appointed location. I waited, increasingly concerned, for some time; finally, upon making inquiries, I learned that he was in his hotel room waiting for me and wondering why I had not kept our appointment. I went to his room and we completed the first of what turned out to be many interviews.

I had been engaged for the Geertz interview on relatively short notice. Given my research commitments at Colonial Williamsburg during the spring of 1991, I didn't have sufficient time to reread Geertz's oeuvre in order to formulate questions about "serious methodological and theoretical issues," to use Schneider's phrase. On the other hand, I was intrigued by what I didn't know about Geertz's career: the sources of his interest in anthropology, the factors that had motivated his choices of field sites and research problems, and so on. I was also practicing a kind of focused or partial life-history interviewing in my museum research, where I structured many interviews by asking people why they had come to work at Colonial Williamsburg, what their job there was, and how their duties had changed over the years. Geertz agreed in advance that an interview focusing on his career in anthropology would be acceptable, and our conversation stuck to that format.

The Schneider interviews, however, came to be structured differently. Schneider approached the task in terms of a set of stories he wanted to tell and topics he wanted to discuss. The mock interview reproduced above closed with a list of "some possible topics to continue":

[George Peter] Murdock and Yale and how I got interested
    in kinship
the origin of the dog
the fetish of fieldwork ([Ronald] Olson on fieldwork)
like castor oil, reading an ethnography is supposed to be
    good for you while writing an ethnography is supposed
    to be Where It's At—the apotheosis of ethnography
Leach on ethnography
and writing écrit inscription discourse and discursive practices
what is anthro all about; Benedict and steeping oneself in a culture
    and the American kinship project
    history??
The Profession and the professionalization of the Association
the terrors of getting tenure and the importance of
    THE BOOK as measured by heft
the joys of the Department Meeting and collegial relations generally

Schneider came to our first interview with a similar list, scrawled on a crumpled piece of yellow paper. Though this one was perhaps less whimsical than the last, it was equally heterogeneous and cryptic, containing such items as "the conversion of the Jews," "the Kroeber story," "the strange case of data," "the George Homans story," "whatever happened to kinship," and "the Rufus Sago story." Schneider's lists seemed rather randomly constructed, but, as I came to realize, they were a shorthand representation of a sustained effort at self-examination.

No doubt Schneider had always been critically reflective about his work and career. In 1989, however, that tendency must have been abetted by the research of Ira Bashkow, which led to the publication, in 1991, of a brilliant essay on "The Dynamics of Rapport in a Colonial Situation: David Schneider's Fieldwork on the Islands of Yap." Bashkow's article focused on how Schneider's fieldwork had been inflected by his informants' responses to colonial politics. To examine that topic, Bashkow ranged widely, summarizing Schneider's intellectual biography, including formative influences and changing theoretical preoccupations, and detailing the political (and military) origins of the Coordinated Investigation of Micronesian Anthropology, the research program under which Schneider went to Yap. Bashkow's research, which included several interviews with Schneider in August 1989, may well have stimulated Schneider to think retrospectively about the trajectory of his entire career. In any case, readers should compare Bashkow's work to Schneider's accounts, as expressed in his interviews with me.[2]

For our first interview (Chapter 1 in this volume), Schneider presented a newly revised overview of his career, one which, he indicated, had been informed, at least in part, by Bashkow's research. But, as readers will see, it was hardly a complete account of his career, nor was it intended as such. Rather, as Schneider stated at the outset, the overview was cast as a moral story, "a cautionary tale for young people." It was also to contain signposts to other narratives, references, and allusions, which he expected us to explore as stories in their own right during subsequent interviews.

From the start, then, there were multiple principles of narrative order implicit in the discussions we planned. The "career" was one such principle, and it, of course, implied a chronological perspective. But the career as a moral tale was crosscut by other autobiographical stories, or stories-within-stories. Moreover, there were topics such as "kinship" and "data" which, though drawing on autobiographical materials, were also intended partly as intellectual history, partly as theoretical critique.

Given Schneider's lists of topics, it was not difficult to organize our interview sessions: once a story had been completed and the questions it provoked answered, we either adjourned or returned to the list to pick another topic, agreeable to both of us at the moment. As the interviewing progressed and we exhausted the topics of Schneider's lists, I relied increasingly on a chronologically informed fill-in-the-gaps principle of narrative ordering; in other words, I asked Schneider about periods in his life and aspects of his work which I thought were missing from the extant narratives.

At the outset, neither Schneider nor I had a clear goal in mind—an idea about what a completed interview or series of interviews would include. The project took on a life of its own, eventuating in five sets of audiotaped interviews conducted over a three-year period.[3] As our work progressed, Schneider and I agreed that it would be my responsibility to prepare the material for publication; he gave me free rein to edit and organize our growing collection of stories. After each set of interviews, I transcribed the tapes and sent the transcripts to Schneider as I completed them; he acknowledged receipt but made almost no corrections or editorial suggestions.

As the interview materials accumulated, I began to think in terms of organizing them as a book-length manuscript. At first I tried to put the many interviews together into one chronologically ordered narrative. This meant taking apart individual interviews and using the pieces to splice together coherent chapters covering the stages of Schneider's career: childhood, Cornell, Yale, Harvard, fieldwork on Yap, Harvard and London, Palo Alto, Berkeley (including fieldwork among Mescalero Apache), Chicago, Santa Cruz. But this ordering principle dissolved too many of Schneider's stories. For example, in our first interview, Schneider presented a highly selective account of his career. As a cautionary tale, it was not primarily conceived as a chronologically framed remembering; rather, it was an exercise of moral judgment, an attempt to grapple with the value of the past choices of its protagonist. I found that interweaving the pieces of that narrative with material from later interviews—everything about Berkeley in one chapter, for example—destroyed much of the significance of the tale.

As an alternative, it would have been possible to present the interviews in the order they occurred. This would have left all of Schneider's tales intact. But the order of the interviews and their particular contents (the tales they happened to include) were to some degree arbitrary, based, as I explained, on spur-of-the-moment choices from Schneider's lists. Interviews sometimes contained two or three complete stories that were not linked chronologically or topically; they also included what we might call fragmentary material, topics that we did not develop or about which little was said. There seemed, therefore, to be no compelling reason to preserve the interview session as a privileged narrative unit.

As a compromise, I have organized these interviews with reference to several ordering criteria: Schneider's career in academia, his fieldwork stints, and the theoretical topics he chose to address. But I have preserved as wholes those stories which, I felt, could not be dissected without seriously undermining the narrator's intent. The audiotaped interviews and unedited transcripts of them remain in my possession and are available to those who wish to consult them.

Editing the interviews sentence by sentence, word by word, has proven less difficult than organizing larger chunks of narratives to form a coherent volume. For the most part, I have presented verbatim transcriptions of the interviews. As Schneider's many students know, he is a wonderful teller of tales. Written language differs in many ways from conversation, and most interviewees are taken aback to read, for the first time, a transcription of what they said. Yet some people are better talkers than others, or, at least, some people are capable of speaking something like an engaging prose. Schneider is one of those. He spoke in complete sentences and, as I have already indicated, he had given a good deal of thought to the larger shape of many of his narratives. Indeed, some of his tales were well established, ones that he had told many times to many people. Thus, though I have "cleaned up" the material presented here, the editorial work was relatively minimal. True, I have eliminated some broken sentences, repetitions, and false starts—my own (perhaps especially my own!) as well as Schneider's. I have also occasionally eliminated colloquialisms and profanity, but, at Schneider's request, have left most of them as spoken:

> Then there are those words like shit and fuck and such like. I am inclined to leave them in as indices of spontaneity, sincerity, honesty, which of course are terribly important when the material is not exactly spontaneous or sincere or honest, but crafted carefully.

This last remark raises a problem that I cannot satisfactorily resolve: how to convey something of the self-critical irony that pervades much of the interview material. As my colleague Susan McKinnon—who, like myself, studied with Schneider in the 1970s—pointed out, upon reading one of the transcripts: those who know David Schneider, who can recall his voice and storytelling, will be able at least to guess at the significant inflections that were so crucial to the oral version of the material presented here. But those inflections are often lost in the translation to print, and I can do little more than caution people to read with a careful ear. Readers can, however, accustom themselves to Schneider's irony by examining the fictional interview that he sent me at the very beginning of our work, and which was presented in this chapter in a complete and unexpurgated version.

One

The Work of the Gods in Tikopia, or, A Career in Anthropology

DMS: I thought that times had changed, and that now you really got where you got on the basis of your merit and your merit alone; and that there were no people behind the scenes pulling strings and colluding, that this business of placing protégés was all over; only to realize—how can I say?—well, I guess it was from 1945 or '46 to 1990 or 1989. In 1989, facts came to my attention that revealed to me how little I understood as to what the hell was going on.

Now that's a story, okay? So I thought I could tell you the story of my career. It started with Cornell and went through I got this job, and I got that job, and so on and so forth, and at various points along the line, we could take off from that—like, What was it like in London?, like, When you came back from London you wrote, you got involved with George Homans's book—then I'll tell you the George Homans's book story. When I was teaching at Berkeley I decided to leave and go to Chicago—then I have the Kroeber story, and along with the Kroeber story, why did I leave Berkeley? and was I right to have made that choice? which is also, I think, an interesting story full of moral—it's a cautionary tale for young people, yes?!

Should we give that a go and see if it works?

RH: Okay. But let me ask one thing. Do you want me to interrupt you, or should I take notes and then ask you questions?

DMS: Either way you want. I don't mind being interrupted.

RH: I think I'll start by taking notes, and see if we can get you to tell this whole story about which you just did a metastory.

DMS: That's it. This will be the first metastory. Then, you see, you can use that as a take-off point. That also implies that I'm not going to tell you about "I was born" and so on. I have another nice story about my relationship to my family, and the fact that my brother was born when I was six, and I saw no need for him around the house, and I fucked up, and all kinds of stuff like that. That's another story.

RH: We can come back to that.

DMS: Okay. I started—I wanted to be a bacteriologist. And I suppose it's of some interest that I read these books by Paul De Kruif—*The Hunger Fighters* and *The Microbe Hunters*.[1] I wanted to study loathsome diseases and cure the world and be good and do good things. But I had no money, and my family had no money. So a very wise cousin said, "Why don't you go to New York State College of Agriculture? and you can learn agricultural bacteriology, and that will be your step into bacteriology, and then you can help rid the world of loathsome diseases."

So I went to Cornell, New York State College of Agriculture, but I never could manage to pass organic chemistry. I got put on probation. I got a D average, and I was told that to get off probation I had to raise my grades. A couple of my friends said, "Take rural sociology. Anybody can get A's."

And they were right. I took rural sociology, I got A's, I got off probation. But in the course of doing that—that was my last two years, my junior and senior years—I took a course from an instructor in economics who was an anthropologist, R. Lauriston Sharp. And that way I got interested in anthropology. He suggested I stay around for one more year, to learn a little more anthropology, and then go on to graduate school.

So I stayed around for one more year and got an M.A. Addy [Adeline Bellinson] and I got married June 17, 1940, which was the day we both graduated from Cornell. She graduated from the arts college, and I graduated from the ag school, and we stayed on that next year, and I got an M.A. in anthropology.

Sharp then told me that the best place to go was Yale. And I went to Yale, but Yale was . . . that's where another whole story picks up. So from Yale I got offered a job in Washington for $1,620 per annum. I took that, because we were broke. It was the Division of Program Surveys of the Department of Agriculture. And I got drafted from there. Now I've left out another whole part, but that's all right.

At Yale I met Geoffrey Gorer, and he was a good buddy of Margaret Mead. Geoffrey Gorer was very friendly, very interested. I had been studying primitive dreams. He sort of revealed psychoanalysis and Freud to me, which I found very interesting, but hard to understand, and I wasn't sure I enjoyed it or felt all that sympathetic. But, you know, he was a nice guy—it was very good.

When I went to Washington, he told me to go see Margaret Mead. I went to see her. We struck up a kind of friendship—very casual, very brief. Then I got drafted.

Meanwhile, Geoffrey Gorer had urged me very strongly that if you really want to be an anthropologist, there's your opportunity to do field-work while you're in the army! Keep notes, all that stuff. So I did.

Margaret Mead, meanwhile, through the Institute for Intercultural Studies, was circulating papers, which I read. These were some of the early studies of culture at a distance. Gorer did one on Russia, [Ruth] Benedict did one on Thai, somebody else did one on—no, Russia or Poland, I'm not sure what Gorer did. Anyway, there were a bunch of those.[2]

So I got drafted. I kept notes in the army, and, indeed, my very first two publications were while I was still in the army, but just getting out. One was "The Culture of the Army Clerk," the other, "The Social Dynamics of Physical Disability in Army Basic Training."[3]

RH: Did you deposit those notes in Regenstein Library?

DMS: No. I believe I still have them. However, interestingly enough, a guy who did a study of gays during the Second World War happened upon my papers—those two papers—and he commented in his book that they were very interesting and revealing. I hadn't realized that I'd been such a sensitive observer![4]

So, I got out of the army. I'd been married—you know, Addy followed me to Camp Roberts and then to Fort Lewis. Then I said, well, if I could get an SSRC [Social Science Research Council] demobilization award, I would go back to school. Otherwise, I was through.

RH: When did you get out of the army?

DMS: 1946. So Margaret Mead told me to apply for it, but I didn't get the demobilization award. When I complained to her that I didn't get it, she said, "Well, you got Geoffrey Gorer to write you a letter of recommendation. In the first place, you've got to get eminent, important, powerful people to write you letters of recommendation. And in any case, you shouldn't get somebody that nobody really respects. I mean, nobody really likes Geoffrey Gorer."

Well, the lesson wasn't much help, because it was too late. Anyhow, so she said, "Go see my friend, Clyde Kluckhohn, at Harvard. He owes me an academic favor. And you tell him that *you* are my academic favor."

So I went to see Clyde Kluckhohn, but I never told Kluckhohn that Mead had sent me. That's a gold star in my favor!

Kluckhohn said, "Fine. We're just starting a new Social Relations Department. I hope you'll be interested. You sound like a natural. Why don't you just go across the street there to the graduate school and fill out the application blank. Everything'll be okay."

So I went out and I filled in the application form and I went back to . . . I was living with Addy's family at that time. Next thing I knew, I got a phone call from Clyde Kluckhohn. "David! You didn't tell me that you had a D average."

"Well, I didn't think it was important."

"Well, of course it's important! Harvard does not let in anyone without an A average."

So I said, "Oh, I suppose I'm done."

"No," he said. "I have managed to persuade them that if they let you in on probation, and you get straight A's for the first year, you may stay."

So I said, "Well, thank you. I'm very very grateful" and so forth. And so I showed up, and, lo and behold, I got straight A's.

RH: Do you know why he did this?

DMS: No, I don't know why he did it. It may well be that he called Mead up, that she called him. I just don't know why he did it. But you see, I assumed that anyone could see that I was a person of great promise, had considerable merit. You see, I had given him those two articles to read, and he'd liked them both. No—he only saw the culture of the army clerk article, but he saw the manuscript of the physical disability article.

So, I got to Harvard and I got straight A's. And then came the opportunity to go to Yap. Now that's another big story. Went to Yap. And when I went to Yap, I sent all my field notes back to the Peabody Museum, but on the very explicit understanding that Clyde Kluckhohn would see them. Now, it so happened that at that time, Kroeber was there at Harvard in a visiting appointment.

RH: When was this?

DMS: 1947–1948. I know that Clyde and Kroeber not only saw my notes—at least, I knew they had access to them—that's really all I knew. But they also watched the movies. I took a lot of movies, and I sent them back, and apparently Clyde and Kroeber would get together on an evening when they had nothing else to do and show my pics!

RH: You took movies?

DMS: That's right. They were Bell and Howell cassettes. All you did was stick it in the camera and point the camera correctly and then, mostly, you got something. Of course, I was really awful. People complained that watching my movies made them seasick—motion sickness, all that stuff.

And this, of course, is where the story really begins. I came back and I started writing my thesis. I went to Yap on the Coordinated Investigation of Micronesian Anthropology, which George Peter Murdock had put together. And there's an interesting story there that goes back to my year at Yale—you see, before I went to Washington, before I went into the army.

Anyway, Murdock and those people were offering a $500 bonus if you wrote up your report real quickly. There were four of us who went to Yap, and I did my part promptly, and the other guys did what they had to do, and in it went. We got our 500 bucks and I started writing my thesis. I had gotten myself involved with the kinship stuff. Well, I didn't find a problem, I didn't find a special topic. I wrote a long narrative called "Kinship and Village Organization of Yap." Kluckhohn didn't know beans about kinship, said he didn't know, said he didn't like it, so he said, "You send the material to Murdock, and if he approves, it's okay with me."

Now, in the meantime, I had thought that I had found double descent on Yap, and I made a big production of that in this preliminary report, and in the final report. And then a few years later, one of the first papers I did on Yap made the point that I thought that it was double descent. You see, previously it had been established by the German ethnographers that they were patrilineal.

Now, unfortunately, I hadn't read much of the literature before I went.

I didn't really know very much. All I had before I went was a course in kinship from Murdock at Yale, which I had not understood, had not liked, had rejected wholeheartedly and completely. Exactly why I got into kinship on Yap, I . . . I can probably figure something out, but I'm not at all clear on it. Leave it.

Murdock, at that point, wrote me a long—I think it was maybe a page, page-and-a-half—letter saying that the material I had presented was unlike anything he had ever seen in any ethnography in his life. It was essentially unbelievable. And he knew that if I'd only go back over my notes very, very carefully, I would be able to put together a coherent account.

RH: So, in other words, he would not approve your thesis.

DMS: He would not. But, he was not asked to approve or disapprove, he was just asked for comments. And Kluckhohn said, "When he makes his comments, we can tell whether he approves or doesn't approve."

Now, the stuff that Murdock boggled at was the kinship terminology. The double descent part he made no mention of. But the kinship terminology part was problematic because I insisted that the Yapese word, for example, for father was only applied to one particular person at one time. But if that person died, there was a kind of reservoir of people from which you could then pull another father out. So there was a kind of active and passive father, and an active father was a live person. He acted the role of father, and then this reservoir was full of other fathers, whom I, of course, ran down to be father's brother, father's younger brother, father's other brothers, patrilineage male ascending generation types.

Murdock didn't like that. Not only didn't he like that, but there were kinship terms for people that were never "used." He said, "It is just logically impossible to have a word which isn't used." You know, in a way, it makes sense.

But I said, "It's used in the sense that they keep them in a reservoir."

And he said, "Look, if it's not used, I don't believe it."

And he didn't believe it!

Well, I stuck to my guns pretty well. Kluckhohn said, "Well, what the hell! Kinship terminology—who gives a shit!" He accepted my thesis, Parsons accepted my thesis, Doug Oliver accepted my thesis, and that was it.

So off I went to the London School of Economics. Raymond Firth gave me a job there. I taught there for two years. But I went there on a senior Fulbright, 'cause that really paid enough money, including passage over and back—the amount of money it paid for the first year permitted me to stay two years.

When it was obvious that I had to leave England—Addy's father died, and everything else, so we had to come back. At that point I sat down and I wrote a letter to, I don't know, fifteen departments saying I had my degree from Harvard, I was coming back, I needed a job. And I got absolutely no replies except for one, from E. Adamson Hoebel, who wrote me a very sweet letter saying, "Dear David, we don't hire people who write us letters this way."

RH: Did you know the people before you wrote them?

DMS: No. I just took a list. But there was nothing. And of course, when I came back—the cliché is, I had a wife and child and no visible means of support.

RH: So Jonathan had been born.

DMS: Jonathan had been born in 1949, just before we went over to England. So I wrote ahead and said to Kluckhohn and Parsons that I was coming back, that I had no job. And I went up to Harvard and saw them. And they were very wonderful—they pieced together bits of money, and they pieced together this and that and the other thing, and they brought me to Harvard to teach for a year. I was a lecturer.

So I stayed there for a year on that money. Then the next year, they put together another piece of money for me. That was 1951–'52 and '52–'53. And there was '53–'54. I've probably got the dates screwed up. I was at Harvard from '51 to '55.

RH: Always on soft money?

DMS: Always on soft money, a lecturer, then assistant professor—I don't know. Then, the last year, I think Kroeber was there on a visiting appointment one of those years again. And by then I had written a paper on American kinship terminology. Now let me go back a minute, okay.

The Yap kinship terminology stuff that Murdock wouldn't swallow, I was absolutely, profoundly, positively, unequivocally convinced that I was dead right on. You know, I didn't speak the language really eloquently. The Yapese when I left complained I couldn't recite poetry, I couldn't make up poetry. They allowed as how I showed the promise of a sort of a young boy. But that, given time, I'd be all right. But, you know, I didn't speak Yapese that fluently, but I spoke well enough to be able to be understood and to understand most of what was going on. But you know, everybody has that fantasy, even if they can't speak the language! But still . . . so I was dead sure of that.

Moreover, I had not liked the way Murdock did kinship, and I hadn't liked the way Murdock did kinship terminology, and I have a feeling that there was, in my mind, a great misunderstanding. You see, the big division in kinship terminology was always between referential and vocative. And since vocative was address, and referential was "I talk to you about that person," it seemed absurd, and manifestly absurd, to me that that was all there was to it. You know, it depended on who I talked to you about. It depended on—even address, if I were addressing somebody in an offensive way, or addressing somebody in a friendly way, there'd be variations.

RH: When you say that this had always seemed absurd to you, were you going all the way back to Kroeber 1909, or had that not entered the picture yet? [5]

DMS: It doesn't really enter the picture because I don't think I read Kroeber 1909 until after I came back from Yap.

But the first real screwup is that there is a technical meaning in the philosophy of language about referential meaning that does not simply confine it to "I talk to you about that." But rather, that this is the formal, proper name for this kind of an object. And I hadn't understood that. I had taken referential in the same—what would you call it?—at the same level as vocative, namely, as a form of address.

RH: But for a different context.

DMS: Exactly. And I had not quite gotten the idea that "referential" also meant the *proper* name for or the *correct* name for. I think referential doesn't just mean the correct name for, but it's very close. So I kept going through this kind of—what would you call it?—action or interaction definition of the situation, and so, coming back from Yap I report to Murdock, "This is what the people really did. These were the many different contexts in which they used the word. Hence, there is no *single* referential meaning, nor was there a single vocative meaning. But it depended on, you know, if your own real father was alive, you called your real father 'real father.' And then if he died, somebody stepped into his shoes." And all that. In fact, if I had really explored ritual contexts more, I would have found other, ritual contexts in which these kinship terms were used. But I didn't. So I think that that was part of it.

So, by the time I got to London, I was pretty well up in arms. I thought that I could definitely and systematically show that *all* these old farts were completely wrong on the way they handled terminology, and that what was worse was that they themselves should've known it by just looking at what they themselves did.

RH: Okay, let me stop you just one minute. "They themselves"—the "old farts"—are epitomized by Murdock.

DMS: That's right.

RH: And what you felt was overly schematized was that referential versus vocative distinction.

DMS: That's right.

RH: And their notion was that there was one set of terms that named the positions, the relationships, and another set of terms that were used when you were addressing somebody, and that's about how much they knew about context.

DMS: That's what I thought. But of course, I didn't really know enough about them to condemn them that grossly out of hand, because they had a theory of meaning that had a lot to do with the philosophy of language. And again, their philosophy of language stuff was not nearly as sophisticated as—well, who does that stuff?—[W. V.] Quine, people like that. For people like Murdock, [A. R.] Radcliffe-Brown, all the guys that messed with kinship terminology—incidentally, Sapir also—their theory of meaning implied that referential meanings were privileged and that all other meanings were in some sense either derivative or at least secondary. And that the derivative meanings always had to "refer back" to the referential meanings.

So when I'm in London, I'm sitting there, I'm working out, on the basis of what I myself know that I as an American *do*. So by the time I came back to Harvard, on my first appointment, I am loaded up with, practically speaking, a lot of stuff about American kinship terminology, and all I really have to do is simply demonstrate to these people that what they're talking about is not what really happens in America.

RH: So in order to think through this intellectual and ethnographic problem, you turned to American data, just playing around with it in your head?

DMS: That's a very friendly and generous way of putting it. But my attitude was sort of crudely simple, and that is, Jesus Christ!—that's not what we do! I mean, I know that I call these different people different things under different conditions.

RH: But what I'm trying to get at is that you didn't try to think it through again with the Yapese material, or *only* with the Yapese material.

DMS: No, no! The trick was to use material that they themselves knew. See, with the Yapese material, they were telling me I was screwed up. But I could point out to them, this is what you do, right?!

So of course, the next obvious step—I come back to Harvard, I begin to talk to George Homans about all this. I couldn't talk to Clyde, because Clyde was repulsed by kinship! And Talcott Parsons's mind was on much higher things. But Homans was interested. So I talked to George Homans about this, and he thought that it was jolly good.

Meanwhile, I had asked for a small piece of research money from the Laboratory of Social Relations. I knew I was absolutely right about all this stuff. But I thought, what is terribly convincing is if you go through all the proper motions. You collect some data, you analyze the data, and you write a formal report! So all right, all right, I'll do it. I asked Social Relations for a small amount of money, and I interviewed graduate students in Social Relations, and faculty in Social Relations, on their use of kinship terms.

And it was fun to interview Fred Mosteller and Talcott Parsons and George Homans and all the graduate students. At that time they had dictaphones with these plastic records. I kept dictaphone copies of the interviews, and I made out little genealogies—not big ones, but just enough genealogies so that you could get "mother" and "mother's brother," and "father" and "father's sister," and "grandfather" and "grandmother," and so on. And of course, I knew perfectly well what I was going to get. And I got it! I even got people to say such wonderful things as, "Well, I don't call him a relative at all. He is a son-of-a-bitch!" I wrote down conscientiously, "call him son-of-a-bitch." Things like that.

So, that was it. George Homans got interested. And I believe he got his name on the paper. Because, then to do further follow-up, we got more money. And the very first time I gave a paper to the American Anthropological Association was on that American kinship stuff, and it *wowed* them. I was absolutely—I don't know what an actor or actress is like when they have their first real success, but I just remember I got into an auditorium that seemed to me to have thousands of people in it. It may have had fifty, I don't know.

RH: Where was this?

DMS: I don't even remember where it was!

RH: Do you remember what year it was?

DMS: It was around '51 or '52—'53 maybe. I can look it up. Everybody loved it, and people wrote and asked for copies of the paper. It was published in the *Anthropologist* with George Homans. He insisted on putting in some psychological crap, but it didn't matter. But it was basically my paper. I had not only done the work on it, I had done the thinking on it. There were about two or three pages at the end that George had a hand in. The reason I say this so firmly is that later on George wanted to reprint the *Marriage, Authority and Final Causes* in a collection of his papers. And we agreed, quite plainly, that that was *his* work, and the other was mine. We agreed at that point that he would take that, I would take this. So all the royalties that came from *Marriage, Authority and Final Causes* he got, and everything that came out of this was mine.[6]

The manuscript of the paper—Clyde said, "Why don't you show it to Alfred [Kroeber]?" So I showed it to Alfred. Alfred said, "Come on over and let's talk about it." So I went over to where he was living, and met Crakey [Mrs. Kroeber], and he really enjoyed it. For example, Kroeber said, "This business about 'father' being a more authoritarian form than 'daddy' or 'pop.' I don't know. I never really had that sort of authoritarian relationship with my children." And then we got off talking about this and that, and somehow it came up that when one of his children was really difficult, he locked him in the closet, leaned a chair against it, and sat on the chair until the child had agreed that it would not be difficult again. And I always thought that that wasn't Kroeber's idea of an authoritarian father relationship, but it sure as hell was mine!

So that was that paper. And out of the Yap stuff came the terminology stuff and all the rest of the business on kinship. I followed kinship pretty thoroughly and consistently, and then the last year at Harvard, there was a chance to have an SSRC seminar. That was the matrilineal kinship seminar with David Aberle, Kathleen Gough, Elizabeth Colson, George Fathauer, Harry Basehart, and a young, promising student named Marshall Sahlins—

RH: —who was the secretary—

DMS: —who was the secretary and who very aggressively and very firmly refused to participate in that book because, being a devout follower of Leslie White and a confirmed social evolutionist, he wanted not to be associated with what he saw was repulsive, archaic, capitalistic structural-functionalism. Therefore he did not. He was invited to participate, to write whatever he wanted. But he didn't.[7]

At that point, sometime in '54–'55, I got a letter from Ted McCown asking if I would be interested in a job at Berkeley. Ted McCown was a physical anthropologist at Berkeley, a student of Kroeber. He was chairman of the department at that time. I wrote back and said I would be very interested in a job, because I had been told by then—at Harvard, there was always this problem of who was going to get the tenured job. David Aberle was there and obviously competing for it; Jack Roberts was there and obviously competing for it; Ben Paul was there and obviously competing for it; Evon Vogt was brought there and was obviously competing for it.

RH: He's the one that got it, right?

DMS: He's the one that got it. But you see, I think it was made very plain to me that I did not even have the chance to compete for it. They all had their degrees before I did, various things like that. So it was a problem. I had to get out. So when McCown writes and asks would I be interested in a job at Berkeley, I thought, great—because Berkeley, it's a major university and a major department.

So I wrote back and said I was interested. There was an exchange of letters: what do I need, how much money, various things like that. And I wrote and said that I was ready to accept the job if it was offered, and I would now wait for a formal letter offering me the job. I didn't understand about bureaucratic problems. If Harvard offered me a job, they wrote me a letter and said, "here it is! You got a job—$4,000 a year."

So I'm waiting, and I'm waiting, and I get no letter. So I write a letter to McCown saying, "if you sent the letter, I haven't received it." No answer. I write another letter and get no answer. I telephone. I can't reach him. I'm grumbling. I tell Clyde. Clyde says, "Very odd. Give it a few days." Clyde finally gets hold of Kroeber. Kroeber says, "I don't understand this." Nobody understands it. Finally, Talcott Parsons is on my back: "We cannot take care of you next year. Tell me what your plans are." So I had to tell Parsons, "I am stuck. Berkeley offered me a job but now they're not sending me a letter to confirm it. I'm up in the air."

And like a knight in shining armor and all the rest of it comes a letter from the Center for Advanced Study in the Behavioral Sciences [Stanford University]. "Would you like to be a fellow next year?" Well, sure as shit I would like to be a fellow next year!

I get to the center in October. We pack everything up and put it in storage. We'd given up Berkeley, we drive out to the center. We now have two kids. It turns out that Kroeber's also at the center. I'm getting on nicely with Kroeber. I like him, he seems to like me. We have pleasant conversations. We talk about my research, about this and that with him. He then takes the initiative and says that when he got back to Berkeley, he got hold of Ted McCown. He got the department secretary. Ted had been a little ill, not feeling well, but it wasn't clear. So they went over to Ted's office. And the desk was piled high with unopened letters. And of course they found my letters. Ted had had a slight nervous breakdown or something. I don't know. He doesn't know. But it was all over, and that was the end of it.

RH: Why did McCown write you in the first place? Was that because of Kroeber?

DMS: I don't know. I assumed that my fame had—

RH: So to this day you don't know why that letter came to you?

DMS: That's the end of the story. At that time, it seemed to me that I'd given this great talk to the American Anthropological Association and that my fame had spread far and wide.

RH: In those days they didn't advertise a position?

DMS: Oh no! It was all done word-of-mouth. So, I'm at the center and Clark Kerr is appointed president of the University of California. He comes around and interviews a lot of people at the center, including me and Seymour Martin Lipset and others. Next thing I knew, David

Mandelbaum calls me up and says, "Would I like to come to Berkeley?" And I said, "Hell, yes! I would be very interested in coming to Berkeley. It almost happened once before." He said, "I think we can get it done this time." And lo and behold, I now have a formal letter, and not only are they hiring me, but they're hiring me as an associate professor with tenure. I thought, "Well, Clark Kerr has gone around to people at the center. He thinks anybody at the center must be the cat's pajamas. I'm at the center. Therefore he thinks I'm the cat's pajamas. Little does he know, but that's okay, I got a job."

So we moved to Berkeley from Palo Alto. I then discovered I had a colleague named Ed Norbeck. Ed Norbeck also had a letter from Ted McCown saying, "Would you be interested in a job at Berkeley? We have a job at Berkeley here for you." Ed Norbeck had sold his house and quit his job at the University of Nevada and moved to Berkeley. Apparently, when he showed up at the department, everybody treated him warmly and cordially, but after three or four days, they were annoyed, because he seemed to want to stay there. They wanted to know why he didn't get the hell out and go home. Well, he thought he had a job there, but nobody in the department thought he had a job there because Ted McCown had done all this by himself.

RH: So what happened to him?

DMS: Finally Ed said, "Look, here is a letter from Ted McCown." So the people in the department gathered together and they went to the administration and said, "Ted McCown fucked up, so what are you going to do?" So they gave Ed Norbeck the job. The university acted responsibly when one of its agents had screwed up. Why Ted McCown wrote to Norbeck I can't tell you either.

So I'm at Berkeley. Kroeber invites me to the house occasionally. I see him. And there's David Mandelbaum, Bob Heizer, and John Rowe, and others. So I'm teaching at Berkeley and it's a bum deal. I don't know—the department was really screwed up. Two of my colleagues had gotten into a furious fight. One was failing all of the other's students. The other guy retaliated by failing all of the first guy's students. They were vicious with each other. Backbiting and nastiness, no cooperation of any kind.

I have a peculiar recollection of all this. There was another guy who used to walk up and down the hall and check to see if everyone was in his office and in his chair by nine o'clock. If you weren't, he wanted to know why. And it wasn't exactly his responsibility, because he wasn't chair. But he was still very officious. It was an awful place!

Then I go to this meeting to decide whether to put Bob Murphy up for tenure. The meeting is held at Ted McCown's house. We're sitting around the living room. Everyone's got their drink. There's a long silence, and Ted McCown says, "Well, we're supposed to be here to discuss Bob Murphy's tenure. What do you think, gentlemen?"

Well, one guy blurts out, "I'll be damned if I'll be in any department where an Irish Catholic gets tenure. I don't think he ought to get tenure!"

I am absolutely flustered, disturbed—I don't know what the hell's going on—and it suddenly comes over me that they hate this poor Irish Catholic more than they hate Jews. It's ridiculous! But I'd been pretty well fed up with the place anyhow. I came home and told Addy about it, and she was upset.

RH: Did Murphy get tenure?

DMS: Of course. Because when push came to shove, the guy shut up, that was all. But he didn't make it any easier on Murphy. Murphy was not reverential toward him. He did not respect his great anthropological works.

Meanwhile, in another part of the forest, Fred Eggan was at the Center for Advanced Study. Fred had been an important person in helping to get the matrilineal kinship seminar—the SSRC—going on that. Dorothy Eggan was very interested in dreams. I still was interested in dreams at that point. Ever since Geoffrey Gorer I had been flirting with psychoanalysis, on and off, here, there, and everywhere. I had meanwhile decided to become a candidate at the San Francisco Psychoanalytic Institute and started a didactic analysis. So I was still in the culture and personality business. I had started my Mescalero Apache fieldwork.

I had met Tom Fallers in London, and he and I got on very well. I respected him a great deal. I had known Geertz back in Harvard when he was at Social Relations. So when I got to Berkeley, I urged very strongly that they try to recruit Fallers and Geertz. Not only did they try to recruit Fallers and Geertz, but I also urged them to recruit Paul Friedrich. Later on, Clyde had written to me or to somebody that Dell Hymes was around and that they should try to recruit him.

So Fallers came and Geertz came, but by that time I was getting very badly disenchanted with Berkeley. So Fred Eggan started with Fallers—wouldn't he like to come to Chicago?—and Fallers said he wanted to stay at Berkeley. Fallers, by that time, had established good relations with Lipset and [Reinhard] Bendix. Fred kept working on Fallers, and Fallers said if he moved to Chicago, they ought to bring me along. When Fred got after me, I said, "If Tom and I go to Chicago, we wouldn't go without Cliff Geertz." Dorothy Eggan did not want Cliff Geertz. Dorothy told Fred that, "no, it's Tom and David, and that's it. Cliff Geertz is very neurotic. He isn't a good public lecturer. He won't attract students."

But we said no, and Fred convinced Dorothy, what the hell, we'll try Cliff. So we pulled up and went to Chicago. Lincoln Constance was dean. He called me in and asked me what it would take to keep me. Instead, all I did was—and this was very rude; it was terrible, and I should never have done it—to tell him what a fucked-up department he had. It was just stupidly naive, because I should have known, and should have understood, that there was nothing he could do about the department. You can't fire a lot of people with tenure. And what he was doing was offering me a chance, for instance, to get out of the department but stay in the university. They had these free-floating positions. So instead of saying, "This is what I want to stay," I was convinced I wanted to leave, and all I did was dump on poor Constance.

We got to Chicago. Sol [Tax] was there, Fred was there, Norm McQuown was there, McKim Marriott, and Milton Singer. Barney Cohn and Ray Smith came in later.

Now, I leave Chicago, I retire, I come to Santa Cruz, I pick up that job, stay in that for two and a half years. While I'm in that job, I get a letter from a woman whose name, I think, is [Grace Wilson] Buzaljko. She turns out to be somebody who was an editor on some anthropological publication. She's writing a history of the department at Berkeley, and she writes to me and asks me a few very simple questions. I look at the material she has sent me, and I am astonished and appalled and I don't understand it.

It tells me that there were letters back and forth between Kroeber and McCown, and then Kroeber and Mandelbaum, and a letter from Clark Kerr to Mandelbaum, and what becomes quite clear to me, suddenly, from the materials she has sent me, is: while I was back at Harvard,

Kroeber had apparently—and I presume this to be the case; I don't have explicit evidence—Kroeber and Kluckhohn decided that they really ought to try to rebuild Berkeley. The first step in rebuilding Berkeley was to get me. Geertz was another step in rebuilding Berkeley. They were happy when I picked Fallers. He met with immediate approval. Not only that—putting three and three together with another twelve and getting another peculiar sum—when McCown screwed up, and I had no place to go, Kluckhohn must have gotten hold of Ralph Tyler at the center and said, "Look, we gotta do something for Schneider. We can't keep him here. Do you—?"

You know what parking stocks and bonds is? If you buy stock but you don't want it to appear in your records, you can park it with somebody else. Well, Kluckhohn couldn't afford to keep me, so he was parking me with the center until Berkeley could get its act together to hire me!

I thought I was earning all of this because of the monumental quality of my intellect. Kluckhohn had gotten me my center appointment. Clark Kerr had had nothing to do with bringing me to Berkeley, until Kroeber said, "You've gotta rebuild the department, and here is the way you start doing it. You start with Schneider and then you bring other people" and so on. There were a few things that went wrong with that.

I had thought that the protégé system was off by that time. I had thought that I had made a big enough impression on Kroeber so that he had said to McCown, "This is a great guy." And he had then hired me. But it turned out that my whole career was being managed by Kluckhohn all this while.

RH: Are you saying that this was just Kluckhohn convincing Kroeber?

DMS: This was Kluckhohn convincing Kroeber, and Kroeber in turn convincing Clark Kerr.

RH: Right, but they were doing this because they respected your work.

DMS: They did it because they respected my work, clearly, but it was the way in which they did it. I didn't have a thing—you see, it's either my own stupidity or their great skilled management, or a combination. I didn't have any notion of what was going on. Nobody said to me, "We want you to go to Berkeley, and we want you to start rebuilding that place. We're trying to fix it up, and we're arranging for you to go to Berkeley. Now shut up and do what you're told!"

None of that. I just get a letter out of the clear blue sky, and I just think that suddenly the magic wand has fallen on me. Naturally, I deserved it, right? Why else?

It gets even more complicated. I had not been happy at Yale at all. I thought Yale was very anti-Semitic. And I still think it was at that time, and it may still be. I thought that Yale was extremely narrow in that Pete Murdock didn't really have any respect for or any kind of feeling for anybody who was not old New England family. My good friend Ward Goodenough and I showed up not at the same time—he went immediately and I came the next year. Ward was immediately the white-haired boy. I formed an alliance with the son of a very wealthy midwestern physician. But, you know, he was from the midwest! And a woman from Texas—although part of Texas aristocracy. So, there were the three of us—an Episcopalian, a Texan (I don't know what her religion was), and a Jew! From Murdock's point of view we were all in the same boat: out, period.

RH: Did those two other people survive?

DMS: They got Ph.D.'s at Yale.

RH: Are they people whose names I would know?

DMS: No. They moved into one of those secret national agencies. They were doing partly code-breaking and partly super-intelligence analysis.

Anyway, I was not doing well with Murdock—didn't like him, couldn't get along with him, and did not like his anthropology. Meanwhile, I had formed a good relationship with Geoffrey Gorer, who liked me, and I liked him. I had no idea he was gay, but that didn't matter. When I got this offer of a job in Washington for $1,620 a year, I didn't think twice. I went into Murdock's office and I said, "Professor Murdock, I have this very good job in Washington, and I am going to take it. So I am withdrawing from the department."

And he, in the first sign of any humanity that I had ever seen, stood up from his desk, put his hand awkwardly on my shoulder, and said, "I know you will be a success at something, Dave, but it isn't anthropology, is it?"

I said, "No, sir, I am quitting anthropology forever." And I left! And I really had no intention of ever going back into anthropology at that time.

At Harvard, I got along very well with John Otis Brew, who was the director of the Peabody Museum. While I was in London, Brew sent me a letter, with a quotation from Murdock, to the effect that the outstanding, the great piece of fieldwork that was done in the CIMA project was done by Schneider. I had never heard anything like that before! I thought, "Gee, that's odd. If he thought that, why didn't he tell me?"

I get back to Harvard, and at this point, Ben Paul comes from Yale to Harvard. Ben tells me this story. Footnote: I now, four or five years ago, remembering all this, go to Ben and say, "Ben, do you remember when you told me this story?" "No, I don't remember anything like that at all." So my version is that Ben tells me that Isidore Dyen has imported a Yapese to New Haven to work on language, and that Dyen is complaining bitterly that he can't get to the Yapese because Murdock is monopolizing him—

RH: —to do kinship terms?

DMS: That's exactly it. So I get the story from Dyen [via Paul]: "Goddamn Murdock! All he does is sit there and say 'unbelievable, incredible, impossible, but the man insists that that's what they do!'" And he's working off the manuscript of my thesis chapter.

RH: What year is this?

DMS: About 1951. I learn this in 1951, but the Yapese was at Yale 1949 to '50, something like that. So once again I'm annoyed, because if Murdock now has checked all my stuff out and finds out that it's not only indisputable, but he's got a native to tell him so, he's still not saying a fucking word to me—and I am really pissed! Because he said the thesis was not possible, that he had never seen any ethnography like this before, that if I would only get my notes together he would be sure that I would see it. And I am now more convinced than ever that I am on the right track. But the right and decent thing for him to do was—"Hey, Schneider, well, maybe I didn't understand it, or maybe you didn't write it up very clearly, but, by God, the guy says something close to what you've said."

That's '51. Now it's '89, and [Ira] Bashkow is coming to visit me, to interview me. Bashkow is telling me that he has read archives at Peabody. He has read all the stuff about the CIMA project, and that there is a long exchange of letters. Very briefly, the story seems to be: a guy named Bill Stevens and I went out as ethnographers; Ed Hunt went out as a physical anthropologist; Nate Kidder went out as a demographer. Murdock has written that he's not interested in and has nothing to say about Hunt's work, the demography he has no problem with, and Stevens's material is too thin to do anything with and is absolutely shameful. The only ethnography that's worth anything at all is Schneider's ethnography, and, remarkably, it's the best piece of ethnography that's been done in the whole CIMA project.

This I have to learn in 1989!

RH: And it's because Ira unearths this—

DMS: —because Ira unearths this in the archives at Peabody. So it turns out that Murdock had conveyed all of this to Joe Brew and, it must have been, before him, to Donald Scott, to Kroeber, and to Kluckhohn. Or he conveyed it very explicitly to the Peabody people, who then must have conveyed it to Kroeber and Kluckhohn.

RH: What was his relationship to Brew?

DMS: When the CIMA project was set up, it farmed out pieces of the work. And Peabody had a contract. So Murdock was telling Peabody that most of the work that had been done was no good, and the only decent piece of work that was done was mine.

So, again, I'm not discovering any of that until 1989. Have I made it clear that Kluckhohn, who didn't know beans about kinship but respected Murdock's opinion on it, is being given an earful by Murdock on what great fieldwork I had done, what great ethnography I'd done?

And now, what I learn from Bashkow is that Clyde had been reading my field notes! Well, I knew he was going to read my field notes, but Bashkow is reporting that Clyde is saying that the field notes are almost like looking into a person's private life, or something like that. And I think to myself, "Was I that transparent? I never knew any of that!"

So whatever Clyde's own judgment was, it was strongly reinforced by Murdock, reinforced by Kroeber, who's also reading the field notes, which is *really* why I got to Berkeley, which is why I was being parked at the center. I was being pushed around like a pawn and didn't know it. And I suppose if I had known I was being pushed around like a pawn, I would've resented it and fucked up somehow—kicked back.

RH: So it was all for your own good?

DMS: It was all for my own good, but, you know, I still have this awful feeling—it's a little like this Greek stuff—you don't know that the gods are manipulating you.

RH: You seem to be very angry about this.

DMS: I am very angry because it takes away from me what I thought I was accomplishing by my own bare hands and my own little, you know . . .

RH: But you were accomplishing it! These people were interested in you because of the quality of your work. I can see your annoyance, but it doesn't take away from the fact that it was your work that impressed them.

DMS: All right, let me give you the rest of it.

RH: Let me ask a question first. Is Murdock anti-Semitic?

DMS: I don't think he's anti-Semitic. Murdock was just a very awkward, uncomfortable guy who had trouble with all kinds of human relations, didn't know how to relate to anybody, much less people, and had a very clear and very obsessive mission that he himself was trying to accomplish, which was at complete cross-purposes to mine.

RH: But my question would be, why is it that Murdock is able to admit, even if only behind your back, that you're doing good work?

DMS: Murdock was a great reader of ethnography. He had read all the ethnography on the whole of the Micronesian area. And Murdock knew that there were a lot of matrilineal places out there, and what was very awkward and disconcerting was these peculiar patrilineal ones that were cropping up. Yap was supposed to be patrilineal. My showing that it was double descent fitted with what he had been teaching about double descent and descent. He could see that. Secondly, it made better sense of Micronesia in terms of *his* understanding of Micronesia. Thirdly, what I was doing was feeding him the kind of data that made it possible for him to confirm the kinds of overall pictures of Micronesia that he found convincing.

What I'm really trying to say is that my work was good work only because it was consistent with his biases. The evidence for that is that however good the work was that I did on kinship terminology, he rejected it flatly out of hand, and never reneged on that. And yet, I think that was *better* work, because later on, you know, I withdrew the double descent business.[8] Double descent according to his definition, but it was not the way Yap culture was built. It was not patrilineal in any way. It was really matrilineal. In an ironic way, it was more consistent with Murdock's impression of a big belt of matrilineal Micronesian places. So that even double descent was out of gear. But double descent was better than simple patriliny.

RH: That's the answer to the question of what motivated Murdock. But I interrupted a further part of the story.

DMS: The further part of the story is this irony that Murdock thought my work was good in some important way not simply because it was good but because it fit his way of thinking. Once again, the horrible irony of the way these gods, who are very human, are pushing you around and your career.

Why am I so moved by those ironies?—you know, the work of the gods in Tikopia, the work of the gods here.[9] See, because even today, with all the job searches, the patronage, the protégé stuff is still operating. They have a big search, for example, at Podunk. They get eighty or ninety applications. People sit and read the applications, but one of the things they read is the letters and who the letters are from. You get a really rave letter from somebody who you think is a klutz, and it doesn't help the candidate! You get a really rave letter from somebody you like and respect, and it helps the candidate a lot. Not only that, there still is the word of mouth. So the patronage system is still really going. It's just harder to keep blacks and minorities out, that's all.

Two
Youth

DMS: I was born on November 11, 1918, Armistice Day. My father [Morris Schneider] used to say that "everyone, everybody came out and demonstrated on the streets the day you were born!" He always thought that was a good joke.

Technically I was born in Brooklyn, but we moved very shortly thereafter to the Bronx. My understanding was that it was because my mother [Pauline Kasman Schneider] couldn't get along with my father's relatives very well. But my father was very closely tied to his relatives, who were mostly his brothers and sisters, and they mostly lived in Brooklyn.

RH: Were these people all first-generation immigrants?

DMS: Yeah, they had all—my mother came over when she was very young, in her first four or five years of life. My father came over when he was sixteen. He was the first one who brought his brothers and sisters over.

RH: They came from where?

DMS: They came from Brest-Litovsk, which half the time was Poland, half the time was Russia. My father came through Canada, I believe, and then down to New York. He was a woodcarver at that time, but he lost his tools. Somebody begged to borrow his tools, and he lent them the tools, and he never saw the guy with the tools again. So he couldn't do any woodcarving anymore, 'cause in those days, you had to have your own tools to do woodcarving.

RH: What did a woodcarver carve?

DMS: They carved all kinds of things: furniture; they carved statuary and ornamental stuff for churches, for restaurants, for homes. One of the things that later on my father contracted for with a furniture maker was a very large cabinet, which had carved figures all over it, and carved things that he designed. Somebody else did it, but he was always very fond of it, 'cause he thought the carving was really beautifully done.

RH: So, he didn't carve it himself. He bought it, he contracted it.

DMS: He contracted to have someone else do it. By that time he was—

RH: —right, he lost his tools, so he was—

DMS: —he lost his tools, and went into one business and then another business. He sold stationery, he sold leather goods, he did this and that. Then for—I'm not sure of the details on this, but my understanding at the moment is that at one point, he lent some people about five thousand dollars, which at that time was a whopping big sum. That enabled them to go into the dress manufacturing business. So, the last time he went out of business, they offered him a job as a salesman. So for the rest of his life—well, when?—I think by the time I was in my mid-teens, just after the Depression, just as the Depression was beginning to lift, about 1934, 1935, he was selling dresses for this company, for the people he'd lent the money to. They essentially said they couldn't pay him back, but that he could be a salesman for them. And that way, he did what he could and he worked on commissions. He never wanted the five thousand dollars back. The job was much more important. Later on, of course, they could have paid him off, because it became a very big and very successful dress manufacturing concern.

So, at one time he had New Jersey as a territory, and he ended up with Pennsylvania as a territory. At one point I'd drive for him and carry his samples for him. That was nice, and pleasant. But by that time, I was well along in high school, and then I think I even carried samples for him when I was in college, once. He had a heart attack, and he was not well, so I drove one summer for him and carried samples for him.

I'm not sure of that, I'm really not sure, because my other recollection is that I worked on farms all the summers. There's some time discrepancy.

RH: What about your mother's family?

DMS: My father had a bunch of brothers and sisters, but my mother was an only child. Her mother was an epileptic, and her father ran a small candy store. Then mother's mother died—I don't remember when, I just remember she died—and then I remember grandfather died while

I was away in high school. He was paralyzed—right arm and right leg, I think. Anyway, I just remember him as being very nice, that's all. And I remember mother's mother being somebody I always regarded with great distance, and I never came near her. Whether it's because she threw epileptic fits around the house, I don't know.

But they didn't live with mother's mother or mother's father. They didn't live with father's parents, either. Father's mother, I can remember, was a very orthodox person. She wore a wig, and she wouldn't eat in our house 'cause we didn't keep kosher. But that's it.

So, I was born, and someplace along the line—I was about six years old—my brother [Herb] was born. You know this story? Haven't you heard it before?

RH: In pieces, but never the whole story.

DMS: Well, briefly, I really didn't see the need for anyone else around the house. I thought it was all well organized the way it was. And I, apparently, resented my brother's appearance with considerable vigor. In fact, I have a very vivid memory of when my brother was born. It was a Jamaican woman who was household help for my mother. Her name was Eva, and I liked her a great deal. Anyway, I can remember Eva dressing me in a snowsuit and sending me out on the street to play. I didn't want to go out on the street to play, and I was told very firmly that I had to go out and play in the snow. So, my vivid memory is standing at the door, triumphantly screaming that I had to come in because I had wet myself. But that's all I remember.

RH: That was after the baby was born?

DMS: It was the day he was being born! That was the beginning of the whole mess, you see. One way or another, I—this, of course, is post hoc rationalization—I figured I had to screw up in order to reestablish my place at the center of attention. And the way to screw up was to screw up at school. So school sent me home and said I clearly had learning difficulties, and I was obviously retarded in some way, and I also had behavioral difficulties. I apparently was not very nice.

RH: You just said that you had to screw up and the way to screw up was in school. Is this your response to the brother's being born?

DMS: That was my understanding. But, you see, my parents wouldn't talk about any of these things. Their response to all of this, of course—

and it's a marvelously ironic story—their response was to send me to a boarding school, which was exactly what I didn't want to do. Instead of sending the younger brother who was unneeded away, and having me reinstated as the dominant person in the household, they shipped me away!

RH: At the age of six?

DMS: No, at the age of nine.

RH: Because for three years you'd been tormenting your little brother?

DMS: No, I hadn't bothered the little brother at all. All I did was, I refused to learn to read, I refused to learn to write, and I refused to learn any arithmetic, which is basically what I should have been doing in those years.

So I got sent away to a boarding school, which, of course, hurt me very badly. I felt I had been rejected; I felt that I was unwanted. I was really unhappy.

RH: Your father must've been doing well at that time, to be able to afford that.

DMS: He was doing okay, but there was something else going on. The boarding school they found was a small place called Cherry Lawn School. It was in Darien, Connecticut, while Darien was still a country town. It was not the big dormitory and suburbia it is now. The Boston Post Road was the main road through it, and the New York, New Haven and Hartford Railroad—and so forth. I can remember, early in my days there, screaming and crying and complaining and wanting to go home. I didn't like the school. And I threatened to ride home on the spare tire of the car. In those days, the car had a spare tire smack on the back of the car. You could sit in it. Of course, this caused people to laugh.

But slowly, that gave way to—you know, if they don't want me, I don't want them. So I stayed at Cherry Lawn from the age of nine to eighteen. From then on it was an ambivalent relationship with my parents. In many ways my mother was not a very—I don't know what you'd call it—well, I'll tell you stories, instead.

Before my brother was born, she used to take me to concerts with her. She wanted to be an opera singer. She had a very good voice. I can remember her singing—turns out I went to the opera two nights ago and heard *Tosca*—nobody has sung "Visi d'arte" the way my mother used to sing "Visi d'arte." She would sing all the time, and she had a piano—and she really wanted to be an opera singer.

But my father, of course, felt that she should stay home with the children, and take care of the house, and feed him, etc. So there was a great deal of tension between them on all that.

She used to take me to concerts, and I am quite sure that that's how I got to be so deeply engaged with music. Not so deeply engaged that I was willing to learn to play anything. 'Cause they tried to give me piano lessons and things like that, but I would never—you know, it was one of those situations: if they wanted me to do it, I wouldn't do it; if I wanted to do it, I would do it. Being so ambivalent, I wasn't going to do anything that would please them, once I got kicked out.

Another problem with my mother was that she was both badly frustrated and not exactly happy in the marriage, and did really have her mind and heart set on opera singing. She didn't relate well with people under any circumstances. For example, another one of these childhood images comes back. This was before my brother was born. There was a cat in the house. I liked the cat. But my mother felt that it was dirty, and it shed hair: she didn't want the cat. So one day she put the cat in a paper bag and took me by the hand, and we went for a walk on the street. She came to one of those trash cans—people put their garbage and ashes and stuff out in the big iron trash cans—she lifted the lid and put the paper bag with the cat into the trash can and put the lid back on it. Well, I am sure that that is, you know, one of those Freudian images that they say have some grave significance; I'm quite sure that for me, that represented me. And, for a long, long while I didn't like cats and would have nothing to do with them. In fact, I was quite convinced that I was allergic to cats. But in fact, it turns out that I do like cats very much, and I've gotten over that. But this image of being tossed in a trash can and having a lid put on and walking away and that was the end of it—I'm sure that was the image in terms of which I understood my relationship to the family.

That kind of scene repeated itself later on. Cherry Lawn School was run by a man named Dr. Fred Goldfrank. The Goldfrank family was related to the Strauss and the Strasser families. They all were very wealthy, well-established German Jewish families from the New York area. One branch of the family was in importing, or something like that. Fred Goldfrank worked along with his mother, and he ran this school. And I'm sure that the family set it up, that they paid for it and took care of it. It was progressive education. It was also outdoors and fresh air. So we had classes outdoors, all the time, winter and summer.

RH: How could you have outdoor classes in the winter?

DMS: We did! They had built an L-shaped thing which was basically like a partly covered patio. It had segments in it. Each little section had a small room in which they kept the books and the paraphernalia like chalk, blackboards, and paper, and we sat in chairs, sort of desk chairs.

RH: The chairs were outside?

DMS: Everything was outside.

RH: When it was twenty degrees in the winter?

DMS: Oh, it was worse than twenty degrees.

RH: And snow was falling on you?

DMS: It was partly covered. You wouldn't sit in the rain, you know. You would go under the eaves, under that roof. But it was all outdoors.

RH: How could you write when it was so cold?

DMS: Sometimes it was too cold to write, you didn't write. And sometimes you just wrote anyway. You had gloves with fingers on them, it was all right. And kids with mittens—I don't know what they did. But I can remember writing, and I can remember doing everything else.

RH: Did anyone consider this cruel?

DMS: No, I thought it was fun. I liked it. And the sleeping porches were all outdoors. There were screened sleeping porches.

RH: Of course, the screened sleeping porch of the 1920s. Sinclair Lewis talks about it.[1]

DMS: Yes, you've got it. So, fresh air, and outdoors, and good food, and plenty of exercise. And we had plenty of exercise. There were forty acres—or was it twenty? Anyway, relatively big. It had a barn. It had cows. It had chickens. It had horses. They raised a lot of the vegetables that we ate. There was a kitchen there.

One of the interesting things, of course, was that a school like that tended to be a dumping ground for very badly adjusted kids.

RH: Would you count yourself among them?

DMS: No, that was the interesting thing. It turned out that I was one of the "more normal" ones. So when my father was really hard-put to pay the tuition, they made a deal with him to charge him a nominal amount because they wanted to keep a number of people like me—and there was another kid called Ted Strongin, and some others. There was one kid that kept trying to drown dogs in the lake. There was another kid that kept going around working some kind of a scissors motion; he kept shrieking about "cut the nipple off." They were rather odd people, many of them.

RH: Were they all Jews?

DMS: Not all, by all means. It was "nonsectarian." The faculty were an odd collection of people, too. Some of them may have been normal, I'm sure.

I immediately gravitated toward the farm, and I used to hang around the barn, and I used to help with the chickens, and help with the cows, and help drive the horse and wagon.

RH: Was this required of students? Was it part of the program?

DMS: No, but it was relatively open, and I found myself kind of happily going that way. That may have had something to do with the fact that one of the kids I became friendly with—he was a little older than I was—was a kid named Sheldon Hart. Sheldon Hart became notable later on, because he was the bodyguard who was seized and abducted at the time they invaded Leon Trotsky's house and killed him in Mexico. They took Sheldon Hart out and killed him; they tortured him and killed him. He was one of my friends at that time. But he was sufficiently older than I was so that I had no idea what his political commitments and interests were. He was a good friend, and he had a dog. I've forgotten its name now, but it was one of those collie-shepherd mixes. He was very strong on animals, so he and I got ringnecked doves, and we kept a bunch of ringnecked doves together. Then he and I found a monkey for sale, and we bought it, and we kept that for a couple of years. I don't know why, but I just found myself engaged with animals and stuff like that at the time. Whether Sheldon was the one who moved me into it, I don't know.

RH: Did you milk cows?

DMS: Oh yes, milked cows, shoveled shit, made hay, cleaned out chicken coops, knew what to do with brooding hens, knew how to feed chickens. But then, of course, we fell afoul, because Sheldon and I trapped a couple of crows, and we wanted to keep them, but the farmer was absolutely livid at the idea of keeping crows. Crows were vermin, for him. So the son-of-a-bitch went in and killed them one night. We were very angry about that.

RH: Was this an all-boys school?

DMS: No, boys and girls—coed. At some point—I must've been more than ten, maybe eleven or twelve, I don't know—I got a dog. Her name was Foxy. She was a smooth-haired terrier plus this, that, and the other. Everybody let their dogs run loose all the time. The farmer had a hard time, 'cause the dogs would chase the cows. And there were all kinds of jokes about how it would make cheese, and all that. But basically, it was a bad scene, 'cause if the dogs chased the cows, it was not good for everybody. So he kept threatening to shoot the dogs. But they prevailed on him, and he didn't shoot the dogs. After a while, the dogs quit chasing the cows.

The dogs all ran loose. The responsibility of the owner of the dog was to just be sure it was fed. After dinner in the evening, each of us who owned a dog would go out to the kitchen, we'd pick up scraps, put them in a plate, put it down where the dog could get it, and go away. It was not what you would call heavy responsibility. I knew which was my dog, but I don't think my dog knew me from anybody else. There were big dogs and little dogs, furry dogs and not-furry dogs. The only thing that was really clear was that if the dog bit, they had to do something. But mostly the dogs didn't bite, and mostly it was training. Kids don't tease the dogs, they don't bother the dogs, they don't give dogs a hard time. It was just that one kid who wanted to: every time he could get his hands on a dog, he'd drag it down to the lake and try to drown it. I don't know why. He was a funny kid, anyway. Had a terrible time. He did not want to wash under any circumstances. So periodically, a couple of teachers would get him and really scrub him down, and then he was good for another month or two. I don't know what ever happened to him.

So my dog shows up with mange.

RH: You're how old at this point?

DMS: I don't know, twelve, thirteen. The vet said, "rub this medicine on the dog." I rubbed the medicine on the dog, did all those things. Well, one vacation the question arose as to what happens: Do I take the dog back to New York with me, or don't I? And my mother said very flatly, "No, you can't do that. The dog has mange. It's very dirty. You have to rub this oily stuff in its skin. The house will be"—etc. So: could not have the dog in the house. All right. But I had left the dog at school other vacations. This time I made arrangements with somebody to feed the dog—one of the people who worked in the kitchen or something. So I went home for vacation.

I came back to school after vacation, and I couldn't find my dog! When I came back from vacation, as usual, my mother and father would drive me back to school. I'm sure my little brother was around, but I have no recollection of him. So they drive me back to school and I immediately went looking for my dog. I couldn't find my dog, and I ran all over looking for my dog, and I went to the person who was supposed to feed it, and I said, "Where's my dog?"

And they said, "Well, don't you know? Your dog is gone."

I said, "What do you mean, gone?"

And they said, "Well, your mother arranged for us to send it to the dog pound to have it killed because it was hopelessly sick with mange."

I got very, very upset. What I can remember is shrieking—I really don't remember what—I shrieked at my mother and father, and I ran as fast as I could, down to the lake. And as I ran, I calmed down and turned around, and there was my father, who was always very fastidious—always very neatly, very perfectly dressed—picking his way gently through the mud puddles, carrying an umbrella, and trying to follow me. All I can remember doing at that point is suddenly breaking out into laughter: Why was he following me? What could he possibly say? It was such an absurd scene—it was the place you couldn't possibly imagine my father to be: in his neatly polished, perfectly kept shoes, and his neatly pressed, perfectly clean and impeccable attire, with his white shirt, and trying to protect himself from this huge downpour that was coming.

I don't remember what I said or what happened after that. I just remember going back to meet him. I think that was one of those things that, once again, made things very difficult between me and my mother. I could never say anything to her, there was no way to talk about any of these things. Now, looking back at it, it was a very stupid way to behave on her part. It was the usual surreptitious . . . have things done and let people work it out. It was a bad scene, and it upset me quite a bit. And I think that was one of the things that really confirmed my feeling that I had to be through with the family: I had to get away; I had to be on my own; I had to be independent; I had to be able to take care of myself.

So from that point on, as far as I can remember, I never wanted to come home for vacations.

RH: Now before then—when you say going home for vacations—does that mean all summer long?

DMS: It meant going home for Thanksgiving, Christmas, Easter, and for all summer long. In those days, my mother had hay fever, so she would take the two of us kids up to Digby, Nova Scotia, one summer, a second summer there, then Bethlehem, New Hampshire, and it was Bethlehem from then on for a while. Later, when I was in my teens, fifteen, sixteen, seventeen, I went up to Bethlehem with her, and I then went hitchhiking. I hitchhiked from New Hampshire to Portland, Maine, and then back. I hitchhiked to various other places around. Somehow, nothing ever happened to me, and somehow I always got there and I always got back. I know it upset my mother and my father. They thought it was dangerous and it was bad, and what was I going to do? and did I have enough money?—and I didn't, but I managed. It was no big deal.

RH: You said that after the incident with the dog, you had to get away. Did you stop going home for the summer?

DMS: As much as I could. What I tended to do was to stay at Cherry Lawn and work on the farm during the summer, for which they gave me room and board. There are funny stories about that. Like: I'm supposed to be weeding the carrots and watching the cows at the same time, and I must have been dreaming about something, 'cause the cows got into the apple orchard. And when cows get into the apple orchard and begin to eat apples, they get drunk.

RH: Don't they founder?

DMS: Yeah, and they break legs, they bash themselves against trees, they walk into barbwire fences. They get drunk. So that was a very bad situation. What else did I screw up there once? I think I screwed up something else. I think I pulled out the stuff I was supposed to be weeding and left the weeds instead. But I did learn a lot about farming there, so that when the time came, I was able to go to the New York State College of Agriculture, where they definitely did not want Jews from New York. Their premise was that Jews from New York don't want to go into agriculture, therefore they have no responsibility and shouldn't admit them. But I claimed I wanted to be a farmer. And they said, "Well, what the hell do you know about farming?" So I was able to demonstrate that I could do all those basic things like harness a horse, drive a team of horses, milk cows, and all that stuff. So even after I went to Cornell, I tended to work on farms during the summers. I got as much as fifteen bucks a month with room and board, some of those summers. That was pretty good, for me.

One of the other elements I'm sure that happened, too, at that time— all connected with my brother's birth and whatever it was in the family situation: somehow, my first premise was that when I got to be sixteen, everything would be better. Because I'd be able to do things I couldn't. And then when I got to be eighteen, then I'd be free of this and that. And when I got to be twenty or twenty-one, you know . . . So I've always had this sort of future orientation, that somehow you can be more autonomous, you can be more in control—but I can remember that as being a very important feature of my thinking then.

RH: Were your years at Cherry Lawn unhappy years?

DMS: No, that, of course is the other—once—well, I was going to say that once I had made up my mind that if the family didn't want me I didn't want them, everything was easy. But it never was, because even after you've made up your mind that if they don't want you, you don't want them, you still do want them. However unpleasant my mother was, however—she did stupid things that were intolerable, like the dog business and the cat business—I basically was still deeply attached to her. And that's about all there was to it. You couldn't really talk to her. I never could talk to her. Long after, married with children and so forth, it was still not possible to talk to her. She was always knocking absolutely everything conceivable. She criticized me, she criticized Addy, she criticized Herb, my brother, she criticized my father, she criticized people in the street; she thought people were dressed badly, she thought people were overweight, she thought people were underweight, she thought people didn't speak politely, she didn't think they spoke good English, and so on. I never heard her criticize musicians. But that was another problem. She was just a very hard person.

RH: So here you are, you've decided that if they don't want you, you don't want them, but you really do want them. So does that mean that there's a kind of undercurrent—

DMS: —oh yeah—

RH: —in your years at—I presume you got along fairly well in terms of daily routines.

DMS: At Cherry Lawn I got along very well. I enjoyed the place, I liked the place, I learned a lot, insofar as I could learn. Like, I took a lot of German, but I never learned any German.

RH: But you learned to read and write and do math?

DMS: Well, I learned to read, but I never really learned to write, and I never really learned arithmetic. And my spelling is atrocious. That's that whole block of things that you're supposed to learn between six and nine or ten. I just can't spell and I can't write—my handwriting is not very legible. And I still can't do arithmetic. But the school was good. We played football, I was on the basketball team, I was a major figure! I was one of the stalwart, best guards that they had on the team. We played all sorts of schools around us, fancy schools in New York, like the Ethical Culture School. And we had a nice gymnasium, and they had folk dancing there, and every year they put on a Gilbert and Sullivan thing. I was always relegated to the very back—"Open your mouth but don't sing, please, David." But I can still sing you songs from *Iolanthe* and from *Trial by Jury*, from *Pinafore* and from *The Mikado*. It was a lot of fun, and I did enjoy it, and there were kids there I liked.

RH: If you weren't doing well with the writing and the math, were they on your case about that?

DMS: There were so many other problems they had! And, you see, it was also progressive education: you gotta let children bloom the way they want to! So they let me alone. It was okay with me. I liked that.

You know, the dogs really were a big thing. The classrooms were built in an L, and in the open part of the L they had gardens for the children. You know, you plant cabbage seeds and you plant carrots and radishes and everything else and you watch them grow. And of course, it was the place where all the dogs in heat, and not in heat, showed up. So we all got a fairly good education in one sense, because we understood about sexual education. I can still hear, if I listen carefully, Adolph Schultz, who was the German teacher, bellowing at the top of his lungs: "Eyes on zee board! Eyes on zee board!" We were watching the dogs fucking, you see!

RH: Since it was coed, did the students fuck each other?

DMS: I don't know. Probably some did, but I was pretty—pretty what do you call it? I was definitely interested in sex, but I didn't get heavily involved with the girls until practically my senior year. And then I "fell in love" with a girl there and went to visit her family. Her family!—her mother—I never knew anything about her father. Her mother worked in Washington, and I visited her in Washington. And that was the end of that. I don't remember what happened afterward. I still remember her name.

But there was a certain amount of groping, petting, feeling. There were two buildings in this place. One was called the Manor House. There was a back stairs, and with a little bit of effort—everybody was supposed to be in bed by nine o'clock—we'd sneak out. A number of us did sneak out. I ran away once. But after about three hours of being away—cold and hungry and there's no place to sleep, and we went into a barn—we turned around and walked back, as I remember. And nobody knew we'd run away.

But girls were not an important part of my high school life there.

RH: When you went to your parents' during the summers, do you remember your brother from those times?

DMS: Hardly. The story with my brother is really very simple. When I was about forty, and he was only about thirty-four, I—I don't know what happened, something happened—I discovered he was really a very nice person. I'm on very good terms with him now. He visits me, I visit him, we call each other. We are now established as brothers. And it really did come to me as sort of a shock, to discover that he was really quite nice.

My father, who doesn't figure as conspicuously in the whole family story, was really a very sweet guy. Given certain problems: I mean, his attitude was that women should take care of children, take care of the house, provide men with food and sex, and otherwise spend as little money as possible. So I can remember him vividly asking my mother, "Where the hell is all the money I gave you last week?"—and she having to account for it, and things like that.

But he was a very sweet, very kind, very generous and loving man. In the end, I am quite sure that both my brother and I identified, in a classic Freudian sense, very heavily with him. When he died, for example, I was absolutely overwhelmed.

RH: When did he die?

DMS: 'Fifty-one, 'fifty-two, 'fifty-three, I'm not sure. I was back from England for a couple of years, at Harvard, when he died. When he died, they had a regular funeral for him, at one of those undertaking parlors. There must've been a couple hundred people came! I was absolutely overwhelmed at how many people came to his funeral, 'cause they all liked him.

But he also had a secret life—he and my mother both had a secret life—which my brother and I were not let in on. They were both very devout communists, very devout Stalinists. I think that my father ran one of the not entirely underground but not entirely open and above-board groups in one of those collections of buildings that the—what do you call it?—Amalgamated Textile Workers, one of those places. It was one of those communist cells, if that's the name for it. I believe that the people who came to the funeral were from that part of his life.

RH: And your mother was also—

DMS: —my mother was also involved, but not as heavily as my father. He apparently did a lot of organizational and administrative work, and she mainly attended meetings and she read a great deal.

RH: If this was secret, how did you find out about it?

DMS: I knew they were communists, I knew absolutely dedicated communists, but I had no idea that he was—it was basically at his funeral that I found out. Because when I asked who the hell are all these people? and what the hell are they doing here? it turns out that my cousin—his sister Rose's daughter—was heavily involved in this way, too. She broke the facts to both Herb and me: that he really had been a major figure in the Communist party at a local level in the Bronx.

I got a great deal of my "political outlook" from them. And although he and I had a big row at the time of the Nazi-Soviet pact—you know, everybody had a big row at that time! You see, he used to walk me past synagogues and say, "Don't ever go into those places. They're houses of superstition." He explained about the importance of reason and the importance of evidence and the importance of weighing the facts and getting the facts and never taking things on faith.

So of course, comes the Nazi-Soviet pact: that was the summer I was driving for him. We were out someplace in Pennsylvania—I don't know whether it was Erie or outside Pittsburgh—and it was one evening, he was through working and we had dinner. And I said, "What about it, Pop? This doesn't look good!" And his only answer was, "Look, David, you've got to accept it. You've got to take it on faith sometimes. They know what they're doing. They know more than we do. They have the facts. We don't. We have to just take it on faith."

Well, I was not so rude to scream at him and tell him that all his life-time he'd been telling me *don't* take things on faith, reason things out, get the facts yourself. I just said, "Come on, Pop. It doesn't wash for me."

"Well," he said, "it washes for me." So he stayed with it, but I got off the wagon at that point. I had a great deal of sympathy and support for the Communist party. I was never a member of it, but I was always— you know, that's where it was, and the socialists were obviously com-promisers, they were really handmaidens of the capitalists—and all that crap. But from then on, I was much more politically independent.

RH: In your travels with your father, did you ever pass through Indi-ana, Pennsylvania, where my parents live?

DMS: Of course, Indiana, he had an account there! Indiana's not far from Pittsburgh, is it? And Scranton, and you name it! It was not just the great big cities, either. Anyplace that had a dress shop.

RH: Were all his clients Jews?

DMS: No, by no means. In fact, that was one of the problems. A lot of the small-town stores didn't like Jews, and they didn't like Jewish sales-men, and they gave them a hard time. They made them wait, and they canceled orders, things like that. The White Swan Hotel—do you know where that might be? Because we still have bits and pieces of—you see, my father then would get even with everybody by stealing silverware, stationery, and soap. So we had collections of stationery, particularly, from the White Swan Hotel and every goddamn town in Pennsylvania.

The driving was not easy, you know. Two-lane roads, and it would get icy and snowy and cold, and the mountains. And the coal towns— Johnstown, I remember Johnstown. That's where the flood was, and the water came roaring down. He and I missed the flood, fortunately.

Three

Addy

RH: Something I'd like to know more about: you've talked about your days as an undergraduate at Cornell. And you talked about marrying Addy on the last day of school. Could you tell me more about meeting Addy, and who Addy was?

DMS: Addy was born in a little town called Montrose, Pennsylvania, where her father bought furs from the local farmers. Her Uncle Max was there doing something, too, and then they moved to—I'm not sure exactly where—but they ended up in Oceanside [NY] when Oceanside was a crossroads and nothing more. Now it's a great big suburb. He had a pocketbook business for a while, and that didn't work. He was in leather goods for a while, and that didn't work. He ended up with another one of these cigar, cigarette, candystore, newspaper places. He sold toys at Christmas time. It had a little fountain with three stools, I think. That was Addy's father. His name was Hyman Bellinson.

Addy has an older sister, Vivian, and a younger sister, Roslyn. So she was the middle of three sisters. Addy had very happy memories of Uncle Max taking them out on a sled with horses, and riding a horse—but not much in the way of riding.

Addy went to Oceanside High School and got a Regent's Fellowship to Cornell. A Regent's Fellowship was one of the real plums in New York State. So she was able to go to the arts college, free. She was very smart. She got good grades and all the rest of it.

She would tell funny little stories—but not very often—about how she and her friend, June Balvin, would steal boys' bicycles, and how the boys would chase them, but they always got away from the boys and they'd hide the bikes, and the boys could never find them—and things like that.

Otherwise, she had a kind of quiet, respectable life. When the hell did I meet Addy? It must've been in the sophomore or junior year. I sort of rattled around Cornell. I didn't know what the hell I was doing or why I was doing it. I was into bacteriology. And someplace along the line—whether it was in the American Student Union, or something; I don't know—but Addy was mixed up with the Zionist crew. And the Zionist crew were really very nice and bright, able—they really were alive, those people. One of them was Laurence Halperin; he's a major landscape architect up here in the San Francisco area. And David Furman, who was killed in an airplane training accident early in the war. Itzhak Hamlin and Igor Rudenko—a whole bunch of those people. They were a really good lot. They used to folk dance and things like that. I don't know how the hell I met Addy.

Anyway, she took Russian history from [Philip Edward] Mosely, and for some reason I decided to sit in on Russian history to see what it was like. I think that's where it began. So I began to hang around, call her up.

RH: Were you sitting in on Russian history because of your communist background?

DMS: I don't remember whether it was because of that or because she was taking it and I wanted to follow her. I sat in on it. Fortunately, I didn't register, so it was not a disaster. She got an A, as usual. Philip Mosely was a very eminent Russian historian. She also opened various things to me; she took government courses, she took various things while I was doing rural sociology—and boy was that a bore. Even the ordinary sociology.

One thing led to another, and we began hanging out together. She was living in the Balch dorms, and each of the dorms had a chaperon. When I went to call on her, I had to get looked over by the chaperon before she was allowed to go out with me. I conned the chaperon, and the chaperon thought I was a very nice young man. So I remember her as a very nice lady, and I had to sit down in the sitting room and talk to her: what was I doing, and where did I come from, and what were my mother and father like, and so on. So she allowed Addy to go out with me, but Addy had to be in by ten every night, eleven on Saturdays.

RH: The fact that you were Jewish and Addy was Jewish: in those days would you expect to date a Jewish girl if you were a Jewish boy? Was that an issue?

DMS: It was an issue in this sense: and that was that there was a good deal of good, plain, open, honest-to-God, unequivocal anti-Semitism at Cornell. I worked in a Jewish fraternity house, in the kitchen; I washed dishes and waited tables. I worked in other fraternity houses, but the Jewish one was just as bad as all the rest of them. I don't know—there were some odd people like Ward and Ruth [Goodenough] who didn't care whether we were Jews or not, and various other people like that. And then, I was fairly active in the American Student Union. And the American Student Union got involved, for example, in a local strike, the waitresses went out in a bunch of restaurants downtown, and we all rallied round and picketed and did things like that. And carloads of us went down when there were some strikes in the coal mines. From Ithaca down to the Scranton area was a couple, three hours driving, at the most. And we would go down there and help support them. And then, when Czechoslovakia was invaded, I can remember going down—I don't remember where the hell we went—carloads of us went to protest. We were protesting like mad. But I don't know who we were protesting to.

So there was a lot of that, and Addy and I went together often, but not always. I, of course, from my communist background, was very unsympathetic to Zionist things. But circumstances were such that it didn't seem worth fighting about. I don't think all the Zionist guys took to me all that wildly, but they tolerated me. And none of them were interested in Addy, which was also a comfort.

One of the nice things about being friends with Addy was that her father had this cigarette, cigar, newspaper store, so she'd get these packages from home. I smoked Chesterfields! And, of course, she had cigarettes galore. They'd send her three or four cartons of cigarettes and two salamis! That would be the package.

RH: Am I right that I can remember Addy smoking at Chicago?

DMS: She smoked—I would have said she smoked the day after she died [November 10, 1982], but actually, she quit smoking two or three weeks before she died. She smoked right up to the end, without any obvious effects. She tried to quit a couple of times, but she couldn't.

RH: Were either of your parents upset at your getting married?

DMS: They were all upset. Her older sister gave her a very hard time: "It was irresponsible, and it was the wrong thing to do." But she and her older sister were always at very, very strong swords' points. They never really liked each other, never got along. Yet, they had this very strong family feeling: no matter how much they hated each other, they were still sisters.

But we both agreed very early, almost from the outset, that we could never work in New York, because if we worked in New York, she'd be exposed to my family, and my mother was absolutely impossible. See, I was off on Yap, and Addy was working in New York, and my mother and father would ask Addy to come over and have dinner with them. So she'd have to go from time to time. All they wanted to do was: "Tell us about our son, David. We don't care about you. What is he writing to you and what is he doing?" They drove her nuts.

And my father, too, could be very difficult. He knew how to get things wholesale. He knew what she looked good in. So he would take her around from one dress concern to another and buy her clothes she didn't want. What the hell was she supposed to do with them? If she didn't ever wear them, it was an insult. So she wore them when she visited them. But she had a terrible time while I was on Yap, for that reason.

We both loved New York. We wanted to live in New York. We would have done anything to be able to. But we both agreed that between her family and my family, it was impossible. So we avoided New York at all costs. And that's the way it was to the very end.

RH: You've just described Addy as being very bright and talented. It seems to me that an undercurrent of this discussion has been the idea that in those days the family roles forced a woman to abandon—

DMS: —oh, didn't I tell you the story about her graduate school?

RH: I don't think so.

DMS: This is a standard story. I've told it a hundred times to hundreds of people. We were pretty much—what do you call it?—an item by senior year. We were going together; it was obvious. We were sleeping together, more or less, insofar as you could sleep together; it was a little awkward. I didn't have a car. I had a crumby apartment with a guy named Charlie Cevick, I think. It was a horrible apartment. She would barely set foot in it, it was so awful. A basement apartment.

Anyway. So, what was I going to do after school? What was she going to do after school? Well, she wanted by then to do Chinese history. Her senior professor was a man named Knight Biggerstaff, whom she thought highly of, up to a point. So she started with her advisor, who was Knight Biggerstaff, and she said she wanted to do postgraduate work in Chinese history. So he sat her down and gave her a simple story: in the first place, Cornell University did not admit women to graduate school in history. Secondly, he didn't know of any other really good universities that did admit women to graduate school. Thirdly, although she might possibly get into a place like Columbia, or one or two others—not many—the fact that she was Jewish made it almost impossible either to be admitted, and certainly not to get anywhere in Chinese history; because Chinese history was a very specialized area, etc., etc.

So she talked to Biggerstaff, she talked to other people in the history department, she talked to people at Columbia, she talked to people all around. And they simply convinced her that there was absolutely no way she could do it. So we talked this over, and she simply gave up. She turned around and she said, okay, she'll put me through graduate school. And that's what happened. We stayed there after we graduated, and I stayed as a first-year graduate student at Cornell, and got the M.A., and she worked as a typist in the Hillel office.

RH: And supported you?

DMS: And she supported me, yes.

RH: And when you went to Yale, I guess she just continued to work.

DMS: I went to Yale, she continued to work. Then, of course, the war broke out and we both moved to Washington. And she got a job in civil service, where she was very successful and very good. And then again, she followed me out, first, to Camp Roberts, which is just down the road [from Santa Cruz], and then to Fort Lewis. Both places, she had very senior, very responsible positions.

RH: How much of a theme was this in your life, her life—or was it just done? Is that what women did?

DMS: Well, it was just done. But I suppose there's something else or, at least, I think there is something else. There are some people who, I'm quite sure—and I know—will sit down and talk things out to the last, gruesome detail. She and I never did. She would make an issue of this or that, we would settle it quickly. She would make a point about this or that, we would settle it quickly. We didn't drag old resentments around. We didn't say . . .

For example, when I made the decision to move from Berkeley to Chicago, she complained that I had not really talked it over extensively enough with her—that I should have talked it over in greater detail before I made the decision. And certainly before I committed myself by telling Fred Eggan I'd come. So, she had a complaint in the sense that major decisions like that should've been discussed, and I agreed that they should've been discussed. But her argument was, and I think it was correct, that I tended not to give her a reasonable chance to make any case. Is there a better way to put it?

RH: That's clear.

DMS: She felt that I really forced the decisions my way. And I, of course, said, "Me, with my halo looking the way it's looking? Oh, no! I am sure I would never have made you do anything you didn't want to do." But, yeah, I'm afraid I did, many times; because I took over, I think, my father's sort of attitude, and that is that men make decisions about work and money and industry and stuff like that.

On money, however, she handled all the finances. I couldn't. I mean, I couldn't balance a checkbook; still don't. Things like that. But "career decisions," I felt that I should make. And I should've talked them over, and I didn't. So she was fairly clear about resenting a lot of those things.

RH: But the role of being a wife and mother—apparently that was just accepted, and she didn't express a lot of resentment about that.

DMS: She didn't express resentment about it in a way like she'd have screaming fits or something. Looking back on it, in many ways you can say she didn't have a lot of courage and she wasn't a big fighter. And looking back on it in other ways, I took advantage of that and it was true. I don't know what else to say.

Four

Surveying the Army

I met Jules Henry when he was working for the Division of Program Surveys in the U.S. Department of Agriculture.[1]

The Division of Program Surveys was run by Rensis Likert and eventually became the University of Michigan Survey Research Center. But at the time it was a sort of free-floating agency in the U.S. government (attached to the Department of Agriculture) which did survey research, public opinion surveys, but was the first to do systematically open-ended surveys (not the "good bad indifferent" kind). Henry, Kai [Katharine] Luomala, Angus Campbell (a Herskovits student who did a thesis on an island in the Carribean), and a variety of other anthropologists and sociologists and psychologists along with some very fine statisticians (if that is not an oxymoron) really pioneered survey work there. Jules was a "study director." That was a senior post, but Likert, Campbell, and others were the top echelon. I was hired as a coder but soon became a "field man"—that is, I did scouting trips and interviews and stuff like that.

My closest association with Jules was on a field trip doing a study of rumors in New Brunswick, New Jersey, near Fort Dix, New Jersey, I believe, directed by John Riley. Riley was in charge, Jules his top aide, and I was low on the pole.

When I quit anthropology forever, Geoffrey Gorer told me to look up Margaret Mead when I went to Washington to work for Program Surveys. I did. She said that Jules was working for Program Surveys, too, and I should look him up. I don't think I did anything about it. So it was really in 1943 (after I had been there most of a year) that I found myself in the field with Jules. Studying rumors. And waiting for John Riley to figure out which way was up.

So I was not very tactful about telling Riley that he didn't know his ass from his elbow and that we should get going. Finally, one day Jules took me firmly by the collar and told me in such clear and unambiguous terms that if I didn't shut up and do what I was told I would find my-self kicked the hell out of the study and probably fired when I got back to Washington. It was probably the first time anybody had ever been that direct, clear, unambiguous, and helpful to me when I was being my usual rebellious, antiauthority self. I never lost the respect and gratitude I had for Jules, although he could be a difficult person to speak with or be with at times. Of course, the study never got off the ground, and we all went home and were distributed onto different studies thereafter. Rumors were, and are, very hard to study.

RH: Do you want to talk about the army?

DMS: Sure. I got drafted while I was in Washington. I was drafted at Fort Lee, Virginia.

Didn't I tell you about how they pulled five of us out, and put us in a barracks, and made us wait three or four days, put us on a train—and I called Addy up from Chicago, said, "I'm going west," and she said, "Well, let me know when you get there"? Then we got to Oakland, got off, and transferred to another train; and nobody would tell us where we were going. We finally ended up here, in Watsonville, where there was a Coast Artillery training station. And that was training for harbor defense. And how we got up the next morning, and how we were welcomed by the camp commander, and the supply sergeant brought out a tripod and transit, put them in front of the five of us—because they had put in a special request for surveyers. Harbor defense, almost all artillery, works on the basis of four guns in a battery, and they're lined up so that you triangulate right onto a target. But you have to be able to survey the line first.

RH: Why did they pick you guys?

DMS: Well, because, when I was inducted in the army they pulled me out as—I was doing public opinion surveying—they put my occupation down as surveyor. I told them I couldn't do this stuff, and they said, well, you'll just have to go with all the rest of them and learn it. So I learned how to do that. It depended on trigonometry and geometry, but much of what I learned I've since forgot. But they never did use us be-cause harbor defense collapsed. The Japanese were obviously not going to land on these shores, so we were all picked up and then driven down to Camp Roberts, which is a little further south here. That's first how I got to this Monterey Bay area, because Watsonville is just below Santa Cruz. We used to sit there on the shoreline and shoot at a target being towed from Santa Cruz to Monterey on Monday and Wednesday and Friday, and back from Monterey to Santa Cruz on Tuesday, Thursday, and Saturday.

RH: Is that where you spent all your time in the army?

DMS: No. That was Camp McQuaid. And from there to Camp Roberts. But in Camp Roberts they determined I was "unfit" for overseas service. So I was thrown into a headquarters detachment, with a large collection of homosexuals and communists and other people they didn't trust.

RH: Why did they determine you were unfit?

DMS: Why? Because I had hemorrhoids and refused to have them surgically removed, and that was another story.

I had had hemorrhoids for some time, and one day on a hike they kind of blew up and got very infected and swollen. I couldn't walk, and they were painful. I was put in the hospital. And at a certain point a doctor came in with a gurney and said, "Get on that gurney, we're going to remove your hemorrhoids," and I said, "The hell you are." So he went away and brought a captain and said, "I order you to come into the operating room," and I said, "Come on, don't be silly. Surgically removing hemorrhoids won't help. They'll be back as fast as you cut them out. I don't want to do it." So he said, "You're just trying to evade combat duty." And I said, "No, you send me the way I am, I'll go." So he stamped up and down and said, "You'll be subject to court martial." Then they brought in a colonel and he gave me the same routine again. But I was pretty pigheaded. I said no. So then the guy with the gurney went away, and he brought me back all my clothes and said, "Get dressed and get the hell out of there before they really get angry with you."

RH: Why did you refuse?

DMS: Because everybody said surgery was not really effective. It made more trouble.

RH: So this was not Schneider being rebellious?

DMS: That's the way it was interpreted. My rationale was that it was an improper medical procedure, it was not really effective.

RH: Is this where you got the idea for the paper on the sick role?

DMS: Well, I had been in three basic trainings in Camp McQuaid and two basic trainings in Camp Roberts—I think it was five. So, following those basic trainings around and around, I was fairly well used to people on sick call. I was on sick call. When I went into the army, Geoffrey Gorer said, "Well, here's an ideal opportunity. You can be an anthropologist. Keep notes and observe." So I observed and kept notes. I still have the notes.

RH: Are they good notes?

DMS: I think so. For example, there was a segment of the army. It was run by Sam Stouffer and Leonard Cottrell, and it had Goodenough on its staff. And they used to write around to different people they knew and ask them—I don't know what the hell it was called—but anyway, I wrote them a long series of papers. And at one point they published a bunch of volumes—the first volume, which was *The American Soldier*— and there I saw my paper appearing verbatim.[2] It was described as "one of our informants" said, quote, and on and on and on it went. It was my work.

RH: Isn't that unethical?

DMS: I thought so. Especially since they quoted me verbatim without giving my name. But, you know, I hit upon this when I was a graduate student at Harvard. And at that point, I didn't care—what the hell! Even now I don't much care.

I wrote a second paper. It was published while I was in the army. It was "The Culture of the Army Clerk." And that was based on all my experience in the headquarters detachment. It was interesting, too. I enjoyed that. They had me entering things on the service records of soldiers—when they got their shots and stuff like that. And God knows how many poor soldiers had to get a second batch of shots because they couldn't read my handwriting. But the headquarters detachment didn't care.

I got into slight but not very serious trouble over that, because there was some rule that you weren't supposed to publish anything without a clearance from the commanding officer. And I never got a clearance from my commanding officer. So, even though it was published while I was in the army . . . Oh, they called me in and said, you're not supposed to have done that, and I said, oh, I'm sorry, I didn't know. And they said, go away and never sin again, and I went away.

RH: When you were writing things and publishing them, even though you had told Murdock that you had quit anthropology forever, you must have still—

DMS: —oh yeah, I was still caught. I was still hooked. And so, when the chance to go to Harvard came, I took it.

RH: What was motivating you to write those papers?

DMS: Well, Geoffrey Gorer, and my interest, presumably, in doing anthropological fieldwork. No, I wanted to be an anthropologist. I just didn't want to be one through Murdock, or get attached to him, or follow his sort of anthropology.

You know, one of the funny things was that goofing off was an important part of the army—learning how to work without appearing that you're not really working. Learning how to be on the job and not work. It was important. So that I could sit in that headquarters detachment, presumably entering things in service records, and look busy—that's very important.

RH: You mean, you were doing your own work?

DMS: No, no, I was mostly goofing off. Sitting there doing nothing and watching other people. And then I was left in charge of the office one day, and a call came through on the teletype saying that they wanted experienced or inexperienced social scientists to help do psychotherapy at Madigan General Hospital. So I sent my name in, and when my name came up and I was transferred, the officer wanted to know how the hell they had gotten my name. And they looked it up and found I had done that. They said, you're not supposed to do that. You didn't have the authority to send your name in. I said, I know. They couldn't do anything about it. It was easier to let me go than to make a fuss.

I got to do psychotherapy. Me and an obstetrician were teamed up to do narcosynthesis; they were giving Pentothal shots. Well, I went to Madigan General Hospital at Fort Lewis, and that was set up specifically for a lot of people who had been caught in the Battle of the Bulge. And they were supposed to be on their way out. We were getting section eights—you know, they're supposed to repair the psyches.

RH: These were people suffering from battle fatigue?

DMS: That's right. And the idea was if they could externalize it through narcosynthesis—

RH: —what's narcosynthesis?

DMS: Well, you give them Pentothal shots, and they often simply talk without remembering what they've said. And then they can reexperience a lot of traumatic material without it hurting them that much, it was said. So me and this obstetrician got assigned to work together, and I worked with him. I don't think anybody got better.

RH: So you were giving people shots and then listening to what they said?

DMS: No, he was giving them the shots. He was the doctor. He was really responsible. But what the hell did he know? He's a goddamn obstetrician.

RH: Were you taking notes on what these people were saying?

DMS: Well, presumably taking notes, and remembering, and talking to them later about it. Things like that. And then I ran group therapy, and that was another charade. We sat around telling stories.

RH: You ran group therapy for soldiers suffering from shell shock?

DMS: Yeah, I was suffering with other kinds of shock.

RH: So, this must have connected to your interest in culture and personality?

DMS: Well, it was in line with my interest in culture and personality. By that time Addy had come out to live with me, and she was with me at Camp Roberts, and she went with me up to Fort Lewis. And she could have stayed in the army with a very good job, but for various reasons I insisted that we get out and go home.

RH: She started working for the army?

DMS: Oh yeah, she was working in the ordnance department, putting together large convoys of trucks.

RH: She was a civilian employee?

DMS: Exactly. She had a good job. It paid well. She had a very good civil service rating, and all that stuff. And she did better at it at Fort Lewis, too.

RH: But you insisted on going back to Washington. You didn't want to stay in the army any longer than you had to, right?

DMS: Yes, exactly, I wanted to get out.

RH: But she could understand that?

DMS: Well, she did understand it, but she had a very good job, and I couldn't promise anything except that we'd go back to Washington and be part of Program Surveys and I would go back to college.

RH: Could she not transfer her civil service work back to Washington?
DMS: Not really. She was working by that time in personnel.

So what else? I met some nice friends in the army whom I still have. I met Lionel Friedman. He got a Ph.D. from Harvard about the same time I did. It was on the whole, for me, a great educational experience. I found I could get along with a lot more people than I thought. And that a great deal of my rebelliousness and peculiarity didn't matter much.

Five

An Education in Anthropology

DMS: Ward Goodenough and I were good friends starting at Cornell. Ward was in Old Icelandic. I was still wrestling mightily with bacteriology. Then when I moved into anthropology with Sharp, Ward did too. Ward had a girlfriend, Ruth Brigette Agnes Gallagher, whom he married and who's now Ruth Brigette Agnes Gallagher Goodenough. I had a friend, Adeline Bellinson, and Ward and Ruth and Addy and I and Joy Agrons and a couple of people on and off were part of a little clique together.

Anyway, Ward went to Yale immediately, but I stayed at Cornell one year to get an M.A. Laurie Sharp very kindly and generously gave me his collection of Yir Yorent dreams to work on, as an M.A. thesis. I didn't know anything else. I'd heard of Freud, and I read it, didn't understand it, and rejected it. So I did a mechanical—anyway, the whole point is that Ward went on to Yale, and Ward became Pete Murdock's white-haired boy.

Now, the straightforward, open, obvious way of interpreting it is that Ward was good. And he is good. He was smart, and Pete recognized it and he rewarded it. The negative, nasty, uncouth, ungenerous way of looking at it is that Ward was old New England, and that's what Pete liked. Not only was he old New England, but Ward's father was an eminent, very important professor of religious studies there. He was the world's leading authority on Josephus. He wrote a long series of things on symbols in Hellenic and Judaic writings. So whether Pete cottoned to Ward simply because he was old New England—you see, I thought Pete cottoned to Clellan Ford because he was old New England, and I thought he cottoned to Johnnie Whiting because he was old New England. But, you know, Johnnie Whiting had talent, but Clellan Ford had nothing.

But Ward and I remained friends, although intellectually we are poles apart. Ward tends to follow a Murdock and Malinowski line fairly closely, whereas I go wildly opposite. When I did the *Critique of Kinship* book, I sent him the chapters—I never sent anyone else the chapters—I did on him. And he got so disturbed, he flew to Chicago and stayed a couple of days and went over it line by line, trying to explain to me what he really meant and what was right and where I'd gotten it wrong. I was in a terrible bind, 'cause I didn't think I'd gotten it wrong at all. I thought he was mainly attempting to get me to agree that he was right. But he kept saying that he was trying to get me to understand what he had to say. So that chapter, I thought, got very badly emasculated by my attempts to maintain warm and decent relations with an old friend rather than attack him.

RH: Is there any sense in which your intellectual opposition to Ward Goodenough could have grown out of your resentment at his being the fair-haired boy?

DMS: No, I don't think so, because I don't think I ever wanted to be fair-haired boy to Pete. I wanted to be, and was willing to be, fair-haired boy to Clyde Kluckhohn.

I told you how I got into Harvard, how Kluckhohn called and said that the D average was not a good thing, and how I had to be on probation for a year. So I was on probation for a year. I believe it was someplace in the middle of that year that I got to be ready to take my oral exams, having passed the written exam. So I went in to take the oral exam, which was scheduled in Emerson Hall. Kluckhohn was there. Ben Paul was there. I can't remember who else was there. There must've been two other people.

There was no formal chairmanship. They just started. They sat me down at the end of the table, and Kluckhohn started by asking a couple of questions that were the equivalent of "Tell us your name, rank and serial number," and "You do know what day of the week it is, and what year," and so forth—it was very simple. And then he started me in on the question of the role of—you know, I was into culture and personality at that time—started me in on the question of the relationship between biology and psychology. Were there inherent tempermental differences?

Were these group associated? Were there kinds of instinctual drives?—
and things like that.

I was fully prepared for that kind of question, because it was a very
important question, and still is, I'm sure, in many ways. So I immediately
unloaded the whole thing. I told him that to the best of my knowledge, and to the best of anybody else's knowledge, biology didn't have
a damn thing to do with psychology. That until they could establish
some kinds of relations between the biological and the psychological
that really amounted to something, that for all practical purposes we
should proceed as if there were no basic biological considerations. Drives
were unnecessary. It was unnecessary to postulate them. Tempermental
differences—oh, I knew there'd been a few studies of this and that, but,
you know, in the end they really hadn't amounted to much. They didn't
really prove very much.

Kluckhohn himself had been involved in a study in which Navajo infants were compared with American infants—the differences in activity,
in reflexes—there were some differences. But, you know, in the end,
what did they do? They had a couple of dozen kids or something, and it
didn't amount to anything.

So, I pressed the whole thing about the fact that, for all practical
purposes, we should just ignore biology. Kluckhohn was leaning over
and listening. And he's looking at me, and getting obviously more and
more upset. Finally, he leans over and says, "Do you really believe that,
David?"

And I said, "Well yes, Clyde, I really do believe that."

And he said, "Well, let's just go on and discuss this a few more minutes,
and see where it leads. Continue to make your case."

So I continued. I had thought about it a lot, and I developed it at some
length. Finally—I was still in the middle of talking—he turned around
so that he turned the whole chair, so that he was sitting more or less
sideways to me, with his back to me. He raised his hand and smote his
forehead—he had a very high forehead—and he said, waving his hand
imperiously, "Ben, you ask him some questions. I'm through."

That is all I remember about that oral exam, because at the end of it I
left, and I went back home, and I told Addy that we'd better start packing, because we were through. My friend Lionel Friedman was there, so

he and Addy took me out to dinner and the movies, and then made me agree that we could start packing in the morning. In the morning, I got Addy to start packing. We both started packing. We began getting everything together. I got hold of the people from whom we were renting the apartment and gave him a forwarding address and so on.

So I said, "I'm gonna go in this afternoon and tell Mrs. Sprague [a departmental secretary] what my forwarding address is. I'll be back in a few minutes, and then we can take off."

So I go in to Emerson Hall, and I'm climbing up the first flight of stairs, and I get to the second floor. At that moment Kluckhohn comes out of his office. He looks at me and glares, and says, "Com'ere." He sits me down, and oh!—did he give me a reaming. "I have never heard such stupidity in my whole life. I have never heard such an asinine position. Do you really mean to sit there and tell me that biology doesn't count?"

Finally I said, "Well, Clyde, the fact of the matter is, I really do believe that."

He said, "That's what I thought. If you hadn't given such a good, careful, systematic defense of that absurd position, you would never have set foot in this place again! Now get out of here! I don't want to see you again for at least a week, till I get over this."

I said, "What do you mean?"

He said, "Well, of course you passed. Don't worry about that. But God, don't give me any more of that crap!"

That was it. But I thought I was done. I was sure I was finished. But that was the kind of guy Clyde was.

RH: Did you call him "Clyde"?

DMS: Yes.

RH: What was your relationship to Kluckhohn like at that time, your first year in graduate school?

DMS: I don't know if it was the time—it was right after the war, the beginning of the social relations department; a lot of people had come back from the army—and though of course we knew that we had to be respectful, there was also a lot of straightforward first-naming. Clyde had parties at his house. He talked to us by first name. There was a lot of fun and joking and things like that. He was very much into having big

intellectual discussions with groups of people. I can remember standing out on the landing—he smoked like mad. You weren't supposed to
smoke in classrooms, and he had just given a lecture and he came out
for a smoke. A bunch of us gathered around, and we were talking about
James Joyce's *Ulysses* and what kind of a book it was. And then from
Ulysses, on to *Finnegans Wake.* Clyde could recite the opening page of
Finnegans Wake—something about the river. I'm not sure I remember it
exactly. But we had a helluva lot of fun talking to him that way. He was
a very open, very accessible, very warm, good guy. So it was all "Clyde"
and "Dave."

RH: During your oral exams, what was it like to be confronted by him
in that way? Did you panic?

DMS: It was when he smote his forehead and turned his back on me
that I knew something was wrong.

RH: Yet, you were able to go on.

DMS: I had made all the case I had to make. And I literally don't
remember what happened, because Ben must've asked me some questions. And not only do I not remember what happened after that, I still
can't remember who else was in the exam, and there must've been other
people.

RH: So it was a traumatic experience.

DMS: It was very traumatic, and I really thought that I had blown
it for good. I wasn't pulling in very much money, Addy didn't really
have a job there. We literally would've had to get out of the apartment
immediately.

RH: Why was your position so uncongenial to Kluckhohn?

DMS: He had written extensively about how culture bears on personality, but it always included a biological stratum, a social stratum, a
cultural stratum, and a psychological stratum.

RH: Did he get this from Parsons? Or did Parsons get it from him?

DMS: This was all part of the climate of opinion, the atmosphere. This
was what was going on at that time. And Parsons was that way, too, and
he and Parsons had talked extensively. It turned out that at that time—
I didn't know it, but at that time, Parsons and [Henry A.] Murray and
a few other people were having these weekly meetings developing Parsons's "general theory of social action." Clyde had written a number of

papers—copies of which I had—for those sessions. Henry Murray and Gordon Alport had written some stuff.

So, to suddenly just—I suppose it represents another one of my fundamental weaknesses, but I should have known that that was no way to ingratiate myself with him. 'Cause I knew perfectly well that he really *did* think that there were—he never said it in quite these terms, but, well, you know, there's a chronic problem with people who are gay. Are they born that way or are they made that way? Clyde was definitely gay. It was not widely known. I didn't even suspect it at the time. And so, in retrospect, this had all kinds of deep and well-embedded meanings for him. And to suddenly argue that it had no bearing at all—when that was one of his fundamental problems: Was this something that he couldn't help? But he was committed [to the position]. And he had a lot of troubles. I did learn he was gay by the time I left. Anyway, that was no way to ingratiate myself with him. I should've known better.

RH: If you didn't know he was gay, why should you have known?

DMS: No, no. I'm *now* thinking that, since he was gay, I can even further understand how he could've been deeply committed to the idea.

RH: But at that moment you wouldn't have known.

DMS: No, but I knew that intellectually he had committed himself, because I read his papers.

RH: What gave you the courage, at that time, to speak your mind?

DMS: It was not courage. It was stupidity.

RH: Are you sure that you're not being too hard on yourself?

DMS: Yes, because I've had this problem again and again. When I went into the emergency room in 1970 with a heart attack, everybody kept telling me how brave I was. The reason they all thought I was brave was that I was blasé, it didn't bother me. And the reason it didn't? I didn't know I was having a heart attack. So, in retrospect, yeah, I must've looked brave, but I was just being stupid again. I thought I was just sicker than hell and didn't know why.

RH: You responded to my question with an example from the realm of sickness and health. But if we talk about your intellectual temperament, why do you want to insist that you were stupid and should've known better? Is this a self-deprecating stance? You went in and made a good enough argument to pass the test. So what's stupid about that?

DMS: The presupposition is that intellectual argument is all that really counts. The fact of the matter is that life isn't run that way. It keeps not being run that way. And everybody knows it's not run that way. You're supposed to ingratiate yourself with your superiors. You're supposed to kiss a certain amount of ass, you're supposed to do things judiciously. There are ways of doing things that are more likely to succeed than others: you catch more flies with sugar than with vinegar!

RH: But you had a good relationship with Clyde Kluckhohn.

DMS: Good relationship!? Anybody in his right mind knows that good relationships have to be cultivated, preserved, kept up, kept warm, and not jeopardized.

RH: Okay, let's put it this way. Supposing you had been smart—you knew what Kluckhohn was after. Would you then have given an answer that you didn't believe?

DMS: You seem to be trying to make me say that I have some kind of intellectual integrity that will permit me to put my head in the oven and then be miraculously spared. But I'm arguing that mostly what I have is a kind of insensitivity to the practical ways of living a successful, happy, and rich life.

RH: Well, I don't know. We don't have to pursue this.

DMS: Well, you see, this also relates to my relations with Murdock. In many ways—and Bashkow was right to ask—I believe it is a not infrequent, faintly paranoid posture that people live better if they have something to fight against. So Bashkow asked if a lot of my motivation wasn't my antipathy to Murdock Which, of course, any good psychoanalyst could then trace back to an antipathy to my father. But you know, in fact, my relationship to my father was not antipathetic. I didn't really dislike him or hate him or anything else like that. So I don't think it can trace that way. Of course, a good Freudian will explain to you that even though I think I was not hostile, deep down, I was unconsciously hostile, because, in fact, he was indeed sleeping with my mother. Yes? What other reason could there be, yes?

So, who knows?

RH: We should talk about Parsons. How did you come to meet him, and what was he doing, and what was his influence on you?

DMS: When I first reached Harvard, I didn't know him, didn't know his name, didn't know anything about him. Somebody said, Why don't you take Talcott Parsons's course on the social structure of the United States? It was basically an American society course. And I did, and it was very good. Or at least I found it very good. You know, you did it in the usual social system way: economics and psychological stuff, and then major institutions—kinship and family, religion, things like that.

RH: What was it like for an anthropologist at that time to be thinking seriously about America?

DMS: At that time, through Margaret Mead and a number of others, I had caught the bug: that interdisciplinary stuff was good. I was, at that time, "interested in" culture and personality. So I fancied myself fairly up on matters psychological, largely psychoanalytic.

RH: And that interest goes back to Sharp at Cornell, right?

DMS: That's right, but the psychoanalytic angle came largely through Geoffrey Gorer. So one of the attractions of Harvard was that it was social relations, interdisciplinary. That's how I started with Parsons.

Another thing was that Parsons was chairman of the department of social relations at that time. So any incoming student would necessarily go to say hello—you know, you paid a courtesy call. I already told you that I got to Harvard through Margaret Mead, who told me to go see Clyde Kluckhohn and tell him that I was one of the credits that she had. So the fact that Kluckhohn was there, and that Kluckhohn was culture and personality, and all that—and at that point, I was making it my business to show everybody that I really was a good student, and promising, and so on. I had already written a number of papers, largely about the army. And I gave my paper—which I originally called "The Cultural Dynamics of Physical Disability in Army Basic Training"—to Kluckhohn. He liked it very much, but urged me to change the title to "The Social Dynamics" because I wasn't really dealing with culture, he thought. I was very agreeable to doing what I was asked to do, so I changed the title. Later, and even now, I think, he was absolutely right, and I should've changed the title. It was okay.

Anyway, I gave that paper to Parsons, and Parsons liked it very much because that was the first time anybody had invented the concept of the sick role as a socially patterned way of behaving—to be sick—and showed many of its ramifications. And he just simply adopted the idea

of the sick role, without crediting me with it.[1] But that was all right—
he had probably had some idea like it himself. And besides, for me as a
young student it was good to be recognized. He did like the paper very
much, and so I knew I stood in very well with him.

There were a number of interesting things about Parsons. You'd go
during his office hours to consult him, and you would sit and listen
to another lecture. It was the source of considerable jokes among the
graduate students, that if you ever got a word in edgewise, it was a mistake, or he was not paying attention. You'd ask him a question, and he
would give you a lecture on the subject. And then you were supposed to
get up and get out.

The other thing about Parsons was that everybody said his writing
was terrible. You couldn't understand—it was always Germanic, things
like that. But when he lectured, when he spoke, it was very clear. I
found him very clear. And also, the ideas—if I found the ideas clear,
they must've been fairly simple—but I liked him a great deal because I
thought he was very clear. And he seemed to be raising and answering
a host of questions which I had only thought about vaguely, but which
were clearly ones that I wanted to be concerned with.

RH: Do you remember the issues that he was concerned with?

DMS: Well, motivation, for example—you see, the old position used
to be, "Why do they do things like that?"—"That's their culture." Well,
what the hell, that doesn't mean much. But Parsons was trying to integrate the whole psychological business of motivation with the social
business of "That's their society" and "That's their culture." And many
of his answers were extremely good and became the "yellow book" in
which he and Shils had a very long paper, which became a sort of basic
and general theory of social science.[2] That was a very good, clear, and
forthright statement. Later on, Shils and Parsons sort of fell out, and
Shils claimed that Parsons was not doing the theory as Shils wanted
him to do it, and Parsons said nothing. But Shils was a very funny guy,
anyway.

So my attraction was: it was interdisciplinary, it did integrate motivation and psychology in a way I understood, and could understand,
and thought was very good and productive. But I was gradually, at that
point, moving away from the psychology and moving toward the social
systems stuff and the culture stuff, rather than motivation stuff.

RH: But the point about taking the course in American culture was that it was simply a way to take a course with Talcott Parsons?

DMS: It was a way to take a course with Talcott Parsons.

RH: And it doesn't really prefigure your interest in American kinship?

DMS: No, but you see, very early, Margaret Mead had come to Cornell and given a talk. And she had made the point—in either the talk or in one of the classes she came to that I heard her; I heard her two or three times that time at Cornell—that anthropology was just as concerned with American culture as it was with "primitive tribes." And that, I thought, was very important. And I still do. So that taking a course in American culture from Talcott Parsons was both a good way of hearing what people had to say about American culture, American society, and a good way for me to continue my interest in applying anthropology broadly.

RH: Would you say that Mead's position was exceptional at the time?

DMS: Yes, Mead's position was exceptional at the time. At the time, I think, the general sense was that anthropology studied the evolution and development of human beings, including the evolution and development of their societies; but anthropology was largely concerned with other societies, small-scale societies, primitive societies, while sociology dealt with big ones. Of course, they left out the whole Muslim area— but that's all right. And, you see, this was one of [Robert] Redfield's big things, that anthropology should be able to do major civilizations like India. He wanted to show that it could. And I think he did, to some extent.

One of the big things that Parsons, Kroeber, and Kluckhohn were doing at the time was worrying about who was in charge of which domain. And that's the famous deal that Parsons and Kroeber made. You see, Kroeber and Kluckhohn had already put together a great compendium of stuff on culture, the 1952 Peabody monograph on culture.[3] There they had come up with the notion that culture was patterns of and patterns for behavior. And, if I understand him correctly, and I think I do, Parsons didn't completely agree with it. It was not patterns *of*, nor was it simply patterns *for*. Those were norms. Parsons was much more concerned with keeping culture confined to the symbolic and meaningful aspects, as major elements in the motivation of actors.

RH: Right, so that norms are at another level, where meaning gets translated into patterns for behavior.

DMS: Exactly. I bought into that very heavily.

RH: Do you remember why? Why would that be attractive to you?

DMS: Well, at least because it's right. What shall I say?—I had indigestion at the time, and so was moved to do that, or I was feeling rebellious, or something? But you see, I had a kind of implicit disagreement with Kluckhohn, because Kluckhohn tended to be very imperialistic. Anthropology controlled everything! Hence, you see, his cliché about patterns of and for behavior. It was both normative patterns and what people did do—practice, in a sense. And I kept thinking that practice was the object—I mean, that's what you had to explain. The question was, how do you explain it?

You see, Parsons was a "neopositivist," and I was a positivist, or a neopositivist, at that time. Except that I didn't know what I was—it was like being able to talk prose. So he was able to fill in all those gaps about what we were doing, and why we were doing it, and how we were doing it. And that also was very useful for me.

RH: It sounds like your dissatisfaction with Kluckhohn's model is that it was too simple. You wanted a more rigorous scientific explanation.

DMS: It was too simple, it was too all-embracingly simple. Culture explained everything.

RH: Why did the all-embracing quality bother you? Was this simply a revolt against arrogance?

DMS: No, because it simply was not an adequate explanation.

RH: Okay, real positivism, then. You were a positivist, you wanted an adequate explanation.

DMS: Yes. So I was very much taken with Parsons. But I wasn't the only one. A large number of the graduate students were, too, and there was a sense that Kluckhohn was competing with Parsons and that if you took sides you were in trouble. Or, at least, I thought so. I was very careful never to really align myself in any simple way with Parsons, but stayed "allied" and loyal to Kluckhohn. And that was okay, that worked out pretty well. But later Kluckhohn died, you know, in 1960. And I felt a great debt to Parsons. And so, when he retired, and he was sort of aimless and wandering around, I got him a visiting appointment at

Chicago and taught a seminar with him, which was a lot of fun and also very useful.

RH: Go back a minute. You mentioned the great agreement between Kroeber and Parsons. What was that?

DMS: That was the paper they published in, I think, the *American Sociological Review,* in which they divided up culture, and gave that to anthropology, and social systems, and gave that to sociology. And motivation went to psychology, and so on.[4]

RH: That sounds like an agreement to divide up institutional turf, as much as it's theoretical.

DMS: That's true. But you had to have some rationale for dividing up institutional turf, so the rationale was very important.

RH: And the scientific rationale was what you've just stated: that Parsons's model was more adequate than Kluckhohn's, in your opinion.

DMS: Yes, I thought so. And apparently Kroeber did at that point, too. You see, Parsons came to that fairly easily, because Parsons was very importantly and significantly influenced by Weber and Durkheim. And both of them very strongly emphasized the moral and meaningful aspects of action as very important determinants of action.

RH: How does this differ from the anthropological tradition out of which Kluckhohn comes? Where is Kluckhohn coming from?

DMS: Kluckhohn should have gone along with it easily, but he was caught in the institutional problems. That is, institutionally, there had always been a low-grade, low-level war between sociology and anthropology, with sociology being heavily Germanic and heavily statistical. So he was always allied with the people at Peabody and the people at Yale—you know, who did "anthropology"—really good, hard, field accounts of small, primitive societies. I think his institutional loyalties kept him from going along.

RH: Where was Kluckhohn trained?

DMS: Gee, I should know. I think he was trained partly at Harvard.[5]

RH: Do you have a sense of how Kluckhohn's anthropology was related to Ruth Benedict's, or to the Boasian tradition?

DMS: Kluckhohn was very close to the Boasian tradition, and he was very much a disciple of Sapir, and very much related to Ruth Benedict. Very close to Margaret Mead, also.

RH: What's the specific relationship?

DMS: Kluckhohn went to Yale to work with Sapir when Sapir was at Yale.

RH: But what did he learn from Sapir? If we read Kluckhohn, where do we find Sapir?

DMS: Patterning, configuration, and, again, the kind of meaningful stuff that Sapir was concerned with.

RH: But again—there shouldn't be much of a conceptual difference between Boasian anthropology and what Parsons was trying to do.

DMS: Oh, absolutely, you're right. There should not be any real difference.

RH: And some of it had to do with institutional—

DMS: —institutional loyalties, yes. And disciplinary loyalties. And it also had to do with the very large anti-intellectual and anti-European sentiment in America.

RH: This becomes complicated, because if I think of your anthropology, it's easy for me to link it to Ruth Benedict. And yet you go more through Parsons. I know that you've acknowledged Ruth Benedict in your work, but it's funny that you should have hit on it by way of Parsons rather than getting it right from Kluckhohn.

DMS: I had hit on Ruth Benedict early, before I went to Harvard, at Cornell. Ruth Benedict and Margaret Mead and Sapir were held up as real models. They *were* real models for me. When I got to Harvard, it was confirmed in a sense, because there was now a place in a wider scheme of things where they fitted exactly. You see, they fitted into the Parsonian scheme by being concerned with patterning, with values, with the cultural and meaningful orientations and so forth.

RH: So that Parsons somehow provides a more legitimate place for these guys.

DMS: Especially if you're a neopositivist.

RH: So there must have been others who weren't neopositivists who would have had no use for Parsons's grand design.

DMS: Absolutely, quite a few of them. [Samuel Andrew] Stouffer, for instance: if Kluckhohn was an imperialist and wanted culture to explain everything, Stouffer tended to want statistics to explain everything. This is the way it was, and this is the way it was going. Stouffer couldn't account for change in any way. You see, one of the big criticisms of Parsons was that he couldn't deal with change—which wasn't entirely true, but it's okay.

RH: If we think about what leads up to Chicago anthropology in the 1960s and '70s, the refiguration of cultural anthropology, it doesn't come directly out of Benedict and Sapir and the Boasians. It comes via Parsons and Harvard. I don't understand why it had to make that detour.

DMS: Yes, it appears to make a detour, in a sense. But it was not really a detour. Because, you see, Parsons's inspiration was Pareto, Weber, and Durkheim. And the Boasian material had a very similar kind of inspiration from Europe.

RH: Yes, Weber and Boas came from the same place.

DMS: Exactly. So it kind of came together there, rather than coming through Parsons, and around. See, the Boasian stuff was also very clearly hooked to that early Weberian and Durkheimian tendency, which exhibited itself primarily through Benedict, in the notion of configuration; and also, you see, Kroeber was of that European intellectual school, too.

RH: Is it fair to say that the Boasian paradigm had begun to dissipate by the 1950s, was under attack from all kinds of scientistic stuff, Radcliffe-Brown, the British functionalists; and that Parsons provides a new authoritatively legitimate site for it to begin again?

DMS: Yes, that there was much of merit in it, and a lot that should and could be saved.

RH: And Parsons provides the place for that to happen.

DMS: A place, and a way of doing it. This is where it comes in, and this is how it says something significant about—you see, it was all bound up with taking a specific kind of problem: How can you explain why people do what they do? It was the problem of explaining social action. And in that sense, the whole notion of culture was transformed, I think, from a kind of vague, general, all-inclusive, including-the-kitchen-sink notion—you know, what people do, what people think, what people act, their representations and everything else—all of that stuff, which generally included a great deal of social action.

RH: So, you have a positivist—the functionalist—attack on the Boasians. Parsons can succeed because it's a positivist assimilation of the Boasians.

DMS: It's a positivist assimilation, and it also was very definitely functionalist. But it was oriented to the specific problem of social action. He didn't try to explain why they think the way they do; he didn't try to explain their history or anything else—

RH: —the question was, why did they act—

DMS: —why did they act that way, yes.

RH: So that Parsons represents the science of the postwar period, but it's an approach that allows you to include—

DMS: —that's right. Now, the really interesting thing is, why did it go out of fashion so quickly? But it's beginning to come back now. People are rediscovering Parsons.

Six

Fieldwork on Yap

DMS: I was a student at Harvard University in 1946. I had been there for a few months when the word went around that there was a possibility of field money through Peabody Museum and Joe Brew. Actually, it was Donald Scott. Joe Brew wasn't director of the Peabody Museum yet. I talked briefly to Clyde Kluckhohn, and he said, yeah, there is money.

I had always wanted to do fieldwork in Africa. However, the jingle of coins attracted my attention.

RH: Why had you always wanted to do fieldwork in Africa?

DMS: I have no idea. All I say is that when I was in school, I did an essay on Africa for some class, which consisted in cutting pictures out of the *National Geographic* magazine, and pasting them on sheets of paper, and either stapling them together or something—I don't know—

RH: We're talking about the school in Connecticut?

DMS: Yeah.

RH: Bare-breasted women and all?

DMS: I think that may very well have played a role in it—"Yes," he said, "very shrewd interviewer here!" No, the men did not attract me at that point—nor since, but that's okay.

My heart was not absolutely set. I'd read some African ethnography, but not much. The idea of getting field money was very important.

RH: Since you'd studied with Sharp, had Australia never been mooted?

DMS: Yeah, but that, again, at that point—you know, I'd been in the army for two years, I was now out of the army, married to Addy, and the career was opening up. I was now "career-oriented" like mad, and the first step in the career was to do fieldwork. I didn't want to go to Africa all that badly.

Anyway, so I had to deal with Carlton Coon and Douglas Oliver. Doug Oliver and Coon were in charge of putting together the team to go to Yap. Bashkow has a lot of the detail on this stuff—has it right. But basically, Murdock gave out assignments to the various universities that were part of the Coordinated Investigation of Micronesian Anthropology, and Harvard got the Yap assignment. And I don't remember whether it was Harvard who specified that it had to be a *problem*—and Harvard took as its problem "depopulation."

So Nate Kidder was recommended by Stouffer as the demographer, Ed Hunt went as the physical anthropologist who was the protégé of both Carlton Coon and Earnest Hooton. I was nominated by whoever it was—I don't know, Clyde probably had a hand in it—and Doug Oliver and Carlton Coon interviewed me and talked to me, and I took a course with Doug Oliver as a result. It was a course in Oceanic ethnography. All I remember about it is being bored stiff.

I can remember doing an awful lot of buzzing around getting ready to go to Yap: putting together a dictionary of Yapese words from Muller's famous two-volume book;[1] Addy and I—Addy, mostly—typing it patiently on onionskin paper, in the form of slips, which we then bound together; and I put them in between two pieces of aluminum, etc. I was gonna learn Yapese—well, the trouble was that the Yapese words were there, all right, but the way to pronounce them was unknown, and I couldn't figure it out. So when I got there, the dictionary turned out to be a total waste of time—a waste of time and effort—but everybody worked on it. Of course, at that point, Addy figured it was also for her as well as for me, and what she was gonna do was not clear, but I suppose the implicit premise was that I would do all the intellectual, ethnographic-type masterminding, and she would pick up the usual women's-type pieces— you know, keep house, make sure that I was properly fed and bathed and so forth. But that all broke up.

RH: You mean, Addy didn't go with you?

DMS: Right. In the CIMA project, which was run by Murdock, Harvard got the Yap assignment. When I was accepted on the Yap team, I asked if Addy could go with me. Harvard had no objection at all, but said it was up to Murdock. And Murdock reported that wives could not go into the field with husbands, because the navy had prohibited it. The navy, according to Murdock, did not permit navy wives into that area yet, and did not want to take the responsibility for civilian women in that area. So Murdock explained that women were not allowed to go. When I got to Yap, of course, there were navy wives there already—not many, but a few. So I screamed loudly and protested, whereupon it became clear that Murdock had himself invented this as an excuse—that he had set the policy: no wives. And this was a source of very serious anger and resentment on my part. Little had I liked Murdock before, and this re-inforced my dislike for him. And it was a source of some concern and tension between Addy and me. I think it made our life different than it would have been, and I think we both would have been considerably happier had she come.

RH: Why was that? Did she want to go?

DMS: Yeah, I think she wanted to go. We were the kind of romantic kids who felt that doing things together was important to our marriage.

RH: Why was it a source of tension if it wasn't your fault that she couldn't go?

DMS: 'Cause it was a whole area of experience and life that we hadn't shared together. The idea was that we were going to share life together.

RH: So you went without Addy.

DMS: Yes. There was supposed to be an assemblage of all the teams going out at the University of Hawaii, and there we would be briefed, etc. For some reason, the Harvard team was late. So the Harvard team flew to California and we stopped off and spent a day or two with Felix Keesing, who was supposed to do something, and instead he drove us around and showed us the view from Skyline Boulevard. That was the end of Felix Keesing, for the time being, and then we flew to Hono-lulu and stayed overnight in the Makalapa Barracks—officers' quarters, I don't know. And from there flew—this is all four-propeller planes— flew to Guam. In Guam, I picked up a couple of barrels. They were small barrels, a little bigger than wine kegs, but they were steel and they had silica gel things in them to keep photography supplies dry. I kept my camera and films, and that was very helpful.

From Guam to Yap, you had to go by boat. And the boat was called an Army A-G. Why the army ran boats was never clear; it didn't matter. So, we got to Yap. There it was! The navy was there. Not a helluva lot of navy, but some navy. They were already established. The problem was to make connections with "natives." So we hung around what at that time was called Yaptown. Before and since it's been Colonia. They had dances—the natives came in and did dances, and things like that. There was much taking of pictures, and so on.

A high chief, named Fithingmau Niga, was brought in. He was not ambulatory. He sat on a litter. We made his acquaintance, and I, I think, on behalf of all the rest of us—it may not have been that—and fortunately, you know, I'm in a good spot now: Ed Hunt has died, I don't think anybody knows where Kidder and Stevens are. So this must be God's truth. Anyway, I talked to Fithingmau Niga through an interpreter, and I asked his permission to come to his village, which elicited peals of laughter from Fithingmau Niga, and the answer was to the effect: How in the hell am I possibly gonna try to stop you?

Keeps happening over and over again. I am pretending that there is no colonial situation. And I *believe* it, you know. And they are saying, what's wrong with you? You're out of your mind. Of course, you can go anywhere you want, and we can't stop you. But I go through all this gymnastics of asking permission.

So after a while, Bill Stevens and I get a—see, Bill Stevens and I are the ethnographers—the game was that Kidder and Hunt would go from village to village and count noses and take somatic-type pictures, whereas Stevens and I would settle in and "do ethnography." Stevens and I got a boat of some kind—one of those small, infantry landing-craft-type things. A motor boat, and the front goes down and you walk out of it, on the beach. So Stevens and I get all our stuff together, and we get the boat, and the boat brings us to Gatchepar, drops us at Gatchepar, unloads us and unloads all our gear, and drives away. And there was absolutely nobody around. Nobody at all.

So we sit there a while, thinking somebody should come and greet us, and somebody should come and help us carry all this junk. Nobody. So we walk inland. We follow a path, and still nobody! We come to a house and there's nobody, but there's a fire burning there. We come to another house, and there's nobody there, but there's a fire burning there. For some reason we feel alone! There's basically nobody around.

So Stevens and I begin to move our junk up from the beach so that water doesn't get to it. We walked inland a little way and we found an abandoned cement—there were one or two steps up—it was a cement platform. Actually, a house had been built on it, and it turned out later it was the Japanese police station. So we loaded all our stuff on top of this cement slab and set up a tent and everything else. And it was, I don't know, hours later, or the next day, finally kids began peering through the bushes. We would spy them, and they would giggle and run away. It was big fun.

I don't remember exactly how it happened, but eventually a couple of people showed up. One of the people who showed up was old Gurewon. Gurewon was an old lady. How old? Who knows. I estimated eighties, but she was probably no more than fifties or sixties. Largely toothless. That's it. She showed up. And a couple of other young men showed up. And gradually people began to come around.

Along with Gurewon, though, very early in the game came Runiol. Now Runiol was clearly an adult and clearly a middle-aged man. He had gray in his beard. Runiol was a regular daily visitor. He frequently came and he sat and stayed with us. Didn't talk a lot, but was willing to talk a little bit. The third or fourth day, maybe, Runiol shows up with a couple of fish. Not very big fish; very small fish, in fact. He gives us the fish. So I turn around and dive into the tent and come up with a pack of cigarettes! So I pressed the cigarettes on Runiol, who, of course, refuses them! But I insist. So he had to take the cigarettes. He takes the cigarettes, goes away, and comes back with more fish. Well, by then, it was too much fish.

It was obviously—the answer is quite clear: if somebody gives you a present, you don't immediately pay for it. You wait and give them a present later. But I didn't know that, and didn't think of it; it was a crude, rude—a totally cloddish way to behave. But that's the way it was.

So Gurewon would—we would cook supper, you know; we'd cook some rice and open a can of sardines or something—and Gurewon was always willing to eat with us. But Runiol would never eat with us. But we had known from the ethnography that there were various complicated food taboos—and didn't know what it was.

I began to try to do something with language, fairly soon. At this point my memory is beginning to get uncertain, as to whether there were groups of people who came in and sat around with us in the evening and in the afternoons—there was a young man and a bunch of kids who came fairly regularly. And then Pitemag came back. Oh my, I forgot Pitemag! Can't forget Pitemag.

While we were on Guam we were introduced to a young man named Pitemag who had been sent to Guam to learn to be a schoolteacher. Pitemag wore a wristwatch and shoes and socks when he came back to Yap. He showed up at our campsite, and he began to "take charge." Pitemag had a friend named Fichibmon and another friend, Defungen, who's still there and still well; Pitemag's still alive, too, I think; so's Fichibmon, and so is Defungen, who became the Yapese anthropologist. But after a while they began taking charge of us.

Again, with my usual inept stupidity, I decided that somehow Pitemag was too highly "acculturated" and that he also was so obviously trying to get control of us, and be the gatekeeper—who we would see and where we would go and what we would do—that I was very anxious to not let Pitemag get control.

But that didn't matter, because Pitemag, Fichibmon, and Defungen, nevertheless *did*. They walked us around, they showed us places, they took us this way, they took us that way. Then they had that big party— but that was fairly late, the big party. The big party was where Bill Stevens got all upset because these guys were sitting on each other's laps, and holding hands—they seemed to be kissing each other—and he had a real, genuine homosexual-panic-type reaction to the whole thing.

Everybody was sitting on everybody's lap, and it looked to the two or three or four of us who were there that these guys were all homosexuals. And suddenly, a great hypothesis began blooming: that the reason for the depopulation was that the men were all homosexual. Right? All right. And there was a good deal of panic among the three or four of us. At least there was among Bill Stevens, and I thought Kidder and Hunt, too. They were very upset.

The Yapese men did—they walked along and held hands with each other. I thought that was odd, also, and—you know, there's a great business of reading into it all sorts of things. So the homosexuality hypothesis was flying around, and Clyde Kluckhohn, who was an honest-to-God, certifiable homosexual, was amused by it all, and laughed. I don't know how he could laugh in a letter to me, but he laughed. So I shut up as fast as I could. And the other guys kept going at it.

RH: Did you ever learn more about it?

DMS: As far as I could tell, there was no homosexuality going on. At least no active homosexuality. But Stevens was convinced that there was.

But this now opens three or four other avenues.

Number one: I really think that I honestly—mostly unconsciously— but I really honestly felt that somehow there was some way of getting true, unacculturated, authentic, untouched, pristine Yapese culture; and that, naturally, I couldn't get it from highly acculturated, Christianized, missionized people. And one of the obvious attractions, by the time I got to Yap, was that it was the most highly conservative, the most resistant-to-innovation island; they still wore grass skirts without shirts; they still wore loincloths; nobody really dressed. Later on, the commander, who-ever was in charge of the navy base, said that "you gotta wear clothes if you come into the navy base." The sailors were getting distracted by all those bare-breasted women, and it wasn't nice, and so forth. So, I really think that more than half unconsciously, I was looking to get the "un-acculturated, untouched, pristine, authentic, ageless, stone-age Yapese culture."

That was also part of my motivation in going up to Rumung, because it was far away, farther away than anyplace. But at this point I had not yet gone up to Rumung. All right, that's that line of thought; that's taken care of for the moment.

Now I'm not sure that Bashkow noticed this, and I may not have writ-ten it clearly in my notes, you see—because, again, you know, you don't really write everything in your notes; you can't—but I must've been sen-sitive enough to the fact that that was really not only a fantasy, but it was a nineteenth-century fantasy. Still, I really feel that was a very important element in my thinking.

Okay, so a guy named Charlie Johnson shows up after a while. He is a geologist, and they're doing a great geological survey. Charlie Johnson was a very nice, very bright, very able—a very pleasant guy. And he would go around with his hammer, banging on rocks. I remember one night, I had been—somehow, Bill Stevens and I were not getting along well. One night when Charlie Johnson was there—cause, you know, he stayed with us—Bill Stevens and I got into a very big, nasty argument. Now again, whether this is before or after the episode with the party, where Bill Stevens got so upset because they were all homosexuals, I don't remember. I could look all this up in my notes, you know.

So I got into this argument with Stevens. And it was really a very nasty argument. I was my usual very nasty self. Stevens said he could teach those buggers English faster than he could learn Yapese. And I knew that that was *not* the way to do it. I said—you know, I'd never been very good at languages, I never really learned languages well enough—I said, "You've gotta learn the language. I've gotta learn the language. I'm gonna have to learn the language." Because at that point, practically nobody in Yap, not even Pitemag, spoke anything like good English. Pitemag knew rudimentary English, so that you wouldn't go totally wrong, but he couldn't really talk English very well. And a lot of the communication was done pointing, and charades, and play acting—act out what you're gonna do.

So Stevens and I got into that big fight. The outcome of all that was that I had been in Gatchepar—by then it was two or three months—too long. I felt as if I was really embedded in the toils of this small, highly acculturated, politically suspect group of Pitemag, Fichibmon, and Defungen. And that I had to get out. And Stevens, in turn, wanted to get out, because he felt that by going back to Yaptown, he could find somebody there and teach him English. And he didn't have to go and shit in the goddamn mangrove swamp. You know, we'd walk into the mangrove swamp to shit; didn't always get that far if you wanted to piss, but you'd go in that direction and then piss when you felt like it. Which of course offended the Yapese, 'cause that wasn't the place to do it.

Eventually, Stevens went off to Yaptown, I went up to Rumung. But before that, I began to try to learn the language—before I had my big argument with Stevens. I tried using Runiol as a language teacher— you know, somebody to learn from. The funny part of the story is that Runiol turned out to be the village idiot. But you know, if you don't know Yapese, you don't know who's the village idiot. And giving him the cigarettes was such a rudimentary faux pas that even the village idiot knew that you shouldn't be exchanging gifts directly. But otherwise, it

turned out that Runiol was the village idiot. He was obviously badly retarded, and although he didn't look like a Down's syndrome, later on it
was quite clear—once I had gotten some control of the language—that
Runiol was just inept, he didn't really understand much.

So, I sat mostly with old Gurewon. And Gurewon, being mostly toothless, would enunciate these things to me with her toothless mouth, with
a great wad of betel quid in it, and I began to talk like a toothless old
woman with a betel quid. Of course, people began to laugh at me, because I talked like a toothless woman with a betel quid. So I began to
give Gurewon a harder time, and she would then spit her betel quid out,
into the palm of her hand, and enunciate it more clearly, as a toothless
old woman without a betel quid would, and then pop the betel quid
back in her mouth. And then I spoke like a toothless old woman without
a betel quid. Which made people laugh as well. But they also laughed for
other reasons.

But you know, it must've taken four or five weeks before even the
kids were willing to laugh. I thought it was a great triumph when the
kids were willing to laugh *at* me, as well as with me. It showed getting
rapport, and it showed that we were being accepted, and all that stuff.

With Gurewon there was the usual sort of thing: when I wanted to
know the word for moon, and I pointed to the moon, and I said, "What's
that?" And Gurewon said something, and I repeated it, and then the
next time the moon came out I wanted to show how smart I was, so I
told somebody. I pointed to it, and I pronounced what I understood to
be the word for moon. Well of course it turned out that she had been
pointing at a star, and I was pointing at the moon! So I said, "star," and
people would correct me. They'd say, "no, no, no." So I would point to
the moon, and they would say, "star," and it went back and forth. That
was also a source of fun.

Then there was the one marvelous day when I learned the word for
bamboo. I pronounced the word for bamboo, and all the children put
their hands up in front of their faces and giggled like mad and turned
around, and everybody said, "poolag, poolag!" Poolag means obscene,
dirty, not good, not acceptable, wrong. And I thought, whatever it is, I
said something interesting. It turns out that the word for bamboo, with
a glottal stop, is bamboo, and without a glottal stop is fart. I, of course,

said fart. And, of course, all the kids thought, that's hilarious; listen to him talk dirty!

But that's how you learn the language.

The Japanese had imported these toads to try to keep the mosquito population down. And the toads made just a riotous noise all night. And of course the toads were all over the roads. You'd drive along the road and it would go pop! bang! pop! bang!—every time you hit a toad, it would explode.

I've left out another big piece, too. We're still staying in Yaptown, and a guy from the *National Geographic* comes, a photographer named Moore. He was the one who explained to us—he was willing to help us out if we'd help him out—and he was showing us a few helpful hints about taking good pictures. He explained very straightforwardly and patiently that the simplest way was to focus on the left nipple—no, it's the right nipple, I think. If you got a good, clear focus of the right nipple, your picture would come out okay. He was the one who coined—at least, for us—the term "tit pictures." I mean, that's what he was there for, to get lots of tit pictures. And enough other pictures to provide some context for them.

So, we got a motorized whale boat, and four of us and him went riding around, and up the Tegerin Canal and back again. This was the first couple of weeks. It was sort of stupid. He was an interesting and a nice guy, but he had a mission, and his mission was to get tit pictures. And he did. And they were all published in the *National Geographic,* and he duly sent us copies of some of his pictures, which were quite good.[2]

I met a navy officer there by the name of Kevin Carroll. Kevin Carroll was really a very interesting person, and in many ways a very nice person. But, as usual, I never really managed to be nice to nice people. There was one commanding officer who—I don't know, his wife got upset and they decided to kill all the dogs they could. For days, they were shooting dogs. Of course, dogs were all over the goddamn place. The Yapese attitude toward dogs was very much like the Arabs'. They were just around, and they were despised because they ate shit. I think I have pictures—and I know I've seen it many times—where a mother would take an infant and turn the infant around on its belly and hold it on its belly with its ass stuck out and call a dog over to lick the kid clean. And the dogs would come over and they'd lick the kid clean. Clearly, there was not much in the way of diapers around at that time.

There was another commanding officer whose wife felt she really should do something. She organized a Girl Scout troop. And the important thing for the Girl Scout troop was that they had to wear bandannas, and they wore the bandanna so that it was knotted at the neck in the back, and the front fell over their breasts, so that there would be some covering. That was her contribution to uplift—is that the right word?

When we got there, the Americans had only been on Yap for some months. The Japanese had been sent out. All of them, except a few—I think a couple of Korean women had ended up marrying Yapese men. And there was a problem of what to do with them, whether they should be repatriated. They didn't want to be repatriated. But when the Americans landed, they said, "Who the hell's chief around here? Who's in charge?" So a Yapese man named Ruwepong presented himself as the king of Yap. He was immediately, therefore, the agent through whom the navy did all their "civil administration." For a while, that was the way it ran.

Kevin Carroll was the boat pool officer. He got himself a native assistant named Pong. Pong was some kind of chief from Tomil. Tomil and Rull were at odds, as they had been traditionally, and they should have been—'cause, you know, that's the way the whole thing was structured—and a good deal of heavy competition. Pong caught English very quickly, and was able to tell Kevin Carroll that Ruwepong was no more king of Yap than he was queen of Romania. Kevin Carroll then began to get a very good idea—at least, a beginning idea—of something about the political situation there, with the natives. Pong was a good instructor.

As time went on—again, it didn't take very long—it was some time just after we got there that Kevin Carroll convinced the commanding officer that he was really doing nothing more than elevating Ruwepong to a position that Ruwepong was not entitled to. And that there were really three high chiefs who should be consulted. Although Ruwepong was clearly one of them, he was not *the* high chief. So Ruwepong was very rudely unseated, Pong became the "éminence grise," and Kevin Carroll was the "expert on native affairs." He was then promoted from boat pool officer to native affairs officer or something like that. He, then, took things over, so I got to know Kevin Carroll fairly well. In fact, well enough so that when Jonathan was born, Kevin Carroll sent Jonathan a silver cup. Kevin Carroll unfortunately ended up in Afghanistan. He and his wife were traveling around in a jeep and some people just shot him and killed him. I don't know if they ever found the people, or why. Just that I remember a newspaper article in which these two Americans were traveling, and he had been killed by "bandits."

Kevin Carroll eventually—again, it didn't take very long; within the first three or four months, at the most—became the commanding officer, or practically the commanding officer of the island. He certainly had major control over what happened with the natives.

Another thing that happened very early in connection with the administration there: I've forgotten the name of the admiral, but there was a definite feeling in the navy circles that somehow the pristine, aboriginal, native quality of Micronesian culture should be preserved. Step one was to prohibit missionaries, insofar as he could. It was hard. Father Bailey was there and a few others got in, but he did clamp down in keeping missionaries out. Secondly, to control trade and traders. That was much harder. But, still, a lot of controls were put in.

Specifically, one of the things about Yap was that the Spanish had brought in a lot of "Chamorros." Chamorros were the descendants of Philippine and Micronesian and Guamanian and Saipanese. The Chamorros had been established on Yap quite a while. A number of the Chamorros spoke very good Yapese. Almost all the relationship between the navy administration and the Yapese was handled through the Chamorros. This is at the same time that Kevin Carroll is learning about what's going on, and they're unseating Ruwepong.

Briefly, the end of the story is that they sent a great big ship down, and they repatriated the Chamorros. Almost none of the Chamorros had been born anyplace except Yap. I'm not sure about that. Many of them may have been born on Saipan or Guam or Tinian. But they moved them all back to Saipan. Having cleaned out the Chamorros, there was literally nobody who could speak with the Yapese, with the possible exception of Pong. Pitemag was still learning English, and not doing very well. Fichibmon was barely able to converse. I, of course, was learning Yapese as fast as I could, and not very fast at that.

I went down to Yaptown to watch the repatriation of the Chamorros. In many ways it was very sad and unhappy, but in many ways it just went along. They took their cattle with them; so there were no cattle left on Yap. They abandoned all the places they had settled in and that by then they had some kind of claim to. But that was it.

By this time I had moved up to Rumung, and I had gotten myself settled. Methegeg and Tithin—you know, the fantasies we live by—I am fleeing from the clutches of Pitemag, Fichibmon, and Defungen, and, of course, I walk straight backward into the clutches of Methegeg and Tithin! But when I did that, I thought, I was choosing them! It was so interesting, because, you know, nobody else presented themselves to be chosen! They were the only ones who presented themselves to be chosen. But, of course, I widened my sphere when I got up there. I found Nifred and old Gilibechuen and Giltemag, a very old man from Fal. I was in his house when the house blew down! Well, I'll remember that, too, one day.

So I'm up there and settled in on Rumung. They had walked me all around: where would I like to live? And they're offering me all sorts of interesting places. But it turns out that the places they're offering me to live—none of them have any dwellings. I ended up on what was called an *unebai tofan*—that is, a place to rest when you're walking along the path. I suppose it's very crudely analogous to a public park. But it was small. It was a lot less than an eighth of an acre, behind which was a taro pit. It was flat, and it was paved, roughly. Paving there was with flat stones. There was about a two-foot drop down to the path.

First I had a small tent. Then the typhoons came along, and I got two sixteen-by-sixteen pyramidals. And that's where I lived all the time. It was twenty-five or thirty feet from the edge of the water. Mangrove swamp to the left, mangrove swamp to the right, but clear to the water. But it was not sandy beach, it was rocky beach. It was really a lovely place, a wonderful place. Like all the rest of Yap, no two Yapese houses were within sight or sound of each other. They liked it that way. They wanted their privacy, or whatever it was. They all had hedges around it, and things like that. So that was where I settled in.

Where do I go from there. Fieldwork? I really think I did a lousy piece of fieldwork.

RH: I've felt that way, too, about my fieldwork.

DMS: Yeah, but you were wrong. I was right. I did not, for example, take genealogies.

RH: I did, and they were useless.

DMS: Well, mine wouldn't have been useless. I could at least have said, "I took 'em but they were useless." I didn't even take genealogies. I did not take texts. I did not ask people to tell me folktales or stories. The result of which was, I never really learned Yapese grammar properly. I learned such elementary things as the difference between singular, dual, and plural, instead of just singular and plural. And then I learned such things as dual inclusive and dual exclusive. But when all was said and done, whatever form I used, the Yapese did their best to catch up with it. I could not ever speak with great subtlety. And although when I left, the highest compliment I got was that I spoke like a promising child—you know, they said, well, obviously, you can't even recite poetry, much less make it up. So, I never really learned the language to speak "fluently." I learned the language well enough to be able to get along, and to be able to understand. When it was clear I didn't understand, most people were kind and decent enough to say, "No, that's not it, you gotta do it this way."

Time and again, I would run into situations where I could see that I had missed all the subtlety in it, and the person talking to me would figuratively throw up their hands and say, "Oh, forget it." So that was not good.

I should have taken texts, if not about folktales, to help learn the language and to help at least get the grammar down. I should've taken texts just to—you know, "tell me the history of this village"—I never even asked things like that.

I never found out how people pissed and shit, or shat. I walked into the mangrove swamp to the left of my tent, which was maybe—oh, what?—twenty, thirty, forty paces away, and I fixed myself up a couple of logs so that when I shat, it dropped into the water and was washed out. And it must've taken me weeks before I noticed that people lined up on the path to watch. But they were always very polite. They never laughed, they never commented, they never went tittering around and saying "Ha ha ha, he's taking a shit." Well, of course, you know in that situation you drop your pants and you don't drop 'em very long, because the mosquitoes assemble instantly. So I didn't hang around, but that was no way to do it. So I never learned things like that.

RH: To this day you don't know how they did it?

DMS: I literally, to this day, do not know how they do it, where they do it, when they do it. I know better about infants, because I was able to watch.

I did a very careful survey of village organization. I went from village to village on Rumung, and "Which is a sacred place?" and "Draw me a map" and "Who is the chief of this part?" and so on. But you know, all that was okay, but it was not enough. Nor was it systematically enough, nor was it in-depth enough. Thus, for example, I never found out whether village offices were consistently succeeded in the lines they were supposed to succeed in. I never found out if the people who presented themselves as this kind of a chief or that kind of a magician or that kind of a specialist were indeed the ones that were supposed to be, or not. I just wrote down what they told me and never asked enough more.

What else did I not do? I didn't do so many things. For example, I knew that personal names were the private property of *tabinau*.[3] But that's all I knew. I never got lists of names for particular *tabinau*. Yet, you know, I could go to another place and they would say, "Who do you know?" and I'd say "I know so-and-so" and they'd say, "Oh, yes, we know so-and-so." And they'd give me his *tabinau* and how he was affiliated and everything else—just from the name.

I think one informant told me how people got their names. People could change their names. I don't know to this day under what circumstances you change your name, under what circumstances you get a new name. It was not good.

Then David Aberle very kindly sent me a copy of the Kinsey report when it came out, and I thought, "That's a jolly good idea; I'm going to ask them about sex." When I was in Yaptown, I palled around with the doctors to some extent. And they were trying desperately to get women to come into the hospital to have their babies there. It was a "good thing," you know? "That's the way it's done in civilized society." But the women wouldn't come and have their babies. So I began asking around:

"Why don't you guys go into the hospital to have your babies?" They then explained that they don't go into the hospital to have their babies because it's better to have your baby at home, in your *tabinau*, where your own ancestral ghosts can take care of it.

But that wasn't quite the end of it, because then, I don't know how I stumbled on this—I think it was a couple of women who told me, "No, no. We're not going to go in and have babies there because these women make you take your skirt off, and they examine your private parts." And I said, "Sure, naturally!" And they said, "No, no! That's awful! You should never let another woman look at your vulva."

So I then pursued that a bit, and it turned out that they would be happy to go have their babies if they would just get those goddamn nurses away and let the doctor do it—'cause the doctors were all men, you see.

All right, that was a piece that was tucked away. Then I go in swimming—you know, I don't give a shit if I've got pants on or I don't have pants on. But everybody I notice is very fussy. And not only that, but when the men jump out of the canoe to take a piss, they do it in such a way that nobody can see. And then when they get back into the canoe, they're always holding their hands over their genitals until they get their loincloth properly adjusted. And then when they're in the water, when they don't have the loincloth on, all the men are standing there with one hand or another holding their penis and testicles.

RH: Even underwater?

DMS: Even underwater.

RH: But you were swimming around naked?

DMS: I'm swimming around, you know—I notice that there's some discomfort, but I don't know what's going on. Finally, I think, old Methegeg must have told me that it is not nice for you to go uncovered. You should always keep yourself covered. Then, when Methegeg had finished that—see, Methegeg was the old man who was my "closest informant" and friend—the younger man, Tithin, said it is not good for a man to see your genitals.

Okay, so men don't let men see men's genitals, women don't let women see women's genitals. And women are telling me that if they'd ever get the women nurses out of there, they'd go in because they don't care if the men doctors see their genitals. So it takes me a few days or maybe a week to figure out, what is it with men, now? And the answer is very simple: what happens when lovers go into the bush together—yeah, they take their clothes off, no problem. Men seeing women's genitals, women seeing men's genitals—no problem. What, then, is the problem? It turns out that the problem is—now this is one informant plus other supporting material; so it's not precise and it's not perfect—but an analogy was drawn between a woman's "estate" and her genitals. *That's* what she has, and that's what she lives by. So she doesn't want to let any other woman see what she's got, 'cause she's competing with other women for men. And men are competing with men for women. So it works, also, with adultery. That is, a man who thinks that his wife is having intercourse with somebody else will try to get the man to stop it, but will leave his wife alone. And a woman who feels that her husband is cheating on her will go to the other woman and get her to stop. But they never attack across sex lines.

So, that is just a piece of it that began to open up after I started on the "sex survey." I started by doing as I usually did after I got going a while, I'd start with old Methegeg and Tithin. I'd say, "Look, I want to inquire into the subject. These are the sorts of questions I want to ask. How best could I ask them? What's the best way to phrase it? Who should I start with? What kinds of problems am I going to run into?" What you might call pre-testing. And I said I want to do sex, and all they would do is freeze up, and they'd say, "Well, I don't know. People don't like to talk about sex." Okay—bug them again and they won't help. Bug them again and they still won't help. So I said, I'll go ahead myself.

So I start interviewing men in private, and I can't get a word out edgewise. I can't get a thing. The men just won't talk.

"How often do you have intercourse?"

"Not very often."

"With your wife?"

"Well, yes, usually. Well, sometimes, doesn't matter."

"Where?"

"Well, we don't—not anymore. We don't fuck very much."

They just did not want to talk about sex. So I gave up. It was hopeless. One day, I was still in the middle of this—now here again, you need some sideways information, that I'll offer in a minute—a woman comes into the tent. As usual, I'm sitting on my folding chair near my table and she squats on the ground, crosses her legs, sits down, arranges the skirt around her and gets her betel quid comfortable in her mouth and looks brightly up at me and says, "You have five knives on the table."

I say, "Yes, I've got five knives on the table."

She says, "Alas and alack, I have no knives at all."

Well, I'd been there long enough to know exactly what that meant. So I said, "Which knife would you like?" Because, you see, if you have none and the other person's got them—you've got to share. It works the same way with babies. If you've got a baby, and you'd get pregnant, people could come to you—but particularly if they have any close relationship to you—and say, "You got one, this next one is for me." And you've got to give it.

So she tells me which knife she would like. Now normally, I would have reached over and handed the knife to her. So instead I said, "Well look, tell me: How often do *you* fuck?"

And she said, "Fuck?"

And I said, "Yes."

So she picks herself up off the ground, moves over closer, arranges her skirt more happily, spits her betel out, puts a little more lime on it, and leers up at me and says, "Let's talk about sex."

I just about fell off my chair! We spent an hour or so just talking about sex! I didn't know what to do. At home, men talk about sex, women talk about sex—but on Yap, men wouldn't talk to me about sex but the women talked to me about sex. Which paralleled, of course, the genitals. So I gave her the knife, she was happy, and she went away with the knife and she had a good talk besides.

So I interviewed a number of women about sex. But then I went back to Methegeg and I told him that and he, of course, was not the least bit surprised. But, you know, it was not my habit to say, "Look, you son-of-a-bitch, you're supposed to help me out. Why didn't you tell me this is the way to do it?"

RH: You said there was some sideways information. Will you come to that, or have you already given it?

DMS: That was the business of sharing. If you've got, and the other person doesn't, you share. But you see, I was always very open with everything. I would go to Yaptown and bring back sacks of sugar and rice and two, three, four cases of beer, and these great big bottles of gin and whiskey—and I gave it out. Tobacco, cigarettes, and I got nylon fish line and everything else. A couple of times I went down there and the commanding officer gave me a very hard time. He said, "You can't be drinking all that beer yourself. You can't be drinking all that gin and whiskey yourself. You know, you're not allowed to give it to the natives. The natives will get drunk."

I said, "I don't ever give it to the natives. This is just for my own consumption. You can come up and look and watch and you can see. Have you heard anybody complaining that I'm giving liquor to the natives?"

Well, of course he hadn't heard anybody complaining, because they didn't want to complain to him. So, sharing I had no problem with. Everybody—as soon as I came back from Yaptown, they'd gather around. You open up the sack of sugar, you open up the sack of rice—

RH: —how self-interested is this? Did you do this just to get them to talk to you?

DMS: No, this is just me. I always grab the check, and I don't need to. I'm always giving people money when they don't ask for it. This is another one of those strange characteristics of my father. He was always giving things to people. If he had an ulterior motive, I don't know.

RH: So you didn't have an ulterior motive?

DMS: Well, I'm sure there's a good Freudian ulterior motive: I want to be liked! Some time later I came back and saw Geoffrey Gorer. We talked about fieldwork. Geoffrey Gorer pointed out that one of the differences between the English and the Americans doing fieldwork is that the Americans want to be loved. And so you do anything to be loved and accepted. And the English doing fieldwork, they want to be respected. They don't care if you like them or not. I hadn't appreciated it, but he drove it home. I knew it was true with me. I wanted to be liked, I wanted to be accepted. So I was just generous with stuff because that's the way I am.

RH: And you had enough funding to do it?

DMS: I had enough money to be able to buy stuff very cheap at the navy base.

So, anyway, that was the sex stuff, or as much of it as I know. No, I never really tried to sleep with any of the natives. I suppose it would be difficult for me to say exactly why. I have never been, as many people seem to be, driven by the idea that the more women you sleep with the better it is for everybody. This has never been a major fact in my life. Nor am I totally uninterested in heterosexual sex. But it's not one of the most pressing and strongest motivations in my life. So, in one way, I didn't really make an effort to. Neither did they, in any way. Apparently, from time to time and place to place, people will make you offers that are hard to refuse. Nobody either tried to—no women approached me, and no men approached to say that I could have one if I wanted one. So the opportunity didn't really arise. And that's really all I can say about that. It was not one of those things that was determined by high moral purpose, although I'm sure there must have been a moral aspect to it, but that was not the main point.

Yet there are millions of marvelous anecdotes about, for instance, an anthropologist who shall remain nameless. He did some ethnography on one of the Pacific islands, and he did it, according to his account, in bed with a woman. That is, he spent all night and most of the days fucking, and in between they would have conversations about island customs.

Ronald Olson used to tell—one of his clever statements was that there he was, and nothing between him and the cold, cold ground but the slip of an Indian girl. I don't know—those things I always found not quite to my liking.

But, there was nothing of that sort. And yet, God only knows, there were a lot of very attractive people there—women. Very attractive, and very nice. And the adolescent girls were afraid of me because I was both foreign and older. The women about my age would talk to me, but they were always fairly careful to do so in situations where they would never possibly be accused of—you see, for a married woman to talk to another man alone out of sight was considered "iling," and iling was the same word for adultery. That is, to sleep with another man, other than your husband, and to talk to another man, other than your husband, was equally iling. So, although they would talk to me, there was no problem, because my tent was pitched literally inches from the path. The sides were always rolled up. Even when it rained we left them rolled up. It didn't matter, because you just stayed more centered.

So there were always people there. I'd go to sleep with people there, and I'd wake up with people there. They were different people, usually, but there were people in and out all the time. And it tended to be very embarrassing, because every so often I would wake up and I'd find I'm holding my penis. I'd look around and there were all these people and, you know, I'm quite sure they saw exactly what was happening. I apparently never could quite manage to arrange that I would wake up not holding my penis. God knows what I was doing when I was asleep!

I had a cot. I slept on the cot. And I had a mosquito net. But the trouble with those mosquito nets is that if you put your elbow against the mosquito net, the mosquito gets you from outside. So my elbows and my knees would end up being mosquito bitten. But the mosquito net, you could see right through it.

So there were always people present, so I was able to talk to women whenever I wanted to. Often they would walk by and they'd stop, and I'd offer them a cup of coffee with a lot of sugar in it. I always had a coffee pot going. I must have had ten gallons of coffee most of the time. And people would stop for coffee.

RH: Ten gallons is a lot!

DMS: Yes it was a lot. That's why I'd get a fifty-pound bag of sugar. That wasn't the only reason. The other reason is that they would take sugar from me. You climb up a coconut tree. You cut the buds off. You pull all the little buds of the coconut thing together, you tie it, and you let it drip into a container. Then you empty that container into these Japanese half-gallon and gallon bottles, and you let it ferment. Well, if you add a little sugar to that, it really helps.

RH: Now when you say they took sugar, do you mean they stole it or they—

DMS: —no, no! They'd ask me for it. I gave. Anybody wanted, they knew they could come and get it. Nobody stole anything from me. And I have a feeling that they never stole, partly because everything was open. They could've stolen my camera, but what would they do with a camera? But nobody even stole the camera. If anyone stole anything, I was unaware of it. But that was also part of the game. You know, I had so much—would I miss it if somebody took a couple of pounds of sugar or rice? There was a bag of it, and every time the bag got half empty, I'd go down to Yaptown and buy another.

So everyone was stopping for coffee. Women would go by, and people would have coffee, and their idea of coffee was to fill it up with sugar. Coffee was a vehicle to get their sugar. And cigarettes—I would give cigarettes away. But after a while I realized that the butts that I had left were valuable, so I would never throw butts away after a while.

RH: At this time you were smoking?

DMS: I smoked like a chimney from about 1936 till 1961 or '62. Never more than two or three packs a day. I used to smoke when I lectured!

RH: Okay, so why were you saving the butts?

DMS: Because if you got a betel quid, and you want to really make it good, you open a cigarette butt on it. There were no filter tips in those days. So you add a little tobacco to it, which adds a little something else to the taste. And if you've been chewing betel long enough, even that hot tabasco sauce, you barely notice it. I mean, it kills an awful lot of taste buds.

So, where was I? Coffee—everybody was getting coffee, and rice. I was living in the open, and everybody was in and out.

RH: So nobody suspected you of adultery—I think that was the drift of our conversation.

DMS: No, nobody did—that was partly why women could come and talk to me anytime, even if we were apparently alone. There were always kids playing outside. I liked the kids. In fact, as I told Addy when I came back, I really took to kids. This one little kid—Tithin's little kid, he's now a full-grown man—who was just a toddler: I used to hold him and play with him. His mother's brother had been away as a sailor and came back. And the kid was sitting in my lap when this strange man appeared. The kid just looked at him and got frightened, put his face in my chest, began to cry. I comforted him and he stopped crying. I thought it was just marvelous, 'cause he didn't even know his own uncle! And he looked like a Yapese and I didn't look the least bit like a Yapese. It was a great thing. So I've always liked kids since then.

The kids were just wonderful—sweet and nice. Well, they played rough, and they were nasty to each other, they killed each other, and they hurt each other. They were systematically exploitative and vicious to low-caste kids—but, that's kids!

And that kid's name?—Figir, little Figir. He was Figir Nichig. Figir

Niga I knew well, but not as well as the little one. Figir Nichig was the one who—did I tell you about the baby being born in my boat?

Tithin and Methegeg were the two who were closest to me. Tithin was married to Genongemeth. Tithin had a son named Figir Niga by his first wife. Figir Niga lived in Riy, with Tithin's father's brother. Genongemeth was clearly pregnant. Were they going to go and have the baby in this hospital, or should they have the baby at home? She got more and more pregnant, and they couldn't decide. One night there was a funny scratching noise. Tithin runs out, and he says, "Genongemeth is here. She's having labor pains! What should we do?"

"I don't know," I said. "You want to have the baby here, or should we go to the hospital?"

He runs out, he runs back. "Let's go to the hospital."

I've got, by this time, my motorboat, which was nothing but a pontoon with a motor attached to it. And it's a good trip—a good three- or four-hour trip. So he says, "We'll get ready," and I say, "Fine, I'm ready, I've got gas, I've got everything."

They finally show up. But they have to wait for this old woman. She is a specialist at catching the child. In we get, and I'm timing her contractions, and I'm not stupid. I'm seeing that they're about five minutes apart. Nevertheless, we take off. And the contractions are still coming at about three, four, five minutes apart. And I know we're never going to make it to the hospital, but what the hell am I going to do.

Meanwhile, I get to hold the older child, Figir. I'm holding Figir and I'm driving the motorboat. Tithin is staying with Genongemeth, and she's having contractions.

Then Tithin says, "Stop the boat!" We stop the boat, he throws the anchor over, and the usual thing—perfect quiet, she never says a word. I can hear breathing, but that's it. And all of a sudden there's this great big thump and I said, "Oh, God! You didn't catch the baby!" And the old woman said, "No, I don't know how to catch the baby!" So I'm holding this little two-year-old. We wait a while, and then comes the afterbirth. The old woman has picked the baby up, put it on her dirty grass skirt. Old women don't change their skirts 'cause they don't menstruate, right? You only change your skirt after you menstruate. Well, her skirt had been on for weeks. It was filthy. So she picks the afterbirth up from the bottom of my filthy boat—you know, dead fish, bare feet, everything!—and plops it on top of the baby.

Then Tithin says, "We've got to stop, because it's important that I get a brand-new drinking coconut for Genongemeth to drink as soon as she's had the baby."

So we go over to the shore. Tithin takes the rope, puts it on this little jetty, and, taking my flashlight, walks in to find a drinking coconut. I watch this light bob around and bob around and suddenly comes a blood-curdling shriek and a scream. The flashlight is jumping all around, and comes Tithin and grabs the rope and jumps into the boat. I say to myself, the poor bastard has seen a ghost. And that's exactly what happened. I get the motor going and we get out away from there as fast as possible.

I asked Tithin what happened, and he said there was a woman's ghost. I said, "A woman's ghost?" He said, "Yes, and she began to chase me." I said, "Did she catch you?" He said, "No, I ran very fast."

Well, he sure did. So, we headed down toward the hospital. You know, I'm not sure he didn't see a ghost. I'm not sure he did see a ghost. I am as scared as they are. It was very tense by that time. But the baby was born, Genongemeth was all right, she said, and everything was okay. We get to the hospital, Genongemeth goes in, I go to the officers' quarters to wake up the doctor, and I say, "A woman just had a baby in my boat. Will you go up to the hospital and check her out and make sure everything is all right?"

He said, "I'm sure everything is all right. Don't worry about it."

I said, "Come on, it's a real good friend of mine. A boat's no place to have a baby. Check it out."

He said, "I'll bet she didn't even make a noise."

I said, "Of course she didn't make a noise."

He said, "These niggers are all the same. They don't feel pain the way we do. I'm sure she's okay."

I said, "Please get up and go see her, check her out. You're the doctor. You're in charge."

He wouldn't get up. This is a guy who's over six feet, and younger than I. I don't know what he was. I was angry and mad and I said, "If you don't get up I'm going to beat the shit out of you." I threatened him with all kinds of things. So he very reluctantly got up, and I don't believe we spoke again after that, ever. But he got up and he went up there and got somebody to interpret: "Did you feel any ripping?" And she said, "No." "Well, let me just look," and it was okay. She was fine.

Twenty years later I went and visited her, and I visited the baby, and the baby had already had two babies of her own. And I said to her, "You know, you were born in my boat." And she said, "Everybody tells me that! Why don't they leave me alone." So that was it.

RH: There's something I don't understand. The old woman didn't know how to catch the baby?

DMS: That's right, and she was brought because she was supposed to be the expert at catching the baby. It was a mix-up. But she was also, you see, from Genongemeth's *tabinau* and that was part of the connection.

. . .

DMS: Have I told you about the "conversion of the Jews."

RH: You mentioned it, but you haven't told the story.

DMS: I got to Yap on a small boat from Guam, called an Army A-G. On the boat was Father Bailey. Father Bailey came from Somerville, Mass., and I came from Cambridge, Mass. And Father Bailey was gonna dedicate his life to converting people to Catholicism on Yap. And that was it.

But, you know, I was a broad-minded, kindly, generous, open, warm person, and Father Bailey and I stood at the rail and puked together. And when you puke together over the rail, you establish a bond with another person.

So, I got to Yap, and we got into the officers' quarters. Father Bailey also got into the officers' quarters, and we both ate in the officers' mess, because Father Bailey's church was—four walls were standing, and that was about all you could say for it. So he was going to build his church up, he was going to learn the language, and he was going to be there the rest of his life.

I was also going to learn the language, and so when I moved first to Gatchepar and then to Rumung, I kept coming down to pick up mail and pick up supplies, and I'd always stop and have dinner at the officers' club. And I always found Father Bailey, and, you know, I would tell him a new grammatical form, another five words I'd learned, and we'd exchange these pleasantries. I liked him, and he liked me. We got along very well. End of phase one.

I go from Gatchepar to Rumung, and everybody is still trying to figure out what the hell I'm doing there. Am I police, am I navy?

"No, I am not navy. I am an anthropologist coming to study customs."

"Oh!—of course!" But they still didn't believe it.

By that time I'd grown a beard. So they were quite convinced that I was a missionary, because all the Spanish missionaries wore beards, whereas the Americans didn't. So a couple of them came along one day and said that they would like to hear me preach. And by now I was pretty sick of establishing that I wasn't any of these things, and I said that I was not a preacher, I was not—so on and so forth.

RH: Are you speaking in Yapese at this point?

DMS: I'm speaking enough broken Yapese to be able to get along, but this is still reasonably early. It couldn't have been more than four months.

RH: But they're not speaking English to you?

DMS: No, they're not speaking English. So as part of the pitch, you see, I am giving it to them that I am not a missionary. And, indeed, I am not even a Christian! I would like to learn customs of the Christians just as I would like to learn customs of the Yapese.

"Oh, ho," they say. "We happen to have somebody who is an expert." Because, you know, I look for the expert on village-this and the expert on magic. "We have somebody who's an expert on Christians." So I said, "good," and I figured, I'll show 'em. I'll interview this person. And I did.

Comes this lovely old woman with a pair of—well, they were spectacles, that is, gold rims but no glass—a set of rosary beads, and an old Spanish catechism, very badly fingered and worn, but still—. So she spreads her skirts and sits down on the ground, and I start in with her, and it was great! "Tell me, who was this Jesus Christ? What lineage did he belong to? What was his authority? What did he do?"—the whole thing. We spent the day. I learned not only what he did, but how he operated and what kinds of prayers to use, and so on.

Extremely useful, extremely good, extremely interesting material. I wrote it all down conscientiously. Not only was I demonstrating to them my ignorance of Christianity, I was even getting good data. 'Cause, you know, by then everybody knew that it was always syncretism—they never took Christianity whole, they always squished it in with their own beliefs.

So she goes away, and as everything else that happened on Yap, there's always a circle of people sitting there and listening. From time to time they interrupted, told her she was wrong, corrected her on this, added another detail—whatever it was.

They all sort of shook their heads and said, "You know, he really doesn't know a thing about Christianity. He really didn't seem to know anything."

I said, "No, I told you, I don't know anything about it. I am not a Christian."

They said, "We thought all Americans were Christians."

I said, "No! Americans are all kinds of people. They are Christians and they are Muslims, and there are Hindus and there are Buddhists and there are Shintoists, and there are Jews, and there are this and that." I told them the whole thing about what a wonderful place America is, the cultural diversity, the religious diversity, and tolerance and blacks and whites and everything else.

They listened to me patiently, and they said, "Well, if you're not a Christian, what are you?"

So I said I was a Jew. They listened to that for a while, they thought about it, and then they said, "Well, when will you tell us about the customs of the Jews?"

I hadn't anticipated that, so I said, "One day we will do it just the way I did it. You ask me about the customs of the Jews, and I'll tell you."

"Good," they said. "Tomorrow morning."

So I thought about it—you know, am I going to go into circumcision, what am I going to do? Yap has an enormously, marvelous, complex set of food taboos, and I thought, oh, good, kosher laws—which I don't really know too well, but, whatever it is—. Of course, you learn in this process that if you're an informant, they must be doing what you're doing to them when they do it to you. And it is unsettling. So, of course, I now am "tailoring" the customs of the Jews to suit the situation, and them, and they interview me the next day, and I give them all the customs of the Jews—the kosher dietary laws and things like that. But I definitely avoid circumcision. I don't know why—my own fastidiousness? I don't know what it was. I just avoided it.

They were fairly patient, but they couldn't last the whole day, which was very much what I had hoped. But I did my best. I hung in there with it, but by early afternoon one after another just sort of slunk away, went away, disappeared into the bushes, had other things to do. And that was it.

So, that was the end of it. I went back to what I had been doing, and I had been doing village organization: what are the different offices of the village, where they're anchored in different plots of land, all that stuff.

A month, the next month—I don't know, time passed. I had to go down to Colonia to pick up more supplies and mail. I go down there. I do the usual thing. I get a good hot shower with real soap. I'm all clean and sparkling and I go into the officers' mess and I sit down next to Father Bailey and I say, "Father Bailey, how are you?"

He will not answer me. "Father Bailey?" No answer. He obviously wants nothing to do with me. So I say, "Father Bailey, did I do something wrong? Did I offend you in any way? I'm sorry. I didn't do it intentionally."

No answer. Finally, he's bolting his dinner down, getting rid of it as fast as he can, and he stands up and he says, "I didn't know the Jews were proselytizing!" And he leaves.

I'm totally confounded. I don't know what the hell's eating the guy. I can't figure it out, but he's gone. I get back in my boat and I go up, the five hours it takes me to get back to my village—you get lots of time to think—and I wonder.

So when I get back to my village there, I start in with Methegeg, the old man, and I say, "Methegeg, a lot of you people used to go to Father Bailey's church. Are you guys going to Father Bailey's church?"

Methegeg says, "No, we're not going to Father Bailey's church anymore."

I said, "Why aren't you going to Father Bailey's church?"

He says, "Dave, if you're Jewish, we're all Jewish, too."

So I left 129 Jews on Rumung, all observing the correct food taboos, which they'd always observed anyway. And there they were. That's the conversion of the Jews.

So I get back. Time passes. Twenty years later, I got a chance to go back to Yap, 1968. And I did, and I got there, and I thought it would be polite—I saw people—I thought it would be polite to go to the church and check in with the priest. Father Bailey, by then, I already know, had gotten ill, had to go home. I don't know if he's still alive or not, but he was gone and there was a new father, who, I believe, stereotypically, was a fat, jolly priest type. He was definitely fat, he was definitely jolly, he was definitely red in the face. And he ho-ho-hoed and I ho-ho-hoed and we talked to each other. So I asked him my question.

Now, after I left, I kept in touch with people on and off. They would write me, and things like that. And it turned out that where I had been, there was a man named Moses Figir, and he had a brother, Isaac Figir. And there was this collection of Old Testament names! And I wondered, what was going on? They had affirmed to me their definite commitment to Judaism, but I thought this Moses and Isaac and Abraham—it was interesting, but it was not believable.

So, I had also heard that the priest tended to do the baptisms, and tends to give names. So, when I got an opportunity, I asked the jolly priest, how did they get their names? these people. And he immediately announced that he gave them their Christian names, but they kept their Yapese names. I thought for a minute and I said, "Well, these people in Fal and Riy and these villages I came from—Moses, Abraham, Isaac, Jacob—?"

"Yes!" he says, "I give them the Christian names. I gave them all those names."

Well, I didn't want to start arguing with him, so I left it alone. He gave them the names. But there was a young man, an assistant of some kind, a seminarian—he caught on immediately. So he plucked—I forget the man's name, Father Whatever-it-was—by the sleeve and said, "Of course, you realize—you know, don't you?—that these are all Old Testament names?"

He said, "Yes, yes, these are all the Old Testament names. I give them those. I confine Old Testament names to the Yapese. When I baptize children from the staff, from the government offices, they usually pick their own Christian names—George, John, Tom, whatever it is. But for the Yapese, I stick strictly to Old Testament names."

So I said, "Why?"

He said, "Well, that's just the way I do it!"

He was a southerner. That's about all I can say. The only thing I can think of is that that's what they tended to do with black people in the South—Sambo, Moses, you know, weird names that come out of the genealogies. And that this guy thought it would be more appropriate for the Old Testament names to go to the blacks. So that's the end of my story on the conversion of the Jews. They clearly were getting their Christian names from him.

RH: So, what looks like a very strange thing happening, didn't really happen.

DMS: The strange thing that happened didn't really happen. For the time being that I was there, they were willing to be Jewish. They were very flexible about those things. Whatever worked, helped—that's about it. But, you know, I felt very good that I had converted 129 people, single-handedly, without actually proselytizing.

RH: When they sat down to interview you, do you remember how that worked?

DMS: They were awkward and uncomfortable about it. They didn't know how to interview. They tried to imitate me as best they could— "Oh!—you really do that?"

RH: But how much Jewish stuff did you know?

DMS: Not very much, so I was making stuff up as I went along, about kosher stuff—for example, I told them it was against the rules to eat pig. And they said, "Oh, that's horrible, that's crazy! Pig is delicious!"

And I said, "Well, but that's the rule."

And then they said, "Why?" and I said, "I don't know, that's the way it was, a long time ago"—and things like that. And, you see, they had the rule that you mustn't cook men's food in pots that women's food comes from, and vice versa. So I did the milk dishes/meat dishes as an analogy. They'd stop and discuss this. Is there any sense to that? That's peculiar. Milk is not a big part of their diet, but on the other hand, milk is a symbolically significant part of a person's "identity"—"I drank milk from her breast" was a phrase about being related to a mother.

RH: Did they know about animal milk—cow's milk, goat's milk?

DMS: Yeah, there were cows there. But the cows and goats had been brought in by the Spaniards and Chamorros later. So it was very recent. But they knew about milk, but it was not integrated well enough to make any real sense. That's one of the reasons it broke up so quickly, 'cause they couldn't think of—also, they didn't have any sense of culture, and they knew I was odd. I'm sure in some sense I was Other. But the idea of systematically exploring the nature of the Other, I don't think was easy for them.

What they really wanted to know about was America, Americans, things American, and what the Americans would do. But I'd been telling them about that all along. They were scared to death that the Americans were going to beat them, tie them to trees—which the Japanese did—throw them in jail, come and put together forced labor parties—things like that. I crossed my fingers and hoped it would never happen. I told them I didn't think it would happen. I told them they wouldn't do it.

RH: And were you right?

DMS: Yeah, I was quite right—at least for the period of my stay. Very late in the fieldwork, I was within about three months of going home, somebody robbed one of the buildings there [Yaptown] and took two thousand dollars and three cases of cigarettes. By that time, all the Chamorros had been sent home. This, you see, is the naive administration, and they never realized that nobody could speak Yapese and that the Yapese couldn't speak English. So they had no way to talk: they were governing this place without talking to the natives. But that didn't bother them. But suddenly, they needed to see if they could catch the thief.

So they sent a boat way the hell up where I was. By motorboat it was at least three hours away—in a fast boat. They sent a boat up, and this sailor comes over and says, "Hey, you gotta come down! The commander says you gotta come and help us. You're the only one who can speak Yap." He told me that the place had been robbed.

So I told him that I can't come down. "You tell him that I will only come down and interpret for them if I have the permission of the village and district chief."

He looked at me as if I were crazy. I said, "I'm just not coming. You go tell that to the commander. Don't *you* worry about it. See what *he* says."

Well, the commander had a fit—I've left out the vulgar term for that kind of a fit. But he was stuck because I was not under his command or

In the Army, 1945 (courtesy David Schneider).

Addy, Jonathan, Michael (in front), and David, August 1955
(courtesy David Schneider).

Cover of the *Harvard Alumni Bulletin,* April 9, 1949. Pictured on
the cover are Schneider and Tithin, seated in native posture at
Schneider's tent site on Rumung (courtesy David Schneider).

Participants in the Wenner-Gren conference on kinship and locality, convened by David Schneider and Louis Dumont, in Burg Wartenstein, Austria, from August 23–September 1, 1969. From left to right: Louis Dumont, Henri Lavondès (in front), James Boon (in back), Stanley Tambiah, Nur Yalmon, Lorenz Löffler, Edmund Leach, Mervyn Meggitt, David Schneider, David Maybury-Lewis, Martin Silverman, Pierre Latouche, Raymond Apthorpe, Clifford Geertz (courtesy David Schneider).

Participants in the School of American Research conference on meaning and culture, convened by Keith Basso and Henry Selby, in Santa Fe, New Mexico, from March 18–22, 1974. Kneeling, left to right: Clifford Geertz, Keith Basso, Ira Buchler, Henry Selby; standing, left to right: David Schneider, Harold Scheffler, Elli Kongas Maranda, Susan Ervin-Tripp, Roy D'Andrade, Michael Silverstein (courtesy David Schneider).

Portrait, mid-1970s (courtesy David Schneider).

Addy and David in Israel, mid-1970s (courtesy David Schneider).

Faculty and administrative staff of the Department of Anthropology, University of Chicago, 1979. Front row, left to right: K. Barnes, R. Tuttle, D. Schneider, S. Tax, M. Sahlins, B. Cohn; back row, left to right: N. McQuown, G. Stocking, P. Friedrich, V. Valeri, T. Turner, R. Klein, R. Smith, R. McC. Adams, M. Nash, Jean

Comaroff, K. Butzer, M. Singer, L. Bisek, R. Braidwood, A. Dahlberg, F. Eggan, R. Nicholas, L. Freeman; absent: John Comaroff, R. Fogelson, M. Marriott, N. Munn, D. Rice, R. Singer, M. Silverstein (courtesy George Stocking and the Department of Anthropology, University of Chicago).

Departmental party, University of Chicago, June 1984, with graduate students
Rafael Sanchez and Eve Pinsker (photo by Bonnie Urciuoli).

With George, Santa Cruz, California, 1994 (courtesy David Schneider).

jurisdiction. I was certain of that. If I had screwed up or if I was having some trouble, he could've done something, but—. So, sure enough, he sent the sailor back, and the sailor told me that he would come with me while we went and asked for the district chief's permission for me to go down and interpret. I took him down to Gatchepar. We went and saw the district chief. The district chief couldn't keep a straight face because he kept laughing and saying, "Of course! Yapese—you know damn well you can go where you want, when you want! Why are you asking me?"

And I kept saying, "No, sir, I'm here with your permission. I'm doing my work, 'cause I have your permission, and I will not do this if you feel that it's in any way a bad thing."

So he finally settled down and said, "Well, what do you think?"

I said, "I don't know. They're not gonna be like the Japanese. They're not gonna really beat people up. They *are* trying to find the stuff. It doesn't look good if some Yapese is pinched. You know, the way I do, that Yapese—some people are thieves."

"Oh yeah, a lotta thieves around here." So he said, "Maybe it will help the Yapese. If you help to find out who is the thief, they won't blame it on everybody."

"Well," I said, "that's certainly a possibility. It's a good idea."

"Okay," he says, "you go."

The sailor's sitting there. He doesn't know what's going on. So I tell the sailor, "I got the permission of the chief. I'll go with you."

So I went down to Yaptown and I stayed there four or five days, interpreting. I did the interpreting in the manner of my own choosing, of course, because, again, they couldn't understand me. I told each person that came in, "You have to understand—I will just interpret. They will ask questions. You tell them what you want to tell them. If you want to tell them anything, you just tell them, and I will tell them what you tell me to tell them. If it is the truth, good. If it is not the truth, it's up to you. You say anything you want. I will not tell them anything."

They had a couple of women in there who'd been sleeping with sailors, and they'd pinched a key from their keyrings—stuff like that. They were terrified. I saw my responsibility as making sure that they didn't get panicked, and that they didn't suddenly confess when they shouldn't, and that they didn't get scared. And to reassure them. But on the other hand, every so often someone would start in on a long harangue about what somebody'd done to them a long time ago. I would listen patiently. All too often it turned out that I would then turn to the navy and say, "He says he doesn't know nothing about it." Well, you know, for six minutes of talk, "He doesn't know nothing about it" doesn't help. But that's the way it was.

I left after five days, and eventually cigarettes began showing up. And they began to pinpoint where they were coming from. It was very simple. They didn't even have to speak Yapese. They found the guy. What's a guy going to do with two thousand dollars on that island? So they got the money back and they threw him in jail for a while. And that was the end of it all. But it sure upset the applecart that I would do a thing like that.

RH: You mean the Yapese got angry at you?

DMS: No, no. It upset the navy applecart that I would not obey the commander's orders and had to ask the district chief. But, it was a kind of a naive, simple-minded conceit on my part—that I'm going to be fair to the natives, that I'm going to do things properly, that I'm not going to be an exploitative, dishonest person. Also, I did definitely want to be dissociated from the administration, the navy or whoever it was, the authority figures. Which was also, perhaps, in keeping with my own character structure.

RH: Why did you leave the field?

DMS: I left the field because our time ran out. We only were supposed to be there about a year.[4] And the navy, and Murdock, running this thing, said it's time for people to go home. So, it was time for us to go.

RH: Were you happy to leave?

DMS: Oh yeah, I was anxious to leave. I was fed up.

RH: Fed up with what?

DMS: Well, being alone. And by that time, I didn't trust the Yapese very much. You know, I had found a lot of fault, but it had to do with the fact that I was lonely, and tired, and I was getting colds and stuff like that. So I began to get a little paranoid about the fact that you couldn't trust these guys. I couldn't trust what they said or anything else. And I just was tired of the job.

RH: Why do you say that by that time you didn't trust the Yapese? Do you mean in the sense that you would ask for information and you really had no way of evaluating what they were telling you?

DMS: Yeah. It was very hard to check.

RH: But when we look back on it, we would expect that to happen, right?

DMS: Yeah, of course. And also take into account. You know, since then, everybody goes into the field, I always advise them a number of things, like take time out in the middle and go and get a vacation. And secondly, write your thesis in the field, 'cause you're right there and you can check all the data clearly, and you can pick up new data as you need it. And come home with a finished thesis. If you write your thesis in the field, you don't have to get engaged in day-to-day work with local people, and so you get a break from the field that way, too. But a vacation in the middle is very important.

You see, an opportunity arose for the navy to fly anyone who wanted to, to Japan. All we had to do was to get to Guam, which was really simple 'cause there was a plane every week. And so, Hunt and Kidder flew to Japan, had a real nice vacation. I should have gone along, and didn't. I think Stevens went, too. I don't remember. But I should have gone and I didn't. I stayed. I wanted to stay and do the work. But I should have gone and gotten a vacation from there.

Did I tell you about the party that they gave me when I was leaving? Well, I was scheduled to fly off the next morning, and so they scheduled a party for the evening before.

RH: The Yapese?

DMS: The Yapese did. We're still up in Rumung. And I'm sitting there, and people are coming in for the party, and they're bringing live chickens and coconuts and things like that as gifts for me. And I'm sore because, you know, what the fuck am I going to do with a bunch of live chickens on an airplane, or coconuts? Huge collections of coconuts and stuff. So, of course I sat there and I redistributed everything. That is, somebody brought three or four coconuts here, and I found somebody else and gave him two of them, and someone else, another one, and the same way with the chickens, and so forth. And eggs. But a couple of the presents were nice. Somebody brought me a shell adze—I don't know where the hell that went. I guess it went to the Peabody Museum. And a model canoe, which broke up later. Things like that. But mostly it was stuff I couldn't possibly use. They brought me bottles of coconut toddy.

RH: Were they upset when you gave it back to them—gave it away to other people?

DMS: No, not a bit. That was normal procedure. But they wanted me to take it with me, to go home. You know, anytime anyone went on an overseas voyage, that's what normally would happen. And then the next day, you'd load all that stuff in the canoe. 'Cause, you know, the coconuts would last, and the chickens would probably last. They used to be able to build fires on the canoes and cook. So from their point of view, it was quite appropriate and proper; from my point of view, it was idiocy. How the hell was I going to drag all that stuff on the airplane? So I paid off all the debts I had by giving people presents all over the place.

But that was the same feeling, see?—that they just didn't understand me, and I couldn't really understand them. It wasn't till later, I was able to figure things out better—that that was the appropriate thing to do when someone went on an overseas voyage. Bring lots and lots of food. And food was so terribly significant, and symbolically significant, because their favorite way of telling you how awful things were was: "Alas, alas, I am starving." You know, they'd be sitting there with food running out of their mouth! But it was like saying, "Oh, I feel lousy." Well, you may not feel lousy, but you've got a problem. "Oh, my aching back," you know. People are always complaining about their back even when they don't have backache.

RH: So, you advise people to write their dissertation in the field, but it took you a long time afterward to figure out a lot of it.

DMS: Right.

RH: So people shouldn't write their dissertations in the field!

DMS: I don't know, I still think it might've been better if I had.

RH: Did you agonize over it at Harvard, or did you just write it up?

DMS: Oh, at Harvard it was very easy. I wrote it up quickly. I used the stuff I wrote for the Coordinated Investigation of Micronesian Anthropology as the core and basis of the thesis. And writing the thesis was easy. I spent more time working on statistics than I did on my thesis. So, no, I had no trouble writing that when I got back. But a lot of people did have trouble writing it.

Seven

From Harvard to England

RH: What did Addy do while you were on Yap?

DMS: She got a job in an office in the Chrysler Building, working for a company that manufactured cigarette paper. It was a very good job. She was very well paid. She could've really made more of a career there. But then I came back and I said, "Well, we've gotta go to school and continue school and write my thesis, and I'm gonna become an anthropologist." So, she quit her job and came up to Cambridge with me, got pregnant, and I failed my statistics exam! It was terrible! I had taken five statistics courses in my life, and I had failed every single one of them. And then I took the statistics course from Mosteller and Stouffer, and it was a requirement for the degree in Social Relations that you pass statistics. So I wasn't going to let that hold my degree up. I had a job at the London School of Economics, and I had a senior Fulbright. I had everything, and it all depended on my getting the Ph.D. in June. I spent that whole year concentrating on statistics, and I took the exam in June or May or April—I don't remember when—and I failed it again. Oh, it was absolutely the pits! It was the end of the world—just impossible.

But you know, it's the same old story: if you owe the bank so much money, you own the bank. Clyde had fixed me up with a job in London, I had a senior Fulbright to go—I was missing statistics. So they said, "Well, never mind, you go to London, you teach in London, and we'll send you the exam and you take it again." So I went to London and we got started, and they sent the exam in February or March. I took it in absentia, and Raymond Firth was supposed to be my proctor. Raymond said generously, "Good God, you don't need a proctor." And I didn't need a proctor. There was no way to cheat. I took the exam and I wrapped it up and I mailed it back to Harvard, and in due course I get this very peculiar letter from Fred Mosteller saying: "Dear David, you have met the requirement in statistics and now they will confer the degree, etc., etc."

So I knew Fred Mosteller fairly well by then, and I wrote back to Fred and said, "Dear Fred, that was a very odd letter. Did I pass the statistics exam or didn't I?" And I got back this very formal letter saying, "Dear David, you have met the requirement in statistics, and let us not discuss it any further."

So, years and years went by, and I discovered, as I knew perfectly well, that, of course I had failed that exam, too, but they had decided, the hell with the requirement in statistics.

RH: Did you fail these exams because you have no aptitude for numbers, or because you can't take tests, or what?

DMS: I don't know. All I know is that I really did learn a helluva lot about probability theory from Mosteller. I am grateful 'cause he was a very good teacher, and I am grateful because I was able to learn from him, which I hadn't been able to do before. And that's about it. I did learn a lot, and I apparently didn't really pass the exam, which may have something to do with the fact that I really couldn't seriously comprehend the ideas involved in standard deviation and things like that.

RH: Tell me about your relationship to the British social anthropologists.

DMS: That's very simple and straightforward. I had come back from Yap. I was writing my thesis. Audrey Richards came through Harvard, and LSE [London School of Economics] was trying to find people to come and teach there. They had to do that because (a) so many of their people had been killed in the war, there was nobody to teach and (b) they had no money to pay anybody. So, they talked to Clyde Kluckhohn, and Clyde said, "Why don't you try David Schneider?" So, I talked to Audrey Richards. I liked her. She liked me. And that was the last I heard of it.

Then Raymond Firth came through and, once again, I talked to Raymond Firth, I liked him, he liked me, everything was okay. And the next thing I know, Kluckhohn is telling me, "Go see Gordon Bowles over in the Peabody." So I went over to see Gordon Bowles. Gordon Bowles was at that point recruiting people for Fulbrights. Again, I really am so incredibly naive. I didn't know what was going on. What must have gone on was that Gordon Bowles had money to give people Fulbrights. Kluckhohn was looking for a job for me.

RH: Did you have a Ph.D. by this time?

DMS: I was getting one in June 1949. So Kluckhohn said, "Why don't you talk to Schneider? He would be a good person to go to LSE. They would love to have him. We would love to send him. All you have to do is hire him."

So I had a very brief interview with Gordon Bowles. I literally only remember that I met him briefly. That was it. The next thing I knew, I had a senior Fulbright to go to England. But of course, it turned out that the senior Fulbright paid me once and a half, or half again—I don't know, but much more than Raymond Firth was earning as a full professor. It was slightly embarrassing, and Raymond made it quite clear that there was some slight awkwardness here, but that was the way it was. So I had the Fulbright for one year, and I stretched the one year's Fulbright out to cover two years of staying there.

RH: So you went in fall 1949?

DMS: I went in fall 1949, with Addy. Jonathan had been born in August 1949. I went over alone, found a place for the three of us to live— which was not suitable, and so we had to find another place—and I started lecturing at LSE. What Firth and LSE had wanted was, in the first place, somebody to teach; in the second place, somebody to teach culture and personality, which was one of my specialties. It was real nice. He had also hired Elizabeth Bott from Chicago. She came on as an assistant lecturer, I think. At the same time, Lloyd Fallers came over as a graduate student to work with Audrey Richards on the way to doing fieldwork in Uganda. So I met Fallers there, I met Bott there. Edmund Leach was at that point teaching at LSE.

Firth was very kind, very generous, took extremely good care of me, was almost beyond belief: good, warm, supportive, generous. For example, he arranged for me to give a talk at the Royal Anthropological Institute. My eyes were absolutely wide—the RAI—wow, that was the greatest! I worked very hard to get a talk on Yap kinship. So I did the very best I could. I really did what I thought was a good paper. I practiced talking it to be sure it fell in the allotted time, and everything else.

We went there. There was, you know, not a big crowd—maybe twenty people at the very most. Some of them I think had come in out of the cold, but I'm not sure. Evans-Pritchard was the chair. Meyer Fortes was there, and Raymond Firth was there. So I give my little paper. Evans-Pritchard was sitting in the chair to the right, behind the lecturn. I moved back to my chair, to the left behind the lecturn.

I sit down, and E-P gets up and goes to the lecturn and says, "Thank you very much, Mr. Schneider, etc., etc. I should just like to point out one or two things." And then he proceeds to explain that Yapese apparently do not have the levirate, as Mr. Schneider said. They do practice, however, widow inheritance. "And I'm not quite sure as to whether there is widow concubinage as well, but still," and so on. And he proceeded to go down the line, to point out that I was wrong about all of these things, because I had not used the proper British forms for them.

RH: Are you saying that he simply corrected your terminology?

DMS: Well, just that I was flat wrong. It was not the levirate, because the levirate was where you raise seed to the dead.

RH: So he wasn't disputing your data, he was disputing the names that you attached to them?

DMS: All he did was to say that what I said was wrong. That's all.

RH: You refuse to answer the question.

DMS: Of course I refuse to answer the question, because that was not what happened. It is true that in American anthropology, what he calls widow inheritance is called the levirate. And it is also true that what he calls the levirate did not really have a special name in general American usage at that time. I mean, this business of raising seed to the dead, (a) I had never read the Bible and (b) I'd never heard of it! And I'd never read very much of it, because I hadn't read any English ethnography. But anyway, the English ethnography is not all that full and well documented. You had to have read E-P's *The Nuer,* and you had to read, before that, E-P's "Marriage and . . ."—a Rhodes-Livingston paper in which he made all these "important" distinctions.[1]

Anyway, after having been put down thoroughly, I was quite willing to drop through the floor, but there was no place to go. So I sat there. When E-P was done—this is why I say Raymond was a great guy; he still is a great guy!—Raymond got up and pointed out how similar the data I had reported were to things generally Oceanic, pointing out how, interestingly, there were one or two differences with Tikopia, but this was a characteristic Micronesian-Polynesian difference, and so on. He talked as if I had given an intelligent, intelligible paper, and put it in a wider context. Which was proper, good, kind, supportive—and was appropriate because he was the senior Oceanist.

I can't remember what else happened, except that, when it was over, Meyer Fortes came up, and Meyer said to E-P and Raymond and me, "Let's go out and have a drink together, shall we?" And E-P said, "Why, no, I think I'll just go off." So Fortes and Firth took me out, bought me a beer. I was not entirely speechless, but I can't remember saying anything, except that that was the first time I'd met Fortes, and that was nice. So that was one of my first introductions to the Brits.

Malinowski had a weekly seminar to which every anthropologist in the London area would come. Sometimes they had it at LSE. sometimes they had it at University College. Raymond was chairing it at that point at LSE. So Daryll Forde came in, and John Barnes came in, from University College, and Firth and Lucy Mair and Audrey Richards and Edmund Leach and Elizabeth Bott and I, and later on Steven Morris and Barbara Ward. That seminar was a good seminar. It was very lively, it was very interesting, and Raymond ran the seminar in a way that I've never seen done since—but he was able to do it all the time. He ran it like a perfect orchestra conductor. That is to say, every so often I would think, "I've got something to say," and I'd either stick my hand up or I'd start talking. And Raymond would quiet me down. Just turn me off and stop me. But I noticed that nobody else did anything like I did, so I shut up. And then Raymond would turn to Edmund or turn to John Barnes or turn to Daryll Forde or turn to me, and either by giving a specific question or just saying, "It's your turn," he would bring us in. For some reason, Raymond always knew what the hell I was going to say. So he timed it so that what I had to say was appropriate to what was being discussed.

I've been in seminars where the game was, you stick your hand up and you just holler, right? It's relevant, irrelevant, appropriate, inappropriate—but, you know, you gotta participate. But Raymond did a beautiful job. So that at the end of a three-hour seminar, you had a feeling that something had really been discussed, something had really moved. You may not have come to any great new conclusion, but, boy, I had a better idea of what was going on. So those seminars were extremely good.

I got to know Daryll Forde. John Barnes was very nice. And almost at the first seminar, Edmund Leach and I had a tiff. Whether this was before or after the affair with Evans-Pritchard, I can't remember. But for some reason, I just wasn't taking any shit from anybody, and I didn't take any shit from Edmund. The result of that tiff was that Edmund and I became very good friends.

RH: What was the subject matter of the tiff?

DMS: I have no idea. It was an intellectual tiff. He said something, I disagreed, or I said something, he disagreed. Edmund was—I don't know how you describe it, but I think everybody who knows Edmund knows it—Edmund would start with a ghastly, ungodly squeak and squeal, and it would gradually coagulate into some kind of coherent English. And then he'd say something. It was his way, especially when he got upset or excited. As I say, he and I became fairly good friends. He went to Cambridge. Fortes had already beat Audrey Richards out of the chair.

Anyway, Audrey Richards gave her manuscript on Chisungu, I think it was—a girl's puberty ceremony in Uganda. I did fine. Raymond then put me up for membership in the Association of Social Anthropologists, which was confined to people who had formal academic positions teaching anthropology in England, or Britain, and the Commonwealth. But nobody said anything.

RH: When you say that you managed to stretch the Fulbright out to two years, is that because they were paying you so well that you were able to save money the first year and stay on the second?

DMS: That's exactly what happened. I got one year of Fulbright money, but LSE was paying me two thousand dollars a year. Nobody could live on that, not even an Englishman.

RH: So the second year, you got a salary for teaching—

DMS: —I got the two thousand dollars from LSE, but it was because of the savings from the first year that we were able to stay on for the second. The reason we came home, simply, was that Addy's father died, and things were looking a little bleak, and we figured it was time to quit. That's it.

So, I got to know Fortes, but I never did get to know Evans-Pritchard very well. I don't think he liked me. I certainly didn't like him, terribly. I got to know Max Gluckman, whom I also did not like very well. He did not like me.

There was a man named Sidney Lee, who, I think, is still alive, still going, and who came from South Africa, who had done a little psychological work with Zulu. He showed up at LSE and gave a talk about Zulu hysteria. It was a perfect opportunity to have a seminar on culture and personality—the sort of thing I was able to do. So he presented a lot of material on Zulu; we all got to reading it; and a woman named Yonina Talmon, who I thought was very bright, very able—I thought a very fine person, a very smart person—she and a man named Philippe Garigue did this seminar on Zulu hysteria. The whole trick was, you read a lot of Zulu ethnography, and you read a lot of this and that, and there was Lee and all of his psychological material. So we began to work some good things out.

But Max Gluckman was the world's leading authority on Zulu. He now has the first chair at Manchester. So we figured, well, we've got this fairly well worked out. Max Gluckman came to London fairly frequently. I saw him at LSE one day and I said, "Max, we've done a lot of work on Zulu. We're not sure, but we'd like to check it over with you and see what you think of it. Tell us where we're wrong, bring us up to date"— which, I think was the proper thing to do: "We've done a little work, you're the authority, help us out."

Max liked grand gestures, big gestures. He invited us to send a team up to Manchester to present this to his group. So we agreed that Yonina and I would go up and do it. So Yonina and I got ourselves put together, we wrote the stuff up, we figured out how to present it. We get to Manchester. To make the story short: we come to the seminar, and we start talking about the Zulu, and we're cut off—told to stop talking about Zulu. It turns out that everybody in the seminar in Manchester has been instructed by Gluckman to take one piece of Margaret Mead or Ruth Benedict and—you know, Yonina and I sat there, and there is the assembled artillery shooting pieces off: "Margaret Mead said this in 1936, and what do you think about that?"

So we were completely confounded. We're coming up to talk about Zulu, yes? We field a few of these questions about the American culture and personality business and Margaret Mead and Ruth Benedict. I finally get—I'm troubled and I say, "Max, we came here to talk about Zulu. I don't want to defend Margaret Mead. Let her defend herself. I want to talk about Zulu. That's what we've come to talk about."

Well, apparently, Max had not told people that that's what we came to talk about. He said, "These couple of Americans are gonna come up and talk about culture and personality. Let's get 'em." So they were all primed to cut us down.

We ended up by doing the best we could to deal with the questions about Mead and Benedict. We got finished with the culture and personality stuff, and then we offered them the Zulu stuff. The seminar, of course, was not interested in Zulu. They didn't know, they didn't care. But in the course of our presentation, Gluckman said, "You're absolutely wrong about this—it's not that way at all," and then he explained how it was. On he went, and in the course of the explanation, the decisive, crucial factor was that the Zulu said this—he gave it as a quotation from an important Zulu chief.

Well, that went fine. They were very polite and hospitable, and I think Max then took us all out and bought us beer. Yonina and I ended up at Max's house and stayed for dinner, and someplace along that time— I don't know whether it was Yonina or I—but we suddenly realized: Max Gluckman had worked in Zululand, and it was a well-known, well-established, well-authenticated fact that all of his field notes had been burned up in an unfortunate fire. He had them all in a little out-house behind—and while he was away doing something, his field notes burned up.

So the next day we said to Max, "Are you sure that the decisive piece of evidence"—we repeated the statement of the Zulu informant.

"Oh," he said. "Absolutely!"

So we said, "Max, if your field notes all burned up, and you don't have any, you have a very good memory—to remember verbatim what was said."

"Oh," he said, "that was not memory, verbatim. That was structurally correct."

So we began to explore what was structurally correct, and he said, "That's what a Zulu informant would have said had I asked him the right question."

So we went back to London feeling that, somehow—very interesting, anthropology, isn't it? That's the way it's done.

RH: Did your dislike for Max Gluckman stem from this trick he played on you with the culture and personality seminar?

DMS: My dislike for Max Gluckman went the gamut from intellectual to purely personal considerations. He was overbearing, overweening, over—everything over. He was a large man. He barged around. He stomped around. He was totally insensitive to everything that I know of. He was a deeply committed Marxist and communist in every respect whatsoever except where it might possibly count: I believe he married a good deal of money, and that was always very important to him. His Marxism, and his being a communist, never really did interfere with the style of life he maintained for himself. That always struck me as a kind of absurdity which I didn't like. He was just, I thought, uncouth and unpleasant.

Intellectually, rituals of rebellion—big deal. Over and above that, he went to Israel and built a—I thought, in my not very humble opinion—a perfectly lousy anthropology department which is still there, at Tel Aviv. He never took any responsibility for it. Meanwhile, Yonina Talmon died; she had breast cancer. He got to Tel Aviv and began building it either when Yonina was still sick or—she had no hand in it; she had nothing to do with it.

He had, I thought, almost no intellectual position of any coherence, and even as a buffoon I think he was pretty bad.

So that was Max. On the other hand, Meyer Fortes and I always got along reasonably well. He kept chiding me, consistently, because I did not really believe in kinship the way he did, because I did not believe in family the way he did. He believed in family. He really did. He lived his life that way. Family and kinship were first and major things in his life. He was obviously deeply in love as long as they were married, with his first wife, Sonia. He lived it. And he also chided me constantly, whenever he got a chance: I was not a good Jew, I didn't go to synagogue—at least on the high holy days I should do something. I didn't think the family was the be-all and end-all, and so on. But we wrote, we corresponded regularly—two or three or four letters a year, at least. He came through the United States—whenever he came through, I saw him. He was in Berkeley when I was there, and Chicago.

He came through Boston while I was still at Harvard, and I spent the whole day with him. He was on his way back to England. England had no sugar, it had no tea—it was hard up. So I went around shopping with him. I knew Boston. I kept urging him to buy this and buy that. He would glare at me and say, "No, no, that's too petty." It was a very good and very pleasant day. I got to know him a lot better. He got to know me a lot better.

That was before I got to England. Then when I got to England, I saw more of him.

RH: You said that Fortes lived his life believing in the family. I don't know much about your relationship to Addy, but my impression is that you were pretty close to Addy for a long time.

DMS: Yes.

RH: So that you, too, had a close and important marriage.

DMS: Yes, that was so. But on the other hand, I don't think either Addy or I thought that kinship and the family as an institution was the be-all and end-all—and Meyer did. That is, Meyer not only lived it, he thought it, intellectually; whereas, for one reason or another, Addy and I did have a long and—what would you call it?—it was a stable marriage. But, I don't think Addy thought that the family was the way to go all the time, for everybody, that the family was the principal institution in society. Neither did she feel that the family had to be the first and only loyalty. She certainly felt that you owed loyalty. But Meyer felt that the family was the *first* loyalty, the primary and predominant loyalty.

This was very closely integrated with his feelings about being a Jew: that that kind of loyalty and commitment—that the two coincided in many ways; that being Jewish and having that kind of family was vital. Whereas Jewishness, for one thing, rested much differently—more lightly, in fact—on me, and fairly lightly on Addy, too.

RH: Did the people in this London circle take a markedly different approach to kinship than the Americans? Were you iconoclastic on this issue even among the Americans?

DMS: I was iconoclastic in the American context to begin with, but, clearly, the English took it very differently than the Americans. In some ways it's very simple. English anthropology, certainly by the 1940s and 1950s, had become comparative sociology. They kept calling it "social anthropology." And although Malinowski talked about "culture," it was a word that—you know, culture for them was ornaments, different hat styles, things like that.

RH: As Meyer Fortes told me in 1973, at Chicago, "I prefer to speak of custom."

DMS: Exactly! I didn't really finish with Meyer. My relations with Meyer became more elaborate when he came to the States and was at the Center for Advanced Study. He had read some of my stuff by then, and his book, *Kinship and the Social Order*, was, to a fairly limited extent, contra me.[2] But, yes, the English were into social structure, social organization, social anthropology. Their notions of culture were, again: it was peripheral, it was ornamental, it was custom. But it was not where it was at.

Whereas the Americans didn't have the same kinds of notions of social structure. Social structure, for the English—from Durkheim, through Radcliffe-Brown—came to be seen as the formal shape of organizations, primarily in terms of major functions. Whereas for the Americans, it was not only custom, it was bits and pieces—you know, [Robert] Lowie's famous "shreds and patches" is always a misquotation.[3] He said that culture was a thing of shreds and patches *with respect to* the historical elements of which it was made, and their diverse origins: things came from hither and yonder in apparently random ways. He did not say, as Benedict later misstated it, that it was not coherently put together. That became a marvelous thing for everybody to poke fun at.

RH: Did the British respect Murdock?

DMS: Murdock was quite different. The answer to your question is, minimally. They didn't see any point in any of that crap. For example, Radcliffe-Brown made a big deal of kinship terminology. That was the end of it. Nobody else really cared. Evans-Pritchard hardly touched it; Fortes paid only brief lip service to it; Firth thought it was—you know, it was like ornaments. Nobody really dealt with terminology until the [Rodney] Needham and Leach papers that began via [Claude] Lévi-Strauss.[4]

But in America, the whole notion of history and evolution somehow being problematically intertwined, Murdock was trying to deal with these hypotheses about Where did it start? How did it start? What is it associated with? So he was doing these big correlations of kinship terminology and kin groups.

So American anthropology was quite different. The kinds of fads that went in American anthropology did not go over at that time in England. Culture and personality was big here, but there they would have nothing of it. Evans-Pritchard made an industry of poking fun at Margaret Mead. He was hostile to women to begin with, and he was hostile to Margaret Mead particularly. So he talked about "the wind in the palm trees" kind of ethnography, and although E-P made all this fuss about anthropology being history or it's nothing, how much history did he do? [William H. R.] Rivers was at least pretending to do history.

Have I told you enough about the Brits?

RH: I'm still interested in that 1963 conference, because Clifford Geertz has said it was such an important moment.[5] He said that Gluckman organized it, E-P boycotted it—

DMS: —that's right. Fred Eggan organized it from the American side, and who were we to make any undue comments about the fact that Fred brought everybody from Chicago who could walk? Marshall [Sahlins] was the only person who came from outside Chicago. Most of them were Chicagoans at that time—Eric Wolf was at Chicago at that time, Geertz, Fallers, me.

Whereas in England, they did take a kind of scattering—Michael Banton, here and there—but E-P definitely boycotted it. He didn't want to have anything to do with the Americans. And he was very right.

RH: Why is that?

DMS: Well, there was a certain amount of Anglophilia among Americans, but I don't think that an awful lot of Americans were as severely Anglophilic. Kluckhohn was very definitely Anglophilic, but by that time Kluckhohn had died. He died in 1960. By then, I was not wowed by the English. Geertz I don't think thought that the English were the greatest things on the face of the earth. Fallers certainly was very polite, very good, very reasonable. But the rest of us were not overawed by them.

RH: Geertz seems to think this was such an important moment.

DMS: I know.

RH: And you don't?

DMS: I perhaps don't appreciate its importance. It was only important for me because I had a chance to write and publish that big paper, which everybody said was a monstrosity—that I should have taken it apart and rewritten it, published it as five different papers.[6] But, you know, that's what I was into. I would've done it even if the conference hadn't happened.

Eight

Mescalero Apache: The Romance and Politics of Fieldwork

RH: Tell me how you got involved with the Mescalero Apache.

DMS: I got involved with Mescalero Apache in the following simple-minded way. I came back from England, got a job at Harvard; second son, Michael, was born. And, you know, fieldwork was the name of the game, so I figured we ought to do some more fieldwork. The best idea is to have fieldwork in a second place that's different from the first place, and that way you have two different areas, and all that, and it was all very proper, and Evan Z. Vogt was at Harvard, and I thought, well, Pacific Islands, sanitation's a problem, getting out there's a problem. I want some field-work now where all four of us can go and do it. So I talked around to various places, and Vogt suggested that the Southwest was a really good idea—lots of good places to work there, lots of important problems—and suggested I consider the Apache.

Well, Western Apache, for some reason, I didn't consider, but considered Mescalero Apache. Nobody else was working there, but Morris Opler had done a lot of work there. So I picked Mescalero Apache.

At the next American Anthropological Association meeting I located Morris Opler, and I approached him—

RH: —is this about 1953?

DMS: That's about right, 1953, '53 or '54. So I approached Morris Opler in the proper, deferential way, and I said, "Professor Opler, I know that you've done a great deal of work on Mescalero Apache."

"Oh, yes!" he said, "I've done it all!" So I said to Professor Opler that I still would like to consider working in Mescalero.

He said, "Well don't worry, there's nothing left to do. I have got it all. I am currently writing it up. I will have it written up and published in no time, and there'll be nothing really left for you to do."

So I said, "Well, look, let me tell you what I'm interested in doing, and see what you think."

He said, "Well, it's not necessary. I just told you that I've got all the data. There's nothing left to collect."

I nevertheless insisted on telling him that I wanted to study the contemporary, present-day, this-very-moment kinship arrangements. To which he replied, "What for?" So, I gave the whole thing up, and decided that I didn't need him anyway. You see, it was courteous to always get the permission of the other person who owned the field before you go in the field. Margaret Mead had been very strong on that, and this was a simple courtesy, and it was proper, and Opler's reply was the standard reply: namely, if I don't want you to go mucking about in my field, I tell you I've got it all taken care of. That's all.

RH: Let me interrupt here a minute, and ask you a question: you asked Opler's permission, but didn't you have to ask permission of the people themselves?

DMS: Oh yeah, but that's the next step. Once I had committed my-self to going there, then I had to get the money to go there. To get the money to go there, I had to have a project, a problem. And *then* I went there. I wrote ahead, and when I got there, I went to see the chairman of the tribal council, and I presented myself at a meeting of the tribal council. I explained what I wanted to do, why I wanted to do it, why it might help them, why it would be good for them, asked their per-mission. I asked *permission,* I didn't ask cooperation or anything else. First I asked permission. I had already, by mail, reached the superin-tendent of the reservation. Here again, I had a very nice arrangement. The superintendent was a fellow named Walt Olsen, who had had a lot of experience with anthropologists and had been extremely helpful to anthropologists when Olsen was working on the Navajo reservation. He knew John Adair, he knew Evan Vogt, he knew David Aberle. He knew a lot of them. So, when I decided I would work in Mescalero, they told me, write Walt Olsen and tell him when you're coming, and see if he can help you out. Indeed, Walt Olsen was very good, very helpful, very nice, and very bright—a very able man. If there is such a thing as a good superintendent in the BIA [Bureau of Indian Affairs], he was it. But the nature of the job makes it almost impossible to be a good superintendent. He arranged for us to have an abandoned teacher's house in a school way out in the middle of the reservation.

RH: Go back a moment. You were saying that Opler wanted nothing of this.

DMS: Not only did he want nothing of it, he didn't want me to go.

RH: How did you make up your mind to do it anyway?

DMS: I just did. I just didn't talk to Opler again. I didn't say a thing. I'm not even sure that I told Evan Vogt that Opler was obviously against the whole thing. I just went ahead. The trick was to apply to the Ford Foundation for a grant. And the Ford Foundation, in those days, was a big operation. They didn't want to monkey with lousy little grants for five thousand dollars! They explained to everybody that they didn't like small grants because the cost of bookkeeping was so great, it was just not economically worthwhile.

However, I had two friends—Frank Sutton and another guy whose name I forget at the moment—both of them in the Ford Foundation. And I was in New York, and I called them up and I had lunch with them, or went and talked with them, and told them my project. They were very sweet. So they arranged for me to have a five-thousand-dollar grant. That's what it came down to.

RH: What exactly was the project?

DMS: The project was a simple one. The Murdock theory of change in kinship systems said that you developed descent rules out of the alignment of kin in a local arrangement. That if, for example, you had matrilocal marriage, and a man moved into the kin group with his wife's kin, then, with the changes in the economic arrangements, that would develop into matrilineality, provided that the economy and so on and so forth worked so well. If, on the other hand, there was matrilocality and the economy was such that it gave way to neolocal residence, then you would rapidly develop a bilateral kinship system. And so on.

Now, according to all the literature, the Mescalero Apache were very much like all the other Apaches, and very much like the Navajo, because they were all Southern Athabascan speakers, and they had all come down from someplace way up north and settled in there. The Navajo and some of the Western Apache were very definitely matrilineal. They had matrilineal clans. But they all had that sort of matrilateral emphasis:

they had a girls' puberty rite. They tended toward matrilocal residence.

So, given a tendency toward matrilocal residence, and given the changed economic circumstances on the reservation, Murdock's prediction was that they would become bilateral. And at that point, and certainly for the sake of the Ford grant, I didn't want to take a position on it. I said, well, Murdock's position is that they're going to be bilateral. They've been around there for, I don't know, fifty, seventy-five hundred years. Let me go see what they are! That was it. It was a problem. It was theoretically interesting. It was a prediction, all that. So that's the way I got the Ford money.

My own plans were to start. It would be a place where Addy and I and the kids could go back year after year. It was not impossible. There were health facilities nearby. It was in the country. It was up at ten, twelve thousand feet—beautiful, high pine forest. It was just great! So we pulled in there in the summer, and we stayed the first summer [1955]. It was not all that easy, but it worked.

RH: Whenever I think about working with Native Americans, it seems to me that, at least today, it would be so difficult politically, that I wouldn't want to brave it at all. What was the climate like in the 1950s?

DMS: The climate in the '50s was not a helluva lot better than it is now. They were definitely hostile. They were definitely unfriendly. They were definitely not interested in anthropology.

RH: And did that make sense to you?

DMS: Sure, absolutely! But, you know, on the one hand I'd read some of the ethnographic material. My friend David Aberle had been working in Navajo for a long time. Vogt had told me something about it. Harry Basehart was up in New Mexico. He had worked in Jicarilla, and so I talked to him. The situation was not easy, and I knew it would not be easy. But my attitude was, what the hell—I was a reasonably decent person, and having Addy and the kids would always help, because I wasn't just going to be a single man catting around. I was more mature. I was serious. I could not only approach old men, I could approach young men. And then I had certain simple advantages, like I had a car. And one of the problems on Indian reservations always is that people need to go places and they've got no transportation. And so you make yourself friendly and useful. David Aberle used to carry around great stocks of canned fruit and things like that in the car, and whenever he stopped and imposed on the hospitality of others, he always was able to leave gifts and things like that, which were appreciated. Watermelons, again, another thing in the summertime—you know, you've got a couple of watermelons and you just drop one off where people had been nice to you, and say, "Oh, hey, I got a couple of watermelons down here. I picked them up, and there's one for me, and I got one for you, if you want."

RH: So in those days, you could just make up your mind to do this, and it didn't seem like a terribly difficult thing to do?

DMS: Well, there were a number of important differences then and now. At that time, Walter Olsen could say, "You can go and live in the teacher's house in White Tail"—that's where we first lived; the next year was in Elk Silver. The tribe had no control over that. Secondly, although the tribe had a kind of court, and had a couple of policemen, they had practically no authority anyplace, and presumably none over whites. They could kick whites out who were living illegally on their land, but I was living in a Bureau of Indian Affairs house. And although the roads were not very good—they were gravel, such as they were—but still, it was not bad.

Since then, not only have—and the Mescalero were one of the first tribes to really establish sovereignty, so that their courts and police control practically everything—it was no longer possible for the BIA to say, "Whether the tribe likes it or not, you can go and have that house." You'd have to get the house from the tribe. So it's much harder now.

RH: Does all that lend credence to the critique that says that anthropology was made possible by a colonial regime?

DMS: Absolutely! I don't argue that anthropology was possible or easy or anything else *without*—let me try it again: colonialism certainly helped. For one thing, they couldn't just up and kill you all that easily. They were not inclined to do it all that easily, although it still happened from time to time. You know, punitive expeditions had gone into all kinds of places to make sure they understood—you know, [Andrew] Cheyne in Belau. They killed some damn beachcomber in Belau, and the British sent in a warship and bombarded the shit out of everything, and then they sailed away. It convinced the Belauans that they ought to be more careful about who they kill next time. That's always been the case.[1]

When I went to Mescalero, the BIA literally let me stay where I wanted. And once the Mescalero established their sovereignty, once the Mescalero established that *they* were able and perfectly free to sell liquor any time of the day or night they wanted, and without paying tax on it—see, when I was there, liquor was absolutely prohibited on the reservation. And Eddie's Bar, just outside the border of the reservation, was making piles of money off drunken Indians. The Indians would drive up there, and they'd leave their car as collateral for the loan that they used to pay for the liquor, and they'd bring bags of groceries there that their families and kids needed, and leave that with Eddie, and go off with a drink. People were drinking like mad, and freezing to death on the roads, getting run over—a Greyhound bus ran some poor Indian over because he was lying, passed out, in the middle of the road.

But then Mescalero got sovereignty. They built that great big Inn of the Mountain Gods. They served liquor, and there's no tax for it. They sold cigarettes and didn't collect tax on it. Now, even today, they're considering putting a radioactive waste dump on their place, for which they'll get a helluva lot of money. Now, at that time, they had a big cattle co-op, and they were doing a certain amount of lumbering, and then they bought a log-peeler, a pole-peeler, and various things like that. And sometimes the Indians were guiding people to hunt bear and do other hunting and fishing. But now, they're doing a lot of it, and it's very big money.

But the point only was that at that time, I could make a deal with Walt Olsen, and he could let me live in the teacher's house. Now, you gotta have permission from the tribe. And, indeed, people have worked in Mescalero since that time. A very capable woman, Claire Farrer, has been working—she's just published a book on them;[2] she had to get permission from the tribal council. She had to make a deal that before she published anything, it had to be reviewed by the chairman of the tribal council, the president, and that if they didn't like what she was publishing, they could literally prevent her from publishing it. She couldn't publish without their permission. She had a lot of trouble, because frequently they didn't like what she was writing.

RH: You said that you, too, went to get permission from the tribal council.

DMS: I went to get permission from the tribal council, but I really didn't need to. I went on the grounds that it was better to get permission and—see, literally, I had no plan for what I would do if they said no. I don't know what I would have done. I just assumed that I would go and ask their permission, and I would be such a nice guy, and they would love me so much immediately, that they'd say, oh, hell, happy day!

But instead, all that really happened was that they said, "We really have no way to stop you. It's okay with us." And a couple of them laughed and said, "You're asking our permission! We can't stop you. Just go on ahead."

So I went. Got Addy and the kids settled into the house. There was a certain amount of strain between Addy and me because the house was filthy and, of course, who had to clean it up? I had to go out and make friends with the Indians, right? So she got the job of cleaning up the house, boiling diapers for Michael, and things like that. But anyway, we worked that out.

So I beetled back and forth in the car, drove here, drove there, picked up hitchhikers, arranged with Percy Bigmouth to give me Apache lessons, arranged with Charlie Smith to be an informant. He lived nearby in White Tail, so that was not so bad. I could just go over there and sometimes take one of the kids with me. And he'd come down to my house. Charlie and Addy and the two kids and I went on a picnic to Three Rivers. It was a lot of fun. He really was a very nice, sweet man. He loved kids, and the kids loved him. He gave the kids Indian names, and the kids *loved* that, and I loved that and I liked Charlie and Charlie liked me.

One day we were sitting around for some reason, and Charlie comes running down, and he's just absolutely tuckered—he was a very old man; I think he was in his eighties. He was absolutely out of breath, and he says, "Come on, come on, you've gotta come, come!"

I said, "What's the trouble?"

He said, "Come on, please, come!"

I said, "What's the matter?"

He said, "Come to my house, just come with me!

I said, "Charlie, *what* is the problem?" I thought he was sick or something. So he gets in the car and I said, "Charlie, what exactly is the trouble?"

And he said, "The Normans are coming!" I was totally nonplussed. I didn't know what the Normans were. So I drove him back to his house, and we sat there, and very shortly came these two Mormon missionaries with their white, short-sleeved shirts and their ties, carrying this large board. And we had to sit and sing hymns with them. That's what the Normans were. "The Normans were coming, the Normans were coming," 1066 and all that, and it turned out to be two Mormon missionaries. And Charlie just didn't want to have to face them alone and sing hymns with them alone. So I had to sit there and sing hymns with him. That's the first and only time I've sung hymns with Mormon missionaries. So that was Charlie.

RH: Did you learn some Apache?

DMS: Well, I actually learned a little bit of Apache, but not enough to do anything with. It's very hard, and of course, Percy Bigmouth was a hunchback. And the Apaches, like so many people, do not treat people with disabilities very kindly. So Percy Bigmouth took care of his old, very, very—used to be called "senile," now it's Alzheimer's—father. His father's name was Bigmouth, and he was a scout, an Apache scout. I don't know whether he was in his nineties, his hundreds, but, you know, he sort of moaned, groaned, muffled, and Percy literally had to mop him up, wash him. Of course, he was incontinent and everything else.

So I would sit on the porch of their house, with Percy, and we did a combination of Apache lessons—how to say this, how to say that—and talked about life in Apache, and what it was like now, and what it was like when he was a kid.

RH: And all the time you were taking notes?

DMS: All the time I'm taking notes with paper and pencil, and of course, came that apocryphal day—everybody encounters this sort of thing—I asked him some question, and he stopped and said, "Just a minute, I'll have to think that over." He walked inside the house, and he came out with the answer. I wrote it down, and we talked some more, and, goddamn, one more time I asked him a question, and "Just a minute," he said; "I'm not sure about that." So he went in the house. But this time I was puzzled. I didn't know what was going on. So I watched as he went into the house. I leaned around in my chair and stuck my neck through the door. And he went over to this table and was looking in a book.

I said, "Percy, what is that book you're looking at?"

"Oh," he said, "I'm just reading Opler's *Apache Life-way*, looking this up so I can give you the right answer."[3]

So I said, "Well, thank you, Percy, I appreciate it." I didn't give him a hard time. I accepted his answers. They were authentic, yes?

He made arrows for the children. He had frequently worked for Boy Scouts telling them Indian lore and things like this. We would sit there and, oh! I had a terrible time learning. I'd be mumbling Apache words driving around, and I learned to say "Hadenya." That is, "Where are you going?" When I picked somebody up, instead of saying, "Hey, where do you want to go?" I'd say "Hadenya?" And they'd always look at me oddly and they'd say, "Well, just take me down to Agency."

RH: They were all bilingual, I suppose.

DMS: Not only were they bilingual, but I could never pronounce it correctly. And they never understood what the hell I was talking about. But that was early on.

So then there was a great big ceremonial of some kind—the girl's puberty ceremony, Fourth of July. We had a station wagon, and we fixed the back of the station wagon up—air mattresses and lots of blankets. We put the kids in the back. They went to sleep, and I went out and stood around the fire and watched people. They did Indian dances, and they were singing, and I stood there. I don't know exactly how it happened, but I found that I had moved away from the fire, and there were these five Indian men standing between me and the fire, and I was very much in the dark.

One of them says to me, conversationally and politely, "I see you're trying to learn to speak Indian."

I said, "Yeah."

He said, "Why?"

I came up with a good, proper, first-year-graduate-student anthropological reply. I said, "I'm going to be here now, and I think it'd be nice—I want to talk to Indians and learn Indian culture, and I think it'd be nice if I could speak Indian language. That's the best way to speak with Indians. Indians like to speak Indian. So I thought I would like to learn Indian."

So he says, "Don't."

I said, "What do you mean, 'Don't?'"

He said, "Look, the white man has taken everything we've got. They've taken all our land, they've taken all our customs, they've given us all kinds of religion that we don't want, we don't need. White men have taken everything we've got. Now, you leave our language alone."

"Oh," I said, "well, if you feel . . ." You know, there were five guys. I'm in the dark. I can see the fire behind them. Each of them appears to me to weigh about seven hundred pounds. They tower over me. I was five feet five, they were like seven feet tall. They were not being hostile; they were being firm: "It's our language. It's the only thing we've got left. You leave it alone, please."

Under the circumstances, I didn't think I had any choice but to say, "Oh, well, gee, I didn't know you felt that way. If that's the way you feel, okay, I'll leave it alone."

"Good," they said. Thereupon the five broke ranks and left an avenue for me to go back toward the fire. And I did.

So, a few days later I'm back to see Percy Bigmouth. I said, "Percy, you know I've been taking language lessons from you." And I tell him what happened.

Percy sits there and listens. He's very quiet, and he says, "Well, you know the store, you go into the store, don't you?"

And I said, "Yeah."

He said, "Did you, when you go in, did you notice the hats there?"

And I said, "Yeah, I did notice the hats."

He said, "What did you see with the hats?"

I said, "There are a lot of hats, but they're not selling very well, are they?"

"No," he said, "they're not selling very well. What kind of hats are they?"

I said, "Well, strangely enough, they're all the same kind of hat."

"Well," he said, "they did sell one hat."

I said, "Really?"

He said, "Yes. That's the Apache. If one person has that kind of hat, nobody else wants that hat. Everybody has to have his own hat, everybody has to have his own opinion, everybody has to think the way he wants to think—and that's the Apache way."

So I said, "Well, what are you trying to tell me, Percy?"

He said, "Well, look, if you want to learn Apache, that's up to you. If they don't want you to learn Apache, that's up to them. *I* want you to learn Apache. They don't want you to learn Apache. What should you do? It's up to you."

The phrase "It's up to you" was absolutely standard there. Every time you'd say, "What are you supposed to call that relative?" they'd say, "Well, it's up to you. You wanna call him this, you can call him this; you wanna call him that, you call him that." Or, you'd say, "Where are you supposed to live when you get married?" "Well, that's up to you. You wanna go here?—that's up to you." It was the epitome of the most extreme individualism.

So I continued taking language lessons from Percy. From time to time I would encounter these five guys. I'd say hello, and most of them never bothered to speak with me at all. They just literally ignored me. That was it. Whether it was the circumstances of that night at the fire—that it was dark, and they were feeling particularly Indian and angry at whites, who knows? They never bothered me again. No particular person bothered me. That was it. So that was Mescalero.

RH: By this time, were you so hooked on kinship that you wanted to keep studying it? After all, you said that originally you hadn't meant to get involved in it.

DMS: It was something I knew about, and knew enough to write a good proposal. I don't think that I had any clear intention of doing more than using the kinship partly as an entree to get the money, partly an entree into—it would be an apparently innocuous thing to study. Where I was going to go from there, I didn't know.

At that point, both Addy and I felt that this was our chance to do the fieldwork that we hadn't been able to do the first time. This was a chance where she could do some work, I could do some work, we could both work together. We were going to see if we couldn't really set up a long-term situation. Lots of people we knew went back summer after summer, year after year. They had ten-, fifteen-, twenty-year contacts with people. The Spindlers [George and Louise] never really did break away from Winnebago. Vogt was always involved with Navajo, one way or another. Aberle was always going back to Navajo. It seemed like a perfect setup. Why shouldn't I do it?

RH: Did Addy want to do anthropology?

DMS: I'm not sure she wanted to do anthropology, but she thought that she would enjoy being in the field and doing what we had not been able to do in Yap. But she liked the Indians. I liked the Indians. The kids were happy there. Maybe it was a terrible mistake, but we got Jonathan a BB gun, and he went out and shot things with it—not very destructive. You know, he'd hit trees, generally. He actually went and shot bats once, shot a few bats.

And then we got a rattlesnake once. We went out and shot a rattlesnake with a BB gun! Have you ever shot a rattlesnake with a BB gun? Jonathan and Michael and I were walking in single file, and there was a distinct rattle of a rattlesnake. I said, "Get back, boys! Hand me the gun!" So I went up to this poor rattlesnake, coiled underneath a bush, and I shot it in the head. Didn't bother the snake one little bit. I shot it in the head one more time. Just made him rattle more. I must've shot it in the head so many times we ran out of BBs. Eventually the rattlesnake just sort of clonked.

RH: Why didn't you just leave it alone?

DMS: Great White Hunters don't leave things alone! So we picked the rattlesnake up, holding it at arm's length, and popped it in the back of the car to drive home and show mother the great snake we had caught. However, before we picked it up, I took the shovel and cut the head off and left it. There was no head, nothing—because I had heard that the worst snake bites come from dead snakes.

So we got home. I figured, okay, I've had it, I'm through with this goddamn snake. Addy says, "No, you can't be through with the snake. You have to skin it!" And the kids said, "Oh yes, we have to skin it and save the skin!"

I said, "Addy, I don't want to skin this snake."

She said, "Well, you shot it. You've got to skin it."

Well, I picked the snake up by the tail, whereupon the empty neck whipped around and smacked me on the hand. Boy, did I drop that snake! Was I glad that I had chopped off the head with the little shovel we carried in the car. So I skinned it, and we had the skin in the house in Chicago for years and years. Gradually the scales fell off, and it flaked. Of course, I had never really cured the skin properly—just rubbed salt on it, lots of it. The kids lost interest, in any case.

That was the summer of '55. When we were finished that summer, we went on to the Center for Advanced Study. The center was flush with money, and they wanted to encourage research. I'm going to work in Apache. I'm still moderately interested in culture and personality, but not irretrievably so. Gardiner Lindzey is interested in doing some research, and he is interested in Indians. Jim March, a political scientist, was a good friend of Lindzey. So the center gave Gardiner and Jim and me money to go back and scout out Mescalero to see if we could set up a good study. The trick would be to set up a study of cultural, psychological, and political aspects of political organization and political problems. We worked out a real nice proposal. We really worked on it, and we proposed it to the Social Science Research Council, and to three or four other places. But nobody would fund it. So we gave it up.

But I still had my connections, so I was going to go back. At this point, I'm getting ready to put in a big proposal to work in Mescalero to NIH [National Institutes of Health], and I meet a psychoanalyst named L. Bryce Boyer. Bryce Boyer and I, with Bryce Boyer's wife, Ruth, put in—well, I put in, as "senior investigator"—through the University of California at Berkeley for funds to do a psychoanalytic cultural study.

We got a great big fat grant. It was a good whopping sum. So we went out that first summer, and Bryce found a medicine man. Once again, we were living in schoolteacher's houses. Bryce found this guy, Woodrow Wilson, who was a chronic alcoholic, but he was a medicine man. And I figured, he's going to do his stuff, I'm going to do my stuff, and that's it. So, we set to work doing household surveys: Who's in the house? Where do you live? etc.

Next summer we go back, and Bryce takes off and goes to the psychoanalytic meetings in Mexico City. All I know is, he's taking off for a week and he's coming back. He comes back and he's very happy. He's really exuberant. He has given a paper, down at the international psychoanalytic meetings, on psychoanalysis of an Apache medicine man!

Well, of course he hadn't psychoanalyzed him, but he had gotten, I think, one or two dreams, from which he had then developed and proposed a whole series of statements about Apache character! So I was very, very perturbed and upset and disturbed, because on the basis of a couple of dreams from a drunken medicine man, and no other information, no other interviewing and no other anything—and just a superficial acquaintance with the ethnographic literature—you don't go around telling an international conference that you've got this great project and you've already got insight into the whole character of the Apache nation.

So we had a slight falling out over that. In fact, we had quite a bit of falling out over that. I said I thought that was a pretty bad thing to do. Now, characterologically me: I have a terrible tendency to not say very much and keep my mouth shut, and then suddenly blow up. And I did. I criticized Bryce, and I said that I didn't think it was proper, I didn't think it was a good idea, I didn't think we were ready to do any of that stuff yet. And he kept saying, "Don't you worry. Never you mind. I know what I'm doing. Everything is under control. You just go ahead and take care of your end. I'll take care of my end."

And I said, "But you're into my end."

And he said, "No, don't you worry."

And there were a few other unpleasant things. He had a young son who was growing up, and he was a great hunter. So he wanted to teach his son how to hunt deer. Well, first, whites are not supposed to hunt on the reservation. Second, it was out of season. Nevertheless, he goes out with his son and he shoots a deer. Well, I don't know where it's easy to get away with shooting a deer. It became known among the Indians. They did not do anything about it. Nobody said a word. I heard about it. And that, I thought, was, again—you know, I do, probably, make something of a fetish of rapport, I make something of a fetish of behaving as properly as I can in the field, and things like that. But that troubled me.

So one fine day I just blurted it out. I got upset, angry. We were driving toward Ruidoso for some reason, and I said, "Bryce, as far as I'm concerned, the project is over. I think you and Ruth ought to pack up and go home, and just quit. It's gone. It's done. Since I'm the principal investigator, and I've got control over the funds—no doubt about it, you get all the money that is coming to you, you get all the money that's due. But you gotta go home, period."

Now, in the meanwhile, they'd had an automobile accident. Somebody had slammed into them and tossed them across the road into a tree. Why none of them were killed, I'll never know. So they were without a car. But it was okay. They could take a train home. That was it. I told him he was through. He argued a bit, he hassled a bit, but I didn't want to discuss it and told him so. So off he went.

However, little did I know, he then went back to Berkeley—well, in the meanwhile, Harry Basehart and two other guys, Ed Rogers and Dick Henderson, had come down to do a study of—I think it may have been on land claims.[4] I think it was Apache land claims. They were working for the tribe. Bryce knew that Harry was working there, so Bryce got on the phone with Harry. Harry, you have to understand, was "an old friend of mine," 'cause Harry had been with us on that matrilineal kinship thing, and Harry had come out of Social Relations, just as I had, and, you know, we were all buddies from way back.

I remember this very vividly. One day, in Berkeley, the phone rang, and Harry's on the phone, and Harry was saying, "Look, I know you're working Mescalero, and it's perfectly good with me, and, you know, I've been working there—no problem. Do you have any special feeling if I continue to work there?"

And I said, "Of course not, Harry. No need to ask me." (You know, back on the Morris Opler problem.) "If you want to work there, you can work there."

So after getting that clear, Harry then explains to me that he and Bryce Boyer are going to put in for a large NIH grant to work there on psychological problems. So I said, "Harry, you know the problems I've been having with Bryce Boyer?"

And he said, "Yes, I know."

So I said, "You're fully aware of all those problems?"

He said, "Yes."

And I said, "You want to work with Bryce Boyer, you want to work there—it's up to you. What do you want me to say about it?"

So Bryce turns around and puts in, with Harry Basehart, for the money to work in Mescalero. So they work together in Mescalero.

RH: They got the money?

DMS: Sure they got the money. Because, you see, what I had done was to turn around and come back to Berkeley, and since I was not going to work with Bryce Boyer anymore, it was my responsibility to return the NIH money to NIH. Minus, of course, what we had spent. That was okay; I called them up, I talked to Phil Sapir [at NIH], explained the whole thing. Phil said okay, he understood, and this is the way to do it, that's the way you send the money back, this is the report you have to write. And he said, "I understand. It's fine." And he adds, "I never had much hope for the project in the first place."

So Harry Basehart then went with Bryce Boyer, and I figured, well, under the circumstances, you know . . . I talked to Addy and we both agreed: the hell with Mescalero. There's no point in going back anymore. Because if Bryce is going to work there, and Harry is going to work there, I don't need to run into them and cross paths with them all the time. I don't want to be a competitor, I don't want to be anything else. It didn't matter to me.

So I pulled out. I've been back there once or twice, just for very brief visits. But that's it.

Needless to say, the tribe got absolutely livid and furious with Bryce. They would not let him stay on the reservation. He bought a trailer. Part of the reservation is called a patent area—land patents. He got permission from—I think it was Mrs. Boldinaro—to park his trailer on the patented land, and he worked out of the trailer.

But the next thing the tribe did was to tell him he could not come onto the reservation. So if any Indian wanted to talk to him, they had to come visit him at the trailer. All he could do was drive up and down the main road or stay around that patent area.

After a while, of course, Harry pulled out, too, because Harry couldn't stand it. And Bryce kept working there, on and off, through that trailer arrangement, but was having more and more trouble because people wouldn't talk to him. One of the things was that they began to find out what he was writing about them—the usual psychoanalytic stuff: they were all repressed homosexuals, and not only repressed homosexuals but they were all alcohol addicted, and things like that. They didn't take kindly to being designated that way. So that was the end of it.

RH: He sounds pretty awful!

DMS: That was my opinion, and my opinion turns out to be shared by a few other people, but that's it. He has become the "expert" on the Mescalero Apache, and he actually has published a book! [5] You can find it in the library, but to the best of my knowledge, I've never seen him quoted on Mescalero Apache character.

RH: And you—you never got enough material to do anything?

DMS: I never got enough material because, you know, I was starting out by "trying to get good rapport." And to just explore a little here, a little there—old stories with Percy Bigmouth, learn the language a little, household survey with Ruth Boyer—which I never really got; she kept the material, which she was certainly entitled to do. I had Charlie Smith, I had Irby and his wife [Roberta]; I had Wayne and Dolores Enjady; I had Mildred Cleghorn for a while, and Mildred Cleghorn's uncle. Anyhow, a bunch of friends. I had long talks with Sam Kenoi, who was one of Morris Opler's informants.

That summer of '56–'57, the BIA started a big program of relocation. They would send Indians to urban areas and find them jobs. The first summer, Willy Magoosh and his wife, Winona, and their two kids were living in South San Francisco. The center gave me a really beautiful, big Ampex tape recorder, and I would go up a couple of times a week to Willy Magoosh and Winona, talk to them, talk Apache, talk about the reservation, talk about Indian life, gossip and stuff like that. You know, part of the business of just gradually developing a circle of friends and a circle of people whom I could talk to, and picking up whatever I could in the way of Apache language.

I did that all that first year. Then the next year, Sammy Cooper, a young man, came also on relocation, got a job driving a bus in Oakland, and he would come and visit us in Berkeley from time to time. He had a Sioux wife, and their kid. And, you know, the usual thing happened: Sammy Cooper began to discover that he was not doing very well financially, and that every bus driver got, I don't know, ten, twenty dollars in change to start his route with, and Sammy was borrowing the change— he didn't have enough change. One day he had to show up with the change, and he didn't have it. So, of course, he called me, and of course, I drove over, and I gave him, I don't know, twenty-five, thirty bucks, something like that, so that he could go in and take his bus out. Eventually Sammy Cooper decided the hell with it, and he and his wife and kid packed up and went back to Mescalero.

Meanwhile, Willy Magoosh and Winona and their kids, they'd had it, and they packed up and they went back to Mescalero. And the whole relocation program never did work out very well for many of them.

So I got to know a lot of them, kept in touch with a lot of them. But that, of course, was another real problem with working with Indians: they very frequently needed a helluva lot of help; they very frequently needed a helluva lot of support; they very frequently got into problems with alcohol, got into problems with drugs, got into problems with domestic discord. Sammy Cooper and his wife fell out a couple of times. You know, try to give them good advice, try to give them support—it gets to be a real problem. It ain't easy.

RH: You were never able to do anything with this stuff? It just kind of evaporated?

DMS: No, simply because—you see, the way I had set it up was to spend a couple of years just developing a position, developing a location, developing a circle of friends, and so on. And at that point, I could then begin to zero in and focus. Some of it was clearly going to be kinship and family. I had thought perhaps of doing something with some of the ritual stuff—the girls' puberty rite stuff. I had *not* wanted to get into mythology, and recovering old stuff and old stories.

And I was definitely interested in politics: how the politics of the situation was working out, relations with the BIA. I got to be fairly friendly with Wendell Chino, with Fred Pelman, who always ran against him for president of the tribe, or chairman of the tribal council. I got as close as I could—but it was not possible to get very close—to Andrew Little, a very smart guy, a person I liked a great deal, but I don't think he had much time for me. I don't think he thought I was either of any use or of any interest to him. So I didn't really make much headway with him.

RH: So, a couple of summers, and you stopped.

DMS: Basically three summers, as I remember it.

RH: And during this time you're also publishing things on Yap?

DMS: During this time I'm publishing things on Yap. During this time I'm now getting half sucked into the American kinship project with Raymond Firth. During this time, Fred Eggan is beginning to seduce me to go to Chicago.

RH: I presume that, having dropped the Apache stuff, you didn't then start looking around for another ethnographic area because you were doing American kinship.

DMS: That's right, exactly, because that was now going to be my next ethnographic effort. You know, if it had been different, it wouldn't have been the way it was!—but the way it worked out, I don't think it was bad. It would have been really nice to have a nice Indian reservation to go to every summer with Addy and the kids. Addy would've been able to do a little something, or whatever she wanted to do. She more than likely would have gone and done some archival, historical stuff. The kids would've had a marvelous time.

But the Indians were not all that friendly. Irby's wife, Roberta, would come over and literally just sponge anything she could sponge off of us, and then go away. Her mother was the same way. She'd come over and "Give me this, give me that; I need this, I need that." Addy would give her and give her and give her, and off she'd go. And then you wouldn't see her again. Then you'd go and visit her and she didn't have much time of the day for you. But, okay, that was the way it was.

In the end, though, when Michael graduated from Beloit, he took off for Santa Fe. He decided he wanted to stay and live in New Mexico for the rest of his life. I asked him once, why? And he said because he'd had such a happy time in New Mexico—New Mexico was the happiest time of his whole life. He wanted to go back and spend the rest of his life there. Well, the only time he'd spent there was those summers in Mescalero. So it did mean something. I could fairly cry, thinking of all those nice times we had.

RH: But it wasn't much fun, though, working with the Indians!

DMS: It was no fun working with those Indians—

RH: —but some of them were nice—

DMS: —well, some of them were nice, but, I don't know, I'd come home, we'd fix dinner, and then one of the things we would do that was fun—it would get dark and we'd get in the car and we'd drive down the road. And as you drive down the road, God, the bright eyes you see!—there's a bobcat, and there's a badger—look at the deer!—there were whitetail deer.

And one wonderful day there was this great big hawk circling up in the air, and it had this huge, big, long black rope attached to its leg. We all went out and we watched it, we watched it and watched it. And finally it came over us. The hawk had caught a snake. It was a big, long blacksnake. And we found a rattlesnake. Not only that, Hereford cattle were all around. We'd sit there on the porch and we'd watch the bulls fight! And we'd say, "Ho, ho, we're at the bullfights." And the kids learned, don't go out into the pasture, stay away from the pasture.

But then, every so often, they'd have a roundup, and clear all the cattle out of the pasture. Then the kids would go into the pasture, and we'd get very worried, because the grass was higher than Michael's head, and he could get lost. So we got a whistle! And if he ever got lost, he was to listen for the whistle. Oh, it was fun!

Then, of course, the water went out. We had to go shit up in the woods someplace. Michael was not fully toilet trained by that time. It was an adventure taking Michael to take a shit, because he would take his shit and you'd mop his ass, and Michael insisted that he had to cover it over with stones, and that he'd mark each place with these stones, so that he could remember all the different places that were his. Well, that's the way the kid wanted to do it—it was fine with us.

And, of course, there was that one day when Addy went out to move her bowels, and she looked up into the bush ahead of her and there was a great big green snake looking at her! She said she finished rather quickly.

She and the kids would go for a walk when I was working, talking to Indians or beating around. And they caught a bunch of horned toads, they caught a bunch of snakes, and we built cages for the snakes. We could only keep them for one week, then we'd let them go. And the horned toads would stay for no more than two or three days, then we'd let them go. Addy and the kids found bear tracks! Oh, that was exciting, and we all went out to see the bear tracks. Then one day, of course, they were absolutely convinced that they had heard a bear growl in the underbrush. They all ran into the house and closed the door. That was exciting for days and days.

And then, every so often, it'd be just one of those days, and every-body'd sit there and look at everybody else and they'd say, "Oh, what the hell, let's go in to Ruidoso." We'd go into Ruidoso, thirty-five miles each way. We'd walk around and shop, buy paperbacks and magazines.

So, you know, the times we were there, we had a lot of fun. And it was a lot of—again, it was very hard work, and a lot of it was unpleasantly hard work that fell heavily on Addy, which was not fair, but that was the way it was. We both suffered for it, and I suffered because she got very upset and angry, justifiably so. It was a source of some tension.

But it was a nice time. And it was beautiful country! The jackrabbits that you get in the headlights at night, and they won't get out of the road—they won't go right, they won't go left, they only go where they can see; and your headlights give them a place to see. So you slow down, you drive slowly behind a jackrabbit, and then, maybe send one of the kids out to see if they can shoo it off the road, and maybe you do and maybe you don't. The owls come swooping out of the trees. Mice and moles and large insects get caught in the front of the car or the wake of the car, and the owls come swooping down out of the trees, either ahead of your car or behind the car. We carried big flashlights so we could see everything.

RH: If it was such hard work for Addy, did she still want to go back?

DMS: I think by the time things blew up with Bryce Boyer, we both didn't want to go back. It had gotten too messy, and particularly—I don't think we had decided not to go back, but when Harry Basehart was willing to front for Bryce, and put in for the money, and Bryce was going to bring Ruth and his three kids—it wasn't worth it. We just decided, to hell with it. And by that time, you see, I was already committed to go to Chicago, and the project with Firth had come up, so everything militated against it. So we never really went back.

I look back on it with a lot of nostalgia. I had a marvelous time. I don't know if I can tell you how nice: you sit on the porch in the evening, and there's still a lot of light, but the sun is mainly down. And there were electric wires, maybe thirty, forty, fifty yards out in front of the house. And those wires would be absolutely covered with purple martins. And purple martins are really wonderful birds. They're very social. They sit on a wire and chatter to each other, and then one of them suddenly swoops off. And they fly magnificently in these great, swooping arcs, around and around. They come buzzing down along the top of the grass, picking up insects, back up on the wire, and chew on them or swallow them—I don't know what they do. The four of us would just sit there and watch the purple martins.

RH: This makes you sound like an anthropological romantic.

DMS: Of course.

RH: Were you like that?

DMS: I'm sure, positively—that's half the trouble with Bashkow's paper. He doesn't ever say it in so many words, flat out, but I was a romantic in the sense that I wanted to be friends with the Indians and the Yapese; I wanted them to love me, I wanted to love them, and I wanted life to be beautiful—all that stuff. Yes, I was a romantic. I wanted to do good science, and come out with important, sound knowledge, and sound, useful, friendly, helpful information. I was into doing everything I could to help individual Indians: I drove them to the hospital, I drove them to Ruidoso, I drove them to Eddie's, I drove them back from Eddie's when they were drunk as a skunk. We went to all the times when they had any kind of gathering. Because mainly, everybody was highly dispersed all over the reservation, which was the way they liked to be. But they would come together periodically—for example, at the girls' puberty rite, which they then rescheduled for July Fourth every year, which was also the time for rodeo, which was the time when they'd make money. They'd get a lot of white tourists, and a lot of other Indians would come to the rodeo, too.

So, yes, I was romantic as all hell—and I think I still am. I had romantic notions about how much I could help them, and it turned out, as usual, that they were a lot better at helping themselves than anyone was able to help them.

RH: Despite the drunkenness?

DMS: Well, no. As usual, everything is uneven. A lot of them were dead drunk half the time, and the other half the time they were recovering from dead drunk. But a lot of them were also very smart, and a lot of them were very politically hep, and a lot of them were interested in taking care of themselves and that's all. A lot of them were into getting political power—and they did. And political power, one way or another, managed to help "the tribe." Wendell Chino was *not* a romantic. He was a genuine, honest-to-God, very smart pragmatist. Whatever would work to do the Indians some good, he managed to pull off.

All kinds of silly, crazy things happened. A guy got thrown off his horse, thrown into a barbed wire fence and, I don't know, one thing and another, and he lost his arm. So he hires a lawyer to sue the tribe, because he was working for the tribe's co-op cattle farm. So the lawyer says, "Fine, I'll be glad to help you. We split the proceeds. I get forty percent, thirty percent, you get the rest, fine." So the lawyer says, "Now tell me what happened," and the guy says, "No, you're the lawyer, you're supposed to find everything out. I'm not going to help you. You go on and find out for yourself!"

The lawyer says to him, "How can I help you if you don't give me the facts. I'm supposed to be on your side."

So the Indian says, "But look, I have hired you. I'm going to pay you this percentage of the money. Why should I help you earn your money?"

Well, in one peculiar sense, it makes rational sense that if they hire a lawyer, the lawyer should do the work. But that kind of thing happened time and time again. It never happened to Wendell Chino. I think Alton Peso knew what was going on, Eric Tortilla certainly knew. But this is the kind of thing that kept happening all the time with those people.

Bernard Little's kids went to college, and one of them became a very good writer. He wrote stories that I read, and I thought were extremely good. They were definitely about Indians, they were definitely Southwest. A number of other kids have gone into law, and I think have done extremely well.

So my romantic notions that I might possibly help them with my anthropology were *really* romantic notions. And romantic in the sense of not really very practical. It might have been that I could have given some practical help on one or another point, but they were perfectly able to take care of themselves. But again, they were able to take care of themselves—not in the way that Rufus Sago was. He was still working out his personal vendettas with any particular white man he could find, whereas the really smart ones—"smart," what do you mean by smart?— the ones who decided that the way in which they could take care of being Indian and getting what they deserved and what they thought they were entitled to, from the white man, was to get themselves organized, to learn the white man's culture, to learn the white man's customs, and to learn how to operate the white man's legal system against him. And they did! And to learn to use the white man's economic system to their benefit, for a change. And when they did that, they did it.

RH: You just mentioned Rufus Sago, and earlier, you mentioned "the Rufus Sago story." I don't know who Rufus Sago was.

DMS: Our second year on the Mescalero Apache reservation. Jonathan is house-trained, knows how to use a toilet. Michael is in diapers. Diapers in those days were large linen things, and you boiled them to keep the kids from getting all kinds of loathsome diseases.

We're out in Elk Silver, a long way from anyplace, in this schoolteacher's house. There were two schoolteacher's houses and an old school. The schoolteacher's house was still habitable. The schoolteacher's house got its water from a big water tank on a hill just behind it, which was in turn fed from a spring about four or five miles away, up the valley. That tank was not only supposed to supply water to the schoolteachers and school, it was also a reserve tank for use in case of forest fires. It was therefore very important to keep it full.

RH: We're talking about a big tank.

DMS: It was so big that it was twice as tall as I was and to climb up on top of it, you had to go up one of these steel ladders that was bolted onto it. It's a big water tank.

The water runs out. No water. I go up to the tank, the tank is empty. I can't find a break in the line. The water is just not running. So I'm carrying water in a cooler—an ice chest, for picnics. I'm carrying maybe twenty gallons each trip. Addy is hard put to deal with dirty diapers, clothes, all those problems. I'm taking clothes into Ruidoso, which is only thirty miles away, to the laundromat. And we're living without water.

I keep going up to that tank and walking around, and I keep looking —"Where the hell could there be a break?" Because as I drove into— to wherever I was going to go to find Indians to talk to—you could drive past the spring, and the spring was gushing. The water was all over. And I walked every inch of that pipe. It wasn't deep underground. It was lying right on top of the ground. There was no break.

So obviously the next step was to go talk to a lot of Indians. "What happened to the water?" They don't know. They said, "Did you walk along the pipe?"

"Yes."

"Is there a break?"

"No."

They don't know. I talked to Indians and I talked to Indians. About five weeks later, I am still brooding about this, 'cause it's miserable. And

I happened to—I don't know what I did, but somehow, there on the ground is a pile of leaves and twigs and stuff, and I'm looking at it, and goddamn it, there's a valve there! I turn the valve. Whoosh—water flows into the tank.

It didn't take me more than three minutes to figure out what that was. Some son-of-a-bitch had gone up there, behind the house—we didn't hear him—and he had closed the valve.

RH: So when you were walking the line, you never noticed that there was a valve?

DMS: The valve was close to the tank, within ten feet of the tank. It was covered over. The valve was set into the ground, and the square box around it was filled with dirt, and over it scattered leaves and twigs. The only inference I could make was that some son-of-a-bitch turned the water off.

Well, that helped, because we could now start flushing water, boiling diapers, and all the rest. So, I'm starting back with talking to Indians, and I talk around. "I finally found the valve, water's running. What the hell's going on?"

And in the course of talking to people, I come upon Rufus Sago. Now, Rufus Sago had met with me a number of times—at least a couple of times. Each time, he had been adamant about what the white people had done to the poor Indians, and how the white people were. There was a phrase at that point: "Lo, the poor Indian!" That was the tag that marked this whole constellation of attitudes and feelings. Namely, we have suffered, and we have been injured, and we have been exploited, and we have been kicked around, and we have been mistreated.

So when I saw Rufus I said, "The water is on. I finally found it. Some son-of-a-bitch turned it off." And Rufus burst out laughing, and laughed and laughed and laughed.

He said, "Most white folks wouldn't have stayed as long. You're pretty tough. I gotta hand it to you. You and your wife, you're okay. White people, you know, they can't go without water for more than a day or two."

So I said, "Rufus, what the hell—what did you do a thing like that for? You know, the goddamn kid's in diapers. Shitty diapers and dirty— what for?"

Rufus gets quite serious. He begins to bang on my chest. "You know what your grandfather did to my grandfather?" And he goes through the fact that his grandfather had been shot by white people.

But, you know, my grandfather—and I explained it carefully to Rufus. I said, "Rufus, look. My grandfather came from Brest-Litovsk. Brest-Litovsk is on the border between Russia and Poland. My grandfather was dead before my father came to this country. My grandfather died in the late 1800s. He never came near this country. My father never came farther west than Toronto. My grandfather didn't bother your grandfather. He had nothing to do with it."

Rufus's answer, obviously, was, "You're a white man, aren't you?"

"I'm a white man, I suppose, but, you know, don't tell me that I did something to you. You did something to me! But I didn't do anything to you. And my father didn't do anything to you. And surely my grandfather didn't. If some son-of-a-bitch of a white man killed your grandfather, that was wrong, and it was terrible, and I'm sorry. But, you know, to turn my water off for this. Come on, Rufus, what for?"

But he was adamant, and he was very clear on the whole thing. "You're white. Whatever I do next time, you'll wait and see—but that's it."

This is an age-old problem, and here it was in microcosm. Not only is there the question of when the enmities stop, but the other question is the important one of reparations. According to tradition, the Jews were held in slavery by the Egyptians; when I was a kid, at one point a bunch of kids gave me a rough time because they said that the Jews killed Christ and gave me to understand, in forceable terms, that I was therefore responsible. Americans imported Africans as slaves and held them in slavery. And they really undertook a genocidal campaign against the natives of North America, whom we now call the "Indians," a misnomer we haven't even bothered to try to change. And Chancellor Kohl of Germany said that the Holocaust happened before his time and he was not responsible for it, or something like that.

The fact of the matter right now, however, is that Native Americans and African Americans, not to mention hillbillies and some others, are given a very hard time. There was a doctor in Ruidoso who we went to a couple of times who was adamant on the fact that these Apache were ignorant savages and needed to be treated with force, that they did not know what to do with their land and that that land should be taken away

from them. His view was that the government coddled them and pro-
tected them, that the women were promiscuous, the men all drunkards,
the children wild and in need of discipline. Some other whites I met
around Ruidoso agreed with him, saying that the land was too good to
be left to the Indians, that it needed proper, experienced people to use it,
and that the Indians were not only ignorant but also inherently stupid
and unteachable. In short, racism, prejudice, open hostility abounded.
People came onto the reservation and swindled them in dozens of ways.
And the government, which was accused of coddling them, had for the
past half-century at least hounded them, swindled them, shortchanged
them, exploited them, imposed paternalistic governance on them, which
in turn made it almost impossible for them to get themselves together
to fight back. So at one level, Rufus Sago had every reason to turn my
water off, and I don't deny the justice of his view. At another level, however, the crucial question is what to do now to change the way these
people are treated, to change the ignorance and prejudice of those who
deal with them, to eliminate the racism, the stereotyping which they
encounter everywhere.[6]

RH: So those are the issues to deal with, not—

DMS: —but how do you deal with those issues?

RH: That's another question.

DMS: But that's really the serious question. It seemed to me that it
was no better way to deal with those questions by his turning my water
off than by my telling him to get his buddy to pull himself up by the
bootstraps. It doesn't help when I tell him, "Well, the reason we treat
Indians badly is because so many of you are drunk." That doesn't help.
And I never did that. But he was certainly doing it to me. He admired
me because I was tough and could go without water, but as far as he was
concerned, I was white and anybody white was collectively responsible.
And so you get into this kind of trap of stereotyping.

RH: That's why I never did fieldwork in a non-Western situation, because I figured that the anthropologist's position is too compromised,
I'm not sure that's the right word. But I simply avoided the issue.

DMS: You're wrong. By doing that, you accept the proposition that
the stereotype holds, and applies. You accept the guilt for what a lot of
other people did, a long time ago.

RH: Well, here's Bashkow's piece about how terribly compromised you were in this colonial situation. Furthermore, by going into the field, whether to Yap or to the Mescalero reservation, you don't do anything to change the situation. At least, one could make that argument. I'm not sure if it's right, but let's try it. You would accept the hegemonic order that gives you this power to go in there and turn those people into your research tools.

DMS: No, that's not quite the way it goes. Go back to Yap for a minute. Take what Bashkow wrote about me, but also the rest of this stuff—which is part of the point of my telling you about the conversion of the Jews and my polished-up version of the American ideology. You know, America's a diverse place; it's culturally diverse, it's religiously diverse, it has religious tolerance—and all the rest of that shit. And it is also a very important part about my identification of myself as being under their jurisdiction, and that I couldn't do things without their permission, and didn't.

I didn't march into people's houses. Another one of these horrible stories: a famous anthropologist came and visited Mescalero when I was there. Harry Basehart sent him down from Albuquerque. I could've strangled the man with my own, two bare hands! He came in, he had his camera, and he wanted me to round Indians up so he could take their pictures.

I said, "I can't do it!"

He said, "What do you mean, you can't do it?"

I said, "I can't do it. I don't do that, and they're not gonna go for that sort of thing. It's not only morally impossible, it's physically impossible."

He said, "In Africa, somebody visits you, you immediately go to the headman to arrange it."

I said, "I may know somebody who will let you take his picture, but you'll have to pay him for it."

Well, he threw up his hands, and he was outraged and annoyed, but he'd come all this far. And not only that, but the man was Geronimo's son. You know?—big deal—Robert Geronimo.

So I drove to Robert Geronimo's house and I said, "Look, Robert, I've got this man. He comes from France, Belgium, I don't know where, and he wants to take a picture of an Apache. If you don't want to do it, it's all right with me. And if you do do it, fine, do it."

He said, "Well, what'll he pay?"

I said, "That's between you and him. What do you want? Ask him."

So he asked him for some sum, and the anthropologist said, "No, no, cut it in half." They bargained back and forth. So, Robert got out his regalia, his fancy hat, bow and arrow and various things and stood in an important posture and the anthropologist took his picture. But not until he paid the cash. Robert Geronimo was a smart man. He'd encountered tourists before. He got the money before he posed. It was as simple as that. So the anthropologist went away, grumbling bitterly about me, about what poor hospitality, and so on, and when anyone came to visit him in Africa, he just had a word with the headman and they lined up. Took their shirts off, I'm sure.

Well, I wouldn't do that. I didn't do that. I was not in a position to do that. But what I was in a position to do with the Apaches, I did. Now I should list all the good deeds I did.

RH: Yes, list all the good deeds you did.

DMS: That'll have to come another time. I gotta think about it. Well, I took people to the hospital. I took people into Ruidoso to visit doctors if they wanted to. I picked people up on the road and took them to wherever they wanted to go. Took them shopping. I did errands. One day we went to Alamogordo. When we went to Albuquerque, we brought things back. Food—we were always giving food away. People were always coming eating in our house.

There were also all kinds of unpleasant things. Wendell Chino, who was a very big operator, a major political figure there, I invited him to come have dinner with us. He said, "Fine."

I said, "Bring your wife and children."

He said, "Fine."

We agreed on some time around six. He showed up around ten o'clock. The food was no good, it was overcooked, all the rest of it, he didn't bring his wife. And he sat and ate and lectured me on what white people had done to offend the Indians. And so we talked about what could be done about it.

The Mescalero Apache—I'm sure I was not significantly instrumental—but they were the first people to break the stranglehold that the state had on liquor. They were able to get a liquor license to build a big resort combination entirely on their own, because they went to court and broke it. I told him that I was sure that was possible.

But that time I was on—I think—the NIMH [National Institutes of Mental Health] committee. In the middle of the Mayflower Hotel, in Washington, I'm about to get on an elevator, and there is Alton Peso and Eric Tortilla and Wendell Chino and one other guy. And I said, "What are you doing here?" and they said, "What are *you* doing here?"

So we went down in the elevator together, and stopped, and talked for a while. They were working in the BIA, I was working in the NIMH— you know, good friends, and better ways to do it than this, and how do you work this, and what should we do about this kind of thing? But they didn't really need me. They were pretty smart themselves, and they hired lawyers who were a helluva lot smarter than I was.

The only things that I really did that were significantly good were on this low level. If I knew somebody was sick, I drove over there and I said, "You wanna go to the hospital? Can I bring you medicine? What should we do?"

Or, when Irby beat up his wife, I got hold of of Irby, and I said, "Come on, go away for a while. Wait till it settles down. Leave her alone. The cops are gonna get you." Then I went to his wife and took her to the hospital. They patched her up.

That's what you do in the field, 'cause you live there. You presume that everybody does it to each other. So after I discovered that I was giving everybody else free rides, taking them wherever they wanted to go—if an Indian needed help, and another Indian had a car, they charged him for the ride! I didn't. All right, but you know, I had money enough to do it. I wasn't suffering, so I did those things. It was not any monumental kind of do-gooding.

RH: What do you make of the critique that says anthropology has been carried out on the back of colonial power?

DMS: I have a complete rap on that. I've thought about it many times, for some reason, since I got to Santa Cruz. The answer is, it's not so simply true, not entirely by any means. And if you read this book of George Stocking's on colonialism,[7] not every anthropologist did those things, not every anthropologist was involved in those things. Many an-thropologists got involved in ways that were not only independent of the colonial organization, but were also antithetical in every way to colonial domination.

But, there's still the crucial question: they couldn't have worked safely except in an atmosphere that was controlled by the colonial administration. That is, the present situation in New Guinea is extremely dangerous. People get killed. People get robbed, they get badly beaten up. Port Moresby and the major cities are very unsafe to be in. Okay, the colonial situation no longer can guarantee safety. That's absolutely true. So if all you're talking about is a condition that enforces a degree of safety, then, definitely, anthropology was done on the backs of colonial operations.

But there are a couple of other considerations. First, anthropology never, never went into anyplace until long after the colonial administrators and missionaries went first, and on the whole, pacified it. So that they were not part of a pacification operation; they were not part of an organization operation; they were not part of an operation that in some sense self-consciously altered a native way of organization. The missionaries wanted to convert them. They wanted to alter a native way of life. The colonial officers and colonial apparatus, with or without police and with or without soldiers, wanted to alter native organization. You know, the British with their indirect rule.

No anthropologist that I know of in the literature really systematically tried to alter existing situations, until development started. And that was way, way into the '60s and '70s. So the idea that anthropology existed on the back of the colonial administration, I think, is empirically wrong.

Secondly, there is a consistent and chronic quality to the anthropological work—with a few exceptions, again, which showed up primarily in the Vietnam War, or around situations like that—where the anthropology could be at worst typified as being laissez-faire. It was almost always altruistic, in some sense. Now whether it was Margaret Mead's condescending altruism of doctoring when she really didn't know a thing about doctoring, or people who were really good at doctoring—it was mainly a kind of altruistic attitude to the whole thing.

My altruism, as you saw, was to some extent to put myself—I am sure they would have laughed themselves silly to think that I was treating them equally.

RH: Are you talking about the Yapese now?

DMS: Yes. I gave off all these egalitarian vibes. They were not egalitarian among themselves. But they certainly saw that I was in no way allied with the navy; for one thing, I provided them with liquor, which was strictly against the law. Again, in interpreting for that theft, I'm sure that the people I dealt with there did not get the impression that I was acting on behalf of the administration. Most of them knew I was protecting them as best I could. I wasn't protecting any guilty people, because it turned out that the guilty people were not there when I was interviewing.

But, it seems to me that, again, even if it's a neutral altruism, of not wanting to fuck the place up, it is directly contrary to the missionary, to the colonial officer, and to the traveler. The traveler—and this is distinctively with reference to Jim Clifford—Jim Clifford is arguing that the missionary and the colonial officer and the traveler all had a great deal of important information, often because their prose is good, to tell us about native life.[8] But that is still radically different from what the anthropologist does. Because the anthropologist goes in to get some customs. But when a traveler goes in to get customs, the traveler picks the customs out, takes them home, and writes a book, which presumably is doing something for him—whether it's making money and improving his standing in the community, or what. And the anthropologist is going in and getting the customs for what?—to get a Ph.D., to write a monograph?

It's true: many, many native groups—the Mescalero are not the least of them—have a feeling that what you're gonna do is to make a million dollars out of the book. And so anthropologists are now falling all over themselves backward to write the book collaboratively with the local people, to give the book—all royalties go to the native whatever-it-is. Those things are happening.

But even before, there was a kind of altruism that, I think, characterized the anthropological endeavor, that never did the colonial or missionary endeavors. The missionaries *thought* they were being altruistic. These people were now going to be saved for Jesus! Well, if you believe that, okay, maybe that's altruism.

RH: But how about this—let me caricature a common critique. The anthropologist uses the natives to further his or her own career.

DMS: That's true. The question is, What's wrong with that? It presumably doesn't hurt the natives. It hurts the natives when, for instance, real secrets are told. It hurts the natives when Griaule goes in there and wangles secrets out of the natives.

RH: In colonial situations, like Yap, weren't you afraid of your information being misused?

DMS: I got a letter from the chief justice of the Supreme Court of Micronesia asking if I would please send him my documents on land tenure and my maps of landholding on Yap so that he could better adjudicate certain controversies that had come up. This was between the middle '50s and the middle '60s. I wrote back and said that the information had been given to me in confidence, and that I would not reveal it. I think I added that, in any case, I cannot vouch for its complete and total accuracy. The first statement was definitely that I had collected this information by assuring everyone of its confidentiality. And, indeed, I don't think I put that kind of stuff in Regenstein Library—I'm not sure.

So I refused to participate in that kind of thing. I'm sure there must've been other situations like that that came up. Oh yeah, one guy that was fairly close to me got killed by his wife's brother, and I got a letter asking if I would have anything to say in the trial. My answer was no—I was out of it, I knew nothing that would be of any use or importance to them. It happened after I left.

Now that you question me, I can think of all these things. One of the first places where I thought I improved my rapport tremendously was when somebody got killed in a village near where I was living. I knew that he'd been killed in a drunken party. Everybody was walking around, so to speak, on tiptoe, waiting for me to report them to the police. And I never said a word to the police. After about a month went by, people began talking about the murder to me; I began discussing it with them. But none of it ever got back to the administration.

Was that an immoral thing for me to have done? The way I saw it, I live in this village, I'm a member of this village, and if this village is going to keep its mouth shut and not report stuff to the town, then if I set myself outside it and stand apart from it, set myself above it, then I can't keep up a pretense of being egalitarian, being friendly, being supportive, being one of the people. So my resolution was to keep my mouth shut.

RH: But you were doing this for instrumental reasons—you wanted to get more data.

DMS: That is certainly one reasonable interpretation. You've got it on tape. But I will argue flatly that it was not entirely instrumental. Instrumentality certainly played a role. If pressed—somebody came up and hauled me down to court—what could I say? I only know about the murder second-, third-, and fourth-hand. I only know what a number of people have been telling me about it. I wasn't there. I didn't see it. All I have is hearsay.

RH: But still, you're torn between claiming to be a good citizen and claiming to be a good citizen in order to obtain information.

DMS: I really should've put it the other way: because I was a good citizen, it improved my rapport. That's the way I tried to put it. But there were a number of situations like that. They knew that I was not squealing on them. And, indeed, at one point, I confronted and got into a terrible row with the senior officer on the base because he claimed that a young woman was coming in and sleeping with sailors. I told him it was none of his business. What he had done was to tell her that she was no longer allowed to come into town. He had called her village chief in and told him that he was to keep her home, that she wasn't permitted to come into town. I told him that that wasn't proper, that he didn't have the authority to do that. He got very upset. He was in charge there, and he had the authority to do this and that. He finally had to fall back on public health issues—spreading loathsome diseases. And I laughed at him. And within two weeks, she was back in town, no problem—'cause he knew he had no authority to do it, and he knew it was wrong. But I figured if he gets away with that, who knows what he'll get away with. It was a minor event, no big deal. But he was furious with me.

RH: So do you think that the notion of anthropology as part of the larger imposition of Western power on non-Western places is misguided?

DMS: It's not totally wrong. But it is considerably less than totally right. It is not totally wrong in that many anthropologists in many circumstances—I keep thinking of Griaule, and some of those French guys before Griaule, the collectors—certainly they were ripping things off right and left, inveigling secrets—and, yeah, I think that was inexcusable.

But I think that this idea that anthropology as a whole is to be totally condemned because it arose at a time and in a place where colonialism and imperialism were essentially the way of life—that kind of condemnation is much too extreme.

Nine

From Berkeley to Chicago

DMS: I was convinced that I should leave Berkeley, and I made a commitment to Fred Eggan to leave and go to Chicago with Fallers and Geertz. I'd known Kroeber, and he'd been very important and very helpful. So I should have talked to Kroeber. It was rude. I didn't. Some period of time went by, and finally I seized the problem and I went in to see Kroeber. I banged on his door, he let me in, and I told him that I was going to leave and go to Chicago.

RH: When you say you banged on his door, you mean his office?

DMS: Kroeber had an office in Kroeber Hall, in Berkeley, and that office was officially allocated to George Foster, because when the building went up and it was named—Kroeber was there at its dedication— the only problem was that they couldn't give him an office in Kroeber Hall because he was retired. The only way they could arrange an office was to allocate it to the chairman of the department. George Foster was the chair. So it was one of those marvelous ironies of the bureaucracy, that the guy after whom the building was named couldn't even get an office in the building.

Anyway, I told him I was going to Chicago, and he said, "Why?"

I said, "It's a split department, they're fighting with each other, they hate each other. It's an impossible situation." I told him the story of Murphy's tenure fuss, and that people were always fighting with each other. There was even a horse's ass who used to walk up and down the hall to make sure everybody was in his office by nine o'clock and didn't leave before five—and stuff like that. Actually, nobody paid any attention to that guy. He just stamped around.

Kroeber listened. He didn't say anything. As I recall, he kept looking down at his desk, and I was standing up. Finally he said, "You have made this as a commitment. There's no going back?"

I said that, no, there was no going back. I had made the commitment. He said, "Well, you could've come and talked to me."

I said that, yes, I was very sorry about that. I could've come and talked to him. I apologized. The deed was done.

He sort of shook his head and said, "Look, you have tenure."

I said, "Yes, I have tenure."

He said, "You have your own work to do, you're doing Mescalero Apache now, you've still got Yap materials."

I said, "Yeah, I've still got a lot of things I want to do."

He said, "You have tenure, you have your own work. It's a big university with a good library and lots of resources. You'll have research money, of course."

I said, "Well, yes, I'm sure that's true."

So he said, "Why do you want to leave?"

I said, "I told you. The department—I find it impossible to live with these people."

"Well," he said, "but you have tenure. You have your own work to do. You have a good university with ample resources and a good library. I don't understand why you want to leave. You don't have to pay any attention to them. You don't even have to go to their meetings. You don't have to have anything to do with them."

And you know, at the time, I really wanted to be in a happy place. I really wanted to be at a place where you would have a community of scholars, always engaged in vigorous, constructive, intellectual interaction.

There's a terrible old joke that's a little like this. This is about the guy who's ready to go to heaven, or he thinks he's going to heaven, anyway. So he appears, and somebody says, "I will walk you down the hall, and you listen outside each door, and then you tell me, behind each door, which place you'd like to spend eternity." So they go to the first door and there's marvelous, lively conversation, but he says, "Not for eternity." The next door, it sounds as though they're having an orgy—"It's tiresome. Not for eternity." They go through various doors and come to the door in which there is a murmur of quiet, peaceful, pleasant, interaction.

So he picks that door, and of course the door is thrown open, and there is this mob of people standing in liquid shit up to their lower lip, and each is saying, "Don't make waves, don't make waves."

Well, the image of a community of scholars is very prevalent. That's what we all keep looking for. And the point of the story only is that Kroeber was absolutely right. I've told the story before, and people always say, "But, you know, you *did* make the right decision, because Chicago did turn out to be great." And in that sense, yes, I made the right decision. But, you know, the fact of the matter was that at that time, I knew what I had at Berkeley. Kroeber was absolutely right. I had my work, I had tenure, I was at a good university with a big library and resources. And I was going for a pig in a poke. Nobody knew what Chicago would turn out to be like. *I* didn't know Chicago would be any good. I didn't know what Chicago really was—a really good, lively intellectual center. And so, in one respect, I really made the wrong decision because it was not a rational decision. It was sheer, blind good luck. That was all there is to it. The moral that a lot of people draw from my story is that, you see, you really should go for it. But I think it's the wrong moral to draw.

RH: I'm not sure I agree with your moral, but I'm not going to argue with you right now. But I will argue with you later.

DMS: I feel very strongly about it. I think that the rational, sensible thing would've been to stay. But, you see, that also feeds back into the irony of Kroeber having set this place up, and tried to bring the new people in to really get it going again, and what did they do?

So Fallers, Geertz, and I went to Chicago, the summer of 1960. That summer Kluckhohn died, Kroeber died—that was it. So we got to Chicago, and that was supposed to have been a great coup on Fred Eggan's part, to wiggle us out of Berkeley. Kroeber was very annoyed.

We got to Chicago. And, as I say, Kluckhohn had died, and the news of it first reached me the day I got to Chicago. Maybe it was the second day, I'm not sure. Anyway, Kroeber had died earlier that summer, coming back from a Wenner-Gren conference.

RH: How did you respond to the news of Kluckhohn's death?

DMS: I was very upset. He had been nice. I owed him a great deal. I liked him personally. He had already begun to back off me, however,

because he felt, I think—I don't know—that he and Kroeber had arranged my going to Berkeley. And that my bringing Fallers and Geertz
in was a good thing. And that Kroeber was trying to rebuild Berkeley
from behind the scenes. And when I pulled out, it got both Kroeber
and Kluckhohn very offended. I mean, there they are, pulling all these
strings and managing everything, and I was screwing things up—for
what appeared to them to be petty reasons—the idea that there could
ever be a happy department. You know, I believed there could be a happy
department, and that being happy in the department was vital to my
work. Naive fantasies, really; it's a long life of trouble, actually. You can't
ever expect to have a good, happy, cooperating department. If you do,
you'd better look and see what else is wrong with it—like, they're not
very smart.

So, there we are at Chicago. Fallers, Geertz, and I tried to establish—
they were trying to redo the curriculum. I was heavily influenced by
Parsons. Fallers was heavily influenced by Ed Shils and Parsons. And
Geertz also had come out of Harvard, where Parsons and Kluckhohn
dominated, or at least were very vital. So we all agreed to put in a Parsonian program. There were two parallel courses, "The Human Career"—
that was essentially done by the physical anthropologists doing human
evolution, and the archaeologists doing what they regarded as history—
and then the social or cultural side. We divided social from cultural, so
you had three "systems" courses: social systems, cultural systems, and
then psychological systems. And that was the introductory curriculum.
We established that.

RH: In addition to "The Human Career?"

DMS: In addition to "The Human Career," yes. Within two or three
years, no more, we made a deal with the physical anthropologists and the
archaeologists that cultural people wouldn't have to take all that stuff,
and they wouldn't have to fuss with all our stuff, except on a selective
basis, whatever they wanted.

RH: Is it worth talking about what Chicago was like when you got
there—in other words, what you were reacting against?

DMS: We were reacting against what we conceived of as the whole
outside field. Chicago itself had very few people. So we were reacting
against what we saw as a classical four-field anthropology: stones and
bones and stuff. We were trying to get social theory off the ground.

RH: What had happened to the legacy of Radcliffe-Brown at Chicago? Was it there when you got there?

DMS: The legacy of Radcliffe-Brown was embodied in Fred Eggan, and that's about all. Sol Tax knew it, but he didn't buy it. And Fred Eggan didn't push it very hard. So, too, the legacy of Redfield was largely embodied in Milton Singer, but he didn't insist on making it a major part of the curriculum: he taught it, and that was it. And the students were able to get it.

So, there was a big vacuum at Chicago.

RH: And somebody, Eggan, was trying to rebuild the department.

DMS: Eggan was trying to rebuild the department, and he started with the three of us. McQuown was chair at first. Eric Wolf was there for a while, but he seemed at loose ends, uncertain as to what was going on. They used to have department meetings regularly. Eric thought they were just ridiculous: endless discussions of picayune problems, like the cost of pencils, or postage stamps, or something like that. So it didn't take him long to hustle around and develop a job at Michigan. He was, of course, partly right. I never found those department meetings terribly exciting, but I didn't find them too dull, either. And when I tried to get from Eric exactly what his objection was, and what should a department meeting be devoted to, I couldn't ever figure out what exactly it was he wanted. But he was unhappy, and he was certainly unhappy with Talcott Parsons, and my concern with Parsons. Tom Fallers—the link was to Parsons through Shils, and Geertz's allegiance to Parsons. He [Wolf] was most emphatically anti-Parsonian. So, when the time came, and he said he was going to leave, nobody got themselves worked up.

As I say, McQuown was chair at that point, and he had been engaged in the Chiapas project for quite a while, with some Harvard people. That year, he had arranged for Julian Pitt-Rivers to be at Chicago, so that Julian could write up a report on the Chiapas project. And Julian did. Julian had also come from Berkeley, but Julian had been—what would you call it?—an inveterate, he never had a job; he always had a temporary job. It wasn't until later that he became more or less securely attached to Lévi-Strauss's organization. But he tended also to fill in on the "very practical level" of the Chiapas project. He was in charge of the field situation there, among other things. He took over the administration of Lévi-Strauss's *laboratoire*. Anyway, Julian was a rather nice guy, with a reputation for being ineffective. He was just too nice and too sweet. You know, he had at one time—I don't know if this is true—it was said he had married the wife of the Spanish ambassador to the Court of St. James. And she turned out to be very nice. She came with him to Chicago from time to time, but that was clearly not her dish of tea. But, as Geoffrey Gorer explained to me at one point, she was trying her best to be a good, loyal, devoted wife. I think she'd be the last one who actually tried hard to be such a thing!

But by the time we got to Chicago, the department was sort of in a hopeless condition. There were very few people there, not much was doing, and it had rapidly lost whatever national reputation it had—'cause there was just nobody left. So Fred took over from McQuown almost immediately, and then I followed Fred as chair. By the time I got in, everything had pretty much improved; things were rolling again. We were building the place up again.

Meanwhile, back at the ranch—now going back in time a little bit: Sherry [Sherwood] Washburn had opened up this whole business of man the hunter and primate studies. He wanted to get out of Chicago 'cause Chicago was not able to provide him with the money and facilities he thought he needed. So he managed to get himself offered a job at Berkeley. And, you know, the courtesies are that the department has to discuss it and make a definite move, even though the [Berkeley] administration wanted him.

At a big department meeting, Kroeber argued very strongly that Washburn was not a good appointment. He didn't think Washburn was worth a row of beans. He wasn't very imaginative; he was much more a kind of good-, routine-, mediocre-, pedestrian-type person. I think Kroeber was right, but that's neither here nor there. Kroeber was opposed, but between the administration that thought they were getting a real hot commodity, and the department getting the money to get a big name, Washburn came to Berkeley.

Let me open a parenthesis here. Before anthropology crystallized as a distinct subject, scripture explained almost everything. But scripture did not fare too well in the eighteenth and nineteenth centuries. Soon evolutionary and developmental accounts began to occupy stage center, and Darwin's views and Darwin-like views were widely held worth a second thought. If scripture was not believable, and people still cared about how things started and how things developed or evolved, then, along with a dash of materialism and a pinch of rationalism, a whole new set of "origins" could be imagined. Furthermore, nobody had to imagine what "primitive man" looked like or how he behaved, since it was believed that there were plenty of them around to be studied. For the age of exploration had, it was believed, turned up many of them, in Africa, the New World, the South Seas, South America.

The question remained: How did things start and how did they get the way they are today? Darwin offered an answer to questions about humankind's physical form, but questions about the origin and development of civilization remained. And the large number of non-European peoples thought to be "savage" or "primitive" seemed to offer a way of discovering what "primitive" or earlier forms of humanity were like, for presumably here were "primitive people" living alongside "us," the Europeans who were the most advanced, least primitive people of all.

Whether the "primitive" people were that way because they were in a state of arrested development, or had degenerated intellectually and/or physically, or were physically and/or mentally inferior to begin with were interesting questions, but did not seriously detract from the assumption that contemporary "primitive" people were just like the predecessors of Europeans, and that much could be learned about how we got to be the way we are by examining these folk, who were presumed to be the way we must have been. And we must have been "simpler" or "simple" and small in scale—i.e., small numbers and largely undifferentiated, without distinct economic, religious, or political institutions.

That was the view from the nineteenth century. And so in the mid-twentieth century, Sherry Washburn took up this discarded idea—proving yet again that if you don't know history you are bound to repeat it, the second time as farce—and applied it to the nonhuman primates, arguing that there were plenty of them around and that if we studied them we could then use that material to learn what early man had been like. It was not so simple as saying that what apes did now was what early man did then, but it was not so radically different, either. Anyway, all sorts of people and granting agencies bought this idea lock, stock, and barrel, and people were watching monkeys and apes all over the globe, which was lots of fun and didn't do much harm and the observations gathered were all very useful to students of nonhuman primate behavior. For students of human behavior, however, the material was of very limited use at best, for even if at one time long ago, humans were very ape-like, they were now different in most if not all significant respects.

What seemed to me to be inexplicable was how so many apparently intelligent people bought this nonsense. People like those at Chicago who should have known better, people at Wenner-Gren and the National Science Foundation, and then those at Berkeley who brought Washburn from Chicago.

There may be an explanation of sorts in the old "help you pack" phenomenon. That is, when Washburn was able to interest the administration at the University of California at Berkeley in his project, which would require space and facilities, and told Chicago of this, Chicago, unwilling or unable to match Berkeley's offer, was instead anxious to speed the parting guest and helped him pack his bags. I did not get the impression when I got to Chicago that Washburn was sorely missed. Instead, I got the impression that a rather disruptive element had left and the scene was much improved. But, clearly, Washburn's exit helped make it possible for Fallers, Geertz, and me to move from Berkeley to Chicago.

RH: So you were at Berkeley at the time the department there was considering Washburn's appointment, and then when he first got there?

DMS: I was at Berkeley. I talked to him, and Geertz talked to him. He got along very well with Geertz. I suppose it was to be expected that he and I did not see eye to eye. The whole point of all this was that his links with Chicago were still fairly strong, so when Fred got Fallers, Geertz, and me to go to Chicago, Washburn apparently told Sol Tax to look out for Schneider—he was very difficult, aggressive, nasty, unpleasant, and so forth. Which of course was mostly true, but that's okay. But I was a little nonplussed when I got to Chicago to discover that Washburn had gotten on the jungle grapevine and told them what to expect. Indeed, at one point, walking back from the Quad Club, Milton Singer complained very bitterly that he had never been consulted about my appointment.

RH: Was the implication that he didn't want you there?

DMS: Well, the implication was that his feelings were hurt 'cause they didn't ask him. But that was Fred Eggan, of course, 'cause Fred did it almost single-handedly—went into President [George] Beadle's office and said, gotta get these people. This used to be one of the leading departments in the country and now it's nothing. So that was that story.

Sol Tax—in many ways, Sol was a tragic person. You see, for a long time, Robert Redfield was the big star in the department. It was his very highly discussed work in Guatemala that was on the front burner. Redfield followed Radcliffe-Brown, and Redfield became the major figure. And then Redfield became dean. In the meantime, Redfield had gotten Sol Tax to go to Guatemala and work there. And Tax's book, *Penny Capitalism,* was supposed to be fairly good, on the economics of a Guatemalan village.[1] But the impression I had when I got to Chicago was that Redfield had used Sol very much as a kind of factotum or—what would you call it? You know, it was Sol's vaunted practicality and efficiency that Redfield found useful—but that Redfield had kind of exploited Tax as his go-and-get-it-done man.

And this culminated in Sol Tax getting the department to buy a farm in Iowa to advance Sol's notions of "action anthropology." It was a farm that was very close to the Fox Indians. And every summer there were some people who'd go and study Fox Indians under Sol's aegis. And the Lichtstern Foundation paid for that. Adolph Lichtstern was a Chicago man and had a lot of money. Fay-Cooper Cole had shaken them down for a nice bit of money, which was given to the anthropology department as a source of research funds. That produced the money to pay for the farm in Iowa. That was perhaps Redfield's way of giving Sol a little something, and Sol gave a lot to Redfield in the way of practicalities and so forth. I don't think it was entirely crudely exploitative, but it had that sort of aspect to it.

The reason I say Sol was such a tragic figure is that Sol very early—partly under the influence of Radcliffe-Brown—wrote some very good kinship papers.[2] That was the direction he should have really taken. It would have been a clear intellectual development. But, instead, he began to get involved with practicalities and go-get-ems, goforism, do things—so he lost a great deal of the impetus to do anything really seriously intellectual. And I have the feeling that it was because he was the first and only Jew around at the time.

RH: Why would that be a factor?

DMS: Well, because it was easy to explain that he was trying his best to be a colleague, to be useful and helpful.

RH: Before we finish with Tax, did you have a sustained personal relationship with him? What was your relationship to him over the years?

DMS: My relationship to him was rather antagonistic. He had been warned against me by Washburn, whom he thought very highly of. Not only was he therefore somewhat cautious and careful of me, but I did not like his practical "action anthropology." Then he started, with Paul Fejos's money, *Current Anthropology,* which I felt was a silly kind of journal. I still think so.

RH: Why did you not like action anthropology?

DMS: How can I put it? First, I didn't see anything "seriously intellectual" coming out of it. Secondly, I didn't even see anything practical coming out of it. It seemed to me to be—and it was, very definitely—an attempt to be good to Indians, help Indians. But I thought it rather condescending. But basically, I just didn't see any intellectual—you know, I was very naive. I think I still am. I want anthropology to be rather "purely intellectual." And that was less than purely intellectual.

RH: And what was your antagonism to *Current Anthropology*—or your criticism of it?

DMS: My first antagonism to it was getting people to comment on the articles—it turned out that many of the comments were, again, not serious. At least, I don't think they were very serious. It all seemed to me very nursery school, kind of kindergartenish. Let's all sit down and talk, fellows, you know?

RH: That's funny, because in principle that should be a good idea, having people comment—

DMS: —in principle it's a great idea, but the way it seemed to me to be working out was no good at all. And I thought again that it had to do with the fact that Sol had abandoned any intellectual pretensions by then. Anyway, I found myself at swords' points with Sol frequently.

For example, as you know, Esther Newton was going through there as a graduate student. She was certainly a very odd duck in many ways. And when the time came for her to do a thesis, and she was going to do a study of drag queens, Sol was one of the first to insist that that was *not* anthropology. And you couldn't have a real discussion about that with Sol. Why wasn't it anthropology? He implied that you had to study "primitive people." But that was an argument that was hard to sustain. So I had a lot of trouble with both Sol and Fred in trying to protect Esther from their definitions that it wasn't anthropology. And it was also very embarrassing for them, because, you know, Fred and Sol were not exactly avant-garde postmodernists. They didn't think that homosexuality and drag queens were nice, respectable.

RH: Was Esther Newton openly lesbian in those days?

DMS: Not openly, but I seemed to be the only person who ever noticed it.

RH: Did you ever discuss it? Did you actually know it, or did you just guess?

DMS: No, I didn't know it. Since then, I can look back and say, yeah, she was having affairs with a number of people, and I was aware vaguely of it, but not seriously. I just treated her as another difficult graduate student. She'd ride on the back of Ben Applebaum's motorcycle, which nice young ladies didn't generally do. And then when the time came for her to defend her thesis, she came over to our house and Addy and I had a long talk with her, and we were trying to convince her to wear a dress. But it was a matter of principle that she not wear a dress. So we finally convinced her that the principle would be better served if she wore a dress during this and didn't get Sol and Fred all worked up. In the end, Sol never came to the exam and Fred didn't care.

RH: Who was her committee?

DMS: Me and—who else?—Julian Pitt-Rivers. He was very helpful and supportive to her.

RH: What was your attitude toward the thesis on drag queens?

DMS: I was all for it.

RH: Just on the principle that a person should study any piece of social life that they wanted to?

DMS: Yep! And that that was a particularly good one.

RH: But you didn't foresee the way it would develop, did you?[3]

DMS: Not only that, but I didn't suggest it to her. In fact, if she had come to me and said, "What should I do for a thesis?" I would have been hard put. She developed that largely, I think, with Julian Pitt-Rivers. He was the one who also insisted that she pay serious, close attention to the theatrical quality.

Now, Fred—I had first met Fred when I was working in Washington. And he was working in Washington also, for the War Relocation Board, it was called, I think. They were the people who were running the Japanese camps. And Fred was staying in the main office and reading these reports of anthropologists who were located in the camps. At one point, it might have been possible for me to get a job there. I wasn't sure I wanted one. It looked too much like spying to me.

RH: So, you met Eggan in Washington.

DMS: Yes. And secondly, I had done my M.A. thesis on dreams, you know, and Dorothy Eggan was very interested in dreams. Dorothy Eggan was—how shall we say? her relationship with Fred was—I don't suppose it was unusual; it was interesting. She appeared to be very dominant, but she wasn't because Fred was quietly stubborn and got what he wanted just by being stubborn.

So I had a good relationship, being interested in dreams and being able to talk about it with Dorothy. And so I had a link with her, and through her, with Fred, too. And when the matrilineal seminar came up, I thought it would be good to get Fred to come join the seminar. And so I got him to come to the seminar, and he came and spent part of the summer with us in Cambridge. Those were my links to Fred, which were fairly good and fairly strong.

But Fred was very odd, too. In many ways, Fred was very conservative and a very old-fashioned anthropologist. And—how shall we say?—I never got the impression that Fred was a great, brilliant mind. But he knew a lot. He studied hard. He read everything. He took his cue from Radcliffe-Brown, so he was finding lineages all over the place. And he made more out of lineages—and when any data was inconsistent, it was immediately ascribed to acculturation.

In many ways, also, Fred was a very nice guy, and Sol was a bit, oh, kind of tight, and somewhat competitive. But we always saw greater competition between Fred and Sol than there was. Actually, they didn't have to compete with each other so much. Each had their own row to hoe. Each was very competent at what they were doing. I thought one of Fred's main troubles was that he had gotten a lot of inspiration from

Radcliffe-Brown, but he hadn't been able to go any further with any of it. He had also been heavily inspired by the old Boasian paradigm, and he wanted to do culture history. A lot of his work was oriented in that direction. And so his "method of controlled comparison" was an attempt to do cultural history, and do it within a wider framework than Boas had ever proposed, and even a somewhat different framework than Kroeber had used. But nobody else took it up.

Fred had a very high regard for Tom Fallers. In one respect, Tom stood against Cliff and me in that Cliff and I were much more oriented to the cultural aspects. But in other respects, Tom and Cliff stood very close together in that both were a lot more politically astute than I was. And they established wide and effective and good allegiances throughout the University of Chicago—partly with the help of Edward Shils, I think, but a good deal of it on their own. And so I always felt as though I were a fifth wheel, sort of trotting along trying to keep up.

But one thing that helped me a great deal was that when the chips were down, Fred Eggan was really just as conservative and old-fashioned as you could expect. He figured that since I was older, I had seniority over Tom and Cliff. But, of course, the tragedy was that Tom had that meningioma. They did head surgery on Tom, and they tried to get rid of a lot of it, but they couldn't get it all. Anyway, he got sick and died of that.

That was really all I was going to say about Fred and Sol. But Sol then essentially left the department to Fred. I began to fall out of Fred's favor in two or three different ways. One was that I began to decide that either I was going to do kinship or I was going to do dreams—I couldn't do both. So I began dropping the dream stuff, and that broke a link with Dorothy.

Secondly, I was doing the kind of kinship stuff that Fred didn't like. I remember very vividly, I was writing—oh, I had decided to try to launch a reissue of Rivers's 1914 *Kinship and Social Organisation,* only to discover that Raymond Firth was doing that. So Firth very generously asked if I would write the introduction. And I, of course, was tickled pink. So I wrote an introduction: Rivers and Kroeber on kinship.[4] And I came out saying Rivers was wrong and Kroeber was right. Well that, of course, got Fred furious. So he tried to get me to change it, to say that

Kroeber was wrong and Rivers was right. But I was adamant. I didn't change it. That led to a good deal of strain, but—nothing too much.

Another source of strain was that Dorothy Eggan wanted very much to play the grande dame. And she used to call Addy up and tell Addy to have a party for so-and-so who was coming through. Well, Addy did that a couple of times, but, you know, there was only so much you could do along that line. After a while it gets to be a burden. So we began to resist Dorothy's attempts to use us as social figures, and that left a bit of a strain, too.

But after a while, Dorothy killed herself.

RH: Do you mean literally?

DMS: Literally. Fred went on a trip at one point, and she took a pile of barbituates, put a plastic bag over her head, and went to bed—after she'd locked all the doors. And Fred came back from the trip and couldn't get into the apartment. So he called the police. And apparently the police broke down the door, and there was Dorothy, quite dead.

RH: Do we know why?

DMS: Why she committed suicide? Well, in one sense yes—ah, she—you know, it's hard to tell how hypochondriacal a person is. But she was always sick with something. She had a lot of allergies, and she had special glasses made, and stuff like that. And she was a very unhappy person in many ways. But that's all I really know.

What else should I say about Chicago?

RH: Well, let's see. You said that there was tension between you and Fred, but you apparently resolved it.

DMS: No, I don't think we resolved it. I backed off and did what I was going to do, and he never called for a showdown, or put undue pressure on me.

RH: This makes it sound like Fred was really the key player there during the late '50s, early '60s.

DMS: Yeah, he really was.

RH: And did you become the key player?

DMS: Well, there's two kinds of keys. One is key with respect to the administration, and the other is key with respect to the intellectual movements of the department. Fred was key in keeping the department together. And he represented the department to the administration. And in that respect he was very effective. Intellectually, his kind of neo-Boasian anthropology didn't get anywhere and didn't have much support anyplace. But he was key in getting Fallers established and keeping Fallers going. But that's it.

My becoming key, I don't think was—I was not—they expected I would be a terrible chair. And I suppose everybody was much relieved that I wasn't as terrible as they expected. I wasn't key in any other respect. I did one other thing, though, that was fairly important.

Bob Adams, Clark Howell, and Bob Braidwood were the people who, at the time we developed "systems," were developing what they called "The Human Career." You know, a course on human evolution and fossil man, and a course on archaeology and history. But by that time it had become fairly clear that both cultural anthropology and those other two things were so highly specialized that you couldn't expect one person to really learn all that. Furthermore, the amount of overlap was relatively minimal.

In the meanwhile, a guy named [Ernst] Goldschmidt, a physical anthropologist, had left and gone to Michigan. Michigan, as you see, was always raiding Chicago. But it was okay. We helped Goldschmidt pack.

So, they brought in Lew [Lewis] Binford. And Lew Binford, of course, had great imperialistic and ambitious notions. He wanted to really move archaeology—and he did! But he needed a lot of money and help to do it. So he wanted to establish a salvage archaeology program. There was a lot of money for that. And I was the department chair at that time. And although Fred had helped to bring him in, and was very sympathetic and supportive, they immediately disliked each other personally. And, anyway, it fell to my lot to try to block Binford from developing a big, ambitious archaeology program.

RH: Because?—Who's motivating this, Fred?

DMS: No, partly I'm motivating it.

RH: And why did you want to block it?

DMS: I didn't want to see archaeology and physical expand. I didn't see any need for it. So, this was the beginning of the bio-archaeology wars, which eventuated in—I think they were taking place across the country. Because there are a lot of places now where, if you are going for a Ph.D. in cultural, you just don't have to take any of those courses, and if you're going for a Ph.D. in physical, or archaeology, you may or may not have to take the cultural courses. But, anyhow, the whole notion of the unified department, I think, has become considerably unstuck.

George Stocking is one of my old antagonists on this. He still believes in the old four-field stuff. But, you know, I say he's a case of arrested development! We're no longer interested in human evolution, or the rise of civilization, or whether race, language, and culture are intimately linked. And that's it.

RH: How long did Binford stay at Chicago?

DMS: He only stayed four or five years. I don't remember exactly how many. Binford had trouble with Braidwood, and Binford had trouble with Adams. And Binford had trouble with—Binford had trouble with almost everybody at one point or another.

RH: Did you and Binford become mortal antagonists?

DMS: Just the opposite! Binford and I became good friends. You see, Binford's question was, somebody was throwing a spoke into his wheels—who was holding him up? He thought it was me for a while. But after a while he realized it wasn't, and he began to blame Adams and Braidwood.

RH: I thought it *was* you!

DMS: Nope!

RH: I thought you said you were trying to block it.

DMS: Well, I was, but not nearly as effectively nor as openly nor as noisily as Braidwood and Adams were.

RH: And why were they trying to block it?

DMS: Well, in the first place, because Binford was attacking them directly. He was saying that their kind of archaeology was outdated and no good and unscientific. And if Binford had his way, they would have been, you know, sort of dumped out with the garbage. You see, obsolete. Binford was all for high statistications, and sampling, things like that. And of course, to some extent he was right. But Adams was more easily able to accommodate to Binford than Braidwood, because Braidwood really was under direct attack. Braidwood's old world archaeology was, you know—it was still very much of the go find important things and throw all the rest of it in the scrap heap. Whereas Binford was very— you had to do careful sampling and, what do you call it? test trenching, things like that. And also Binford was very much more closely concerned with the ecology. In fact, Binford's archaeology became absolutely the rage for quite a while.

On the whole, the department was one of the nicest departments ever. They didn't fight with each other. And if they did, it was all very soto voce, in quiet tones. There were never any real open feuds, or massive kinds of problems. The important thing was for everybody to get their own work done. In any way they could help do that, they did. Each person tended very much to take care of their own problems and try not to bump into others. And when there was a problem that one person encountered, the department generally got together and helped with it. And the administration was extremely good, too. They supported almost any kind of research endeavor with time off, and extra funds—things like that. And so, at least from my point of view—I think everybody else felt it, too—it was a very happy department. I don't mean it was ecstatic all the time. I just meant that it was free from many of the strains and stresses of internecine warfare.

Now where do I go from there? But there was a small problem that arose. As I said, the place had been pretty well decimated until Fred Eggan brought Fallers, Geertz, and me in. It was short of help. And then Eric Wolf left. So, about the first thing that happened was that Fallers had decided he was going to be doing major research in Turkey, and he decided he really needed Nur Yalman. So Nur Yalman was hired, because Tom wanted him. And that kind of ethos began to take place for a while. Clark Howell decided that Russell Tuttle was indispensable to Clark Howell's work. But of course, Clark Howell got up and left, leaving Russell Tuttle at Chicago.

Not only that, but then Fallers and Geertz got together. They had met Mel Spiro at the center, and they decided they wanted him. So, they put on a big push—but it didn't take a helluva lot of effort—and we hired Mel Spiro. But Mel Spiro decided he needed Ray Fogelson, and so, you know, to please Mel, Ray Fogelson was hired. And then, as I said, Binford had been hired earlier, and that was to "beef up" the archaeology program. And then Ray Smith was hired. I largely pioneered that effort. But it was okay.

Oh yeah, and then Michael Silverstein was hired, too. Silverstein was hired partly through the efforts of Paul Friedrich. You know, he felt he had to have somebody. And Barney Cohn was hired largely at first because Milton Singer pushed it. But it became clear almost immediately that Barney was his own man. And, of course, Silverstein was his own man. Friedrich had no control over him. But, you know, there's always that sort of folklore or myth that if you bring somebody in, you will control them. But it just never worked.

The other side of it was the less desirable side, and that was, if you hire somebody just because one person wants him, that's a pretty poor reason. If they can't do their work without that person's help, they ought to go and find another way.

Nur Yalman only stayed a while. [Stanley] Tambiah came. And he was very good for a while, but when Nur went to Harvard, Nur then pulled Tambiah to Harvard.

RH: Who hired Tambiah?

DMS: Tambiah—it was Vic Turner and Terry Turner who hired Tambiah. All I have is a recollection that almost everybody was enthusiastic about Tambiah. And, indeed, he did turn out to be very nice, very good, very congenial.

Vic Turner, who was apparently unhappy at Cornell—the people in Social Thought wanted him very badly. And Social Thought said, shouldn't we do a joint appointment with Anthropology—'cause I think that was what Vic wanted. And we did a joint appointment. And Vic said he wouldn't come without Terry.

RH: For those of us who were students there, it seemed like a place with so many undercurrents and crosscurrents. But when you talk about it now, it seems very straightforward and simple.

DMS: No, it was full of crosscurrents.

RH: Well, let's try this for crosscurrents: how did the Vietnam War affect the anthropology department?

DMS: It affected it very directly. A number of us—Adams and I, and a number of the others—were very definitely against the war, and wanted it stopped. Efforts were made by the government to try to get records on students. So we instructed the secretarial staff that they were not to give out any information to anyone without approval by faculty. Over and above that, some of the senior faculty, and the older faculty, were very "strong supporters" of the government, and supporters of the war, in fact.

RH: On what grounds?

DMS: Who knows! You know, there were a lot of people who supported the war. You had to stop communism wherever it appeared.

RH: That doesn't sound like anthropologists, though.

DMS: No, it doesn't. But the thing came to a kind of a head a few years later when the university decided to give out a prize of some kind— a peace prize, I think, of some sort—and it elected Robert McNamara to receive the prize. He came, and there was a lot of fussing then. Fred Eggan and Joan Eggan were invited to the dinner at which McNamara would be given the award, and they marched in a procession going to the dinner, and a number of anthropology people stood watching the march go by. And Fred came in for a lot of very severe criticism. There was also some disruption—somebody was arrested. I don't remember the details.

Otherwise, the Vietnam War didn't really bother the department at all. Fallers and Geertz were generally regarded as somewhat to the right of center, and I generally tended to take far left of center positions. That's about all.

I think Geertz and Fallers both, along with Shils, who was pretty far right, too, were upset by what they called the politicization of the university. And they said it was going to go the way South American universities went: it was going to be dominated by local politics and other such things. It would lose its scientific objectivity and independence, and so on.

You see, I fell out with Fallers and Geertz very sharply over the situation in the Congo. Fallers was, of course, our local expert on Africa. And he had had it from authoritative sources, he said, that [Patrice] Lumumba was nothing but a small-time rabble-rouser, and that by killing Lumumba, the CIA had done the right thing. So Fallers felt that Lumumba getting pushed out, and the CIA having a heavy hand in putting Mbutu in, who was really a simple and honest man—ha! ha!— was a good thing. And I didn't think so. But, you know, I wasn't the local Africa expert, and so I really hadn't—but anyway, I fell out with him, and with Geertz too, very emphatically and clearly at that point. There was never any resolution of that. Fallers died, Geertz left, and the whole Congo situation "sort of went away"—was no longer of immediate, local interest.

RH: When you say you fell out with Fallers and Geertz, does this mean you didn't talk to each other, or did you segregate political disagreement from your everyday, personal relationships, or did it affect everything?

DMS: Well, it clearly affected personal relationships to a great extent. Fallers frequently commented that my special talents had to do with small, primitive tribes—you know, classical, old-fashioned anthropology—and that he and Geertz were on the Committee on New Nations, and they dealt with major, worldwide movements and stuff like that. So that was really the most prestigious and important task. Fallers and Marg Fallers used to invite Addy and me and our two boys over to their house on various occasions. And, you know, we'd known each other a long time. And the kids—oh, Fallers and the girls had a puppet show they put on, and we were invited over there a couple of times for that. But that sort of stopped when the political situation got touchy. And I definitely was very angry. I didn't want to be put down as being only interested in "primitive tribes and small societies." And Fallers and Geertz, being on the Committee on New Nations, were—what would you call it?—I thought they were very possessive of that.

RH: Often in anthropology, you have to have credentials in a "primitive" society to count as a "real anthropologist"; this makes Chicago sound like a funny kind of anthropology-on-its-head place.

DMS: Not really, 'cause, you see, Fallers had Uganda, and Geertz had both Bali and Java. So they had good credentials. But the other side of the story, of course, was that I fancied I was just as cosmopolitan, just as worldwide, as they were.

RH: But you were working on American kinship, so why shouldn't you be counted as a person working on a—

DMS: —exactly.

RH: They didn't see it that way?

DMS: No. Because they saw themselves discussing world politics in a way that I didn't really do. Well, it's okay. These are small prestige fights that are of no real consequence.

RH: Brush fires!

DMS: Yes, brush fires.

What else could we say about Chicago? Well, very simply: Chicago was one of the happiest times of my life. I really felt I was happy there. The children certainly grew up, and became adults, by the time I left. I felt I had established myself as an anthropologist very well during the Chicago period. The Berkeley period was a kind of a prelude, a getting-ready-for. In terms of the life cycle, Chicago was a period of maturity for me. I did some of my best work at Chicago, really.

RH: *American Kinship* and the *Critique?*

DMS: *American Kinship* and the *Critique.* But, you see, the *Critique* really started in London.

Ten

Studying Kinship

RH: Let's take another topic. Whatever happened to kinship?

DMS: First, until recently, kinship had ceased being a major popular subject in anthropology. Papers on kinship clearly fell off. They became fairly rare. Now, of course, phoenix-like, it's risen from its ashes. This is due to people like Marilyn Strathern with her marvelous book on English kinship, and the new work in gay and lesbian studies, like that of Kath Weston and Ellen Lewin, and to feminist work, from people like Sylvia Yanagisako.[1]

But before this new work, old-style kinship studies had begun to fall off by the early 1970s, certainly by 1975.

Why did it happen? I asked Roy D'Andrade why he thought it happened. He agreed it had happened. He explained that it happened, at least for him, and, he thought, for most of the cognitive anthropologists, because they had solved all of the problems. There really were no interesting problems left. There were just no more questions of any real interest. So they moved on to other things. That was certainly marked clearly by Berlin and Kay going into color categories.

So that was Roy D'Andrade's answer. I haven't asked many other people. In fact, I can't remember asking anyone else.

Another answer is that it isn't just kinship. It's the whole idea of discrete, functionally specific institutions—that is, the whole idea that institutions are the major things of which society is made up, and that the cultural categories of institutions are really what it's about. That, I think, was abandoned. So it was not just kinship that evaporated. Primitive religion evaporated, although there's still a good deal of talk about religion. But religion, kinship, political organization—that pretty much broke down.

RH: So, categories like kinship, politics, and religion have been "deconstructed"—is that what you're getting at?

DMS: That's right. That's the beginning of my answer. People don't believe the system that much. Now, they're still writing on economics. And that has a lot to do with the fact that Marxists argue strongly that political economy is where it's at. But the institutional notion has been going, too. So that "topics" in anthropology now tend to be gender, political economy, race, and class. Even myth as a subject has gone away, to a large extent, though people are still doing analyses of myths.

Under that, I would add something else. In part, the institutional notions that obtained from the 1920s, maybe the 1910s, through the 1960s broke down, first, because the kinds of problems changed. At the same time, what is held to be the nature of social and cultural life changed. Along with these came a shift in the theoretical orientation, and these changes were all, of course, closely intertwined.

Let me go back to the nature of social and cultural life. There was a predominance of the sort of structuralism that was well established by the time of Malinowski—it was well established through the sociologists, like Talcott Parsons—where the social scheme of things, social life, was made up of a set of major institutions and their interrelations. But with the breakdown of the notion that it was all a bunch of institutions came the shift to "practice" orientation. That is, structure moved to practice. And as structure moved to practice, so it also moved to discourse, and so forth.

Here I should add a parenthetical. There had always been this constant back-and-forth between structure and process, between static and dynamic analysis—

RH: —between norms and social action—

DMS: —exactly. This had been going on and on. But by the late 1960s, certainly by the early 1970s, there had been a massive shift away from structure.

RH: By the early 1970s?

DMS: I think so. The question is, how do you date things? Do you date things by when they peak or do you know that they're over when they peak? Lévi-Strauss was very heavy in the 1970s, very popular. By the time a thing gets popular, all the avant-garde people have left it!

So when was it really over? I would say that by the time Lévi-Strauss was really popular—there had been a lot of intellectual and academic discussion of structuralism—that's when Bourdieu was getting his act together. Bourdieu was not the only person who was going to move toward process, toward practice.

So, the back-and-forth between dynamic and static, between structure and practice had been going on for quite a while. But the point I'm trying to make now is that I don't really know how long the practice stuff is going to be in ascendance. By this time, I would suspect, people are beginning to get a little fed up with practice, too.

With the shift away from structure, with the shift away from structures like institutions, kinship began to lose on those grounds. Another important ground on which it began to lose was that kinship had been significant theoretically because from the beginnings of the evolutionary and developmental lines of thought, the argument had always been that everything went from the simple to the complex, that the simplest kinds of social arrangements were those that centered on biological reproduction, and that the earliest social forms must have been familial and kinship forms. This was not universally true. Fustel de Coulanges argued that the earliest form was the coresidential group bound around a common hearth through a common set of ancestors whom they worshiped.[2] So that the earliest social form was a religious group. But nobody really took Fustel too seriously. All the rest of them argued that it was a familial group.

This in turn is closely related to the fact that in Victorian times— whenever that was—everybody thought it was sex that made the world go round. So, it was not only a family form. They envisioned sex as being both terribly powerful and terribly dangerous. I have a marvelous collection of quotations from Malinowski that express this beautifully— real lurid phrases, like "the untrammeled" this and that, "sex-rears-its-ugly-head" kind of thing. And "competitive wooing!" I thought that was very pretty. Can you picture competitive wooing—these people batting each other over the head, while the innocent maidens stand by who are the objects of all this stuff?

So with sex as a major obsession of the time, and the family as the only way to control sex, that's where kinship came in. My point is that with the shift in—and nobody believed that crap anymore—all that was left of that, certainly by the 1950s, was that kinship gave the outlines of a complete social structure. Closely connected with that was the idea that it was out of kinship that other social organizations developed, so that political and religious organizations developed out of kinship organizations. Economics was first isomorphic with kinship and then only gradually became different.

Certainly by the late 1960s, nobody was interested in evolution anymore—except for the primate-study people, and biological anthropology—that's their problem. So, most social and cultural anthropologists were no longer interested in evolution. They no longer believed in the institutional organization of society. They no longer believed that kinship was at the core of all of that. A whole new set of problems had begun to arise.

When I say "new problems," I don't mean it quite as emphatically as that. Rather, old problems got recast. For example, the problem of race got recast into much more contemporary terms than had been the case with Boas. Boas was interested in demonstrating the independence of the cultural definition of race from its presumed biological basis. People were largely no longer—not entirely, but largely—seriously assuming that the biological problem was a problem. They were now much more sharply focused on the social consequences of race and the injustices that were connected with it. Oh yeah, a few people are still hollering that, in fact, race really mattered and that there were real biological differences. But mostly nobody pays too much attention to that.

RH: Of course, Boas was also concerned with the social issues around race. But you're saying that he had to establish the fundamental scientific terms about what race is and isn't.

DMS: That's right.

RH: But you're saying that the problem was solved for the mainstream.

DMS: Well, they believed it was solved. They just didn't assume that the biological differences were that important. And along with that, of course—and here is where the "sexual revolution" came in. It was not simply as a sexual revolution. Sex was no longer seen as a threatening, potentially disrupting, violently uncontrollable thing that had to be dealt with in the severest terms. So the notion of the family as the preserver, etc.—which, of course, still survives on the far right, and did at that time, too—but in these largely intellectual circles that wrote papers about kinship, that was no longer in.

I can remember giving lectures on the incest prohibition when, at the time, people thought that, oh, that's an interesting subject. And then giving papers on the incest prohibition when people thought, what the hell, who cares. Now, parenthetically, did that change of interest come at the same time that it became openly apparent that an awful lot of incest went on—whereas before it was believed practically not to happen—and child abuse and stuff like that became a major social problem, whereas before it was always swept so completely under the rug that people didn't even believe it was there? Maybe it wasn't there; who knows?

So that's another set of changes that made kinship study, you know, like "Who needs it?" But the main point is the way in which problems change. Not only did people give up the idea of these institutions as the basic framework of society, but race became very largely a problem of justice, equal justice. That kind of move hooked up and was largely associated with the civil rights and feminist movements. And much of this was, very importantly, post–World War II. World War II gave a great impetus to it.

One other element needs to be woven in here: the "democratization of the intellectual enterprise." When I went to high school, the idea that I could go to Harvard was unthinkable. In fact, one of the kids in school with me—I just didn't understand how it had happened—did go to Harvard. I never did find out how or why or what the arrangement was.

RH: By "I couldn't go to Harvard," do you mean that a Jew couldn't go to Harvard?

DMS: A Jew couldn't go to Harvard. You needed money to go to Harvard. All of that. So I went to the New York State College of Agriculture. Tuition was free, etc. When I came back from the army, [James] Conant had started the big revolution at Harvard. He opened it up, partly on the grounds of geographic distribution. He wanted to get people from all over the United States, not just the New England area. At the same time, he opened it up in the sense that you didn't really need money anymore to come to Harvard. Nor was there a Jewish quota or anything like that. So all kinds of people were turning up at Harvard in 1947, when I got there.

The point is that there was that democratization that went with the G.I. Bill of Rights. A large number of people came into the academic system who would not have been able to get in earlier. They, or some of them, in turn, brought in kinds of problems and approaches which—I suppose the technical term now is—"destabilized" the earlier arrangements. There had certainly been Marxists and communists before. But they had been few and far between, and they had a helluva hard time. City College of New York and Columbia—Nicholas Murray Butler was famous for being a vigorous anticommunist. But just the fact that all these people had come in, a wide variety of people, brought something that made for a change in the kinds of problems that were of interest: problems of race, of poverty, of justice, of equality.

Where the upper-middle-class and upper-class intellectual establishment tended to be concerned with the stability of social systems, as something they wanted desperately to defend, establish, and maintain— and the problem was to prevent any kind of instability—so Durkheim was concerned in that connection, as were Radcliffe-Brown and Malinowski. But with the democratization of the intellectual establishments through the universities, stability wasn't seen as the be-all and end-all. In turn, social theories began to get opened up. So the view of a society as an essentially equilibrated organization built around a kinship system just did not make sense anymore. Not only was it unbelievable—and it was unbelievable because by that time, people knew that things changed faster—you know, they used to talk about people still living with the same stone-age customs they always had. Well, they still say that to some extent, but to a great extent, that's gone. And certainly to a great extent it's gone in anthropology. Nobody really believes that these things have been stable for eons and eons. Nobody believes that they still have the same kinship terminology for eons and eons. But, Radcliffe-Brown believed that, and all those people believed that.

So that, with the democratization, all that stuff began to open up.

RH: The Boasians had already argued that history had been going on for a long time, that there were no primitive, in the historical sense, peoples. What was the difference between their sense of history and this new interest in social change that you've just described?

DMS: People like Malinowski, Radcliffe-Brown—whatever their class origins—people like Meyer Fortes, Evans-Pritchard, Ralph Linton, even Margaret Mead, tended, I think, to agree that the major "social problems" were problems that required that we do everything we could to maintain stability. With the democratization came lots of people who were less committed to what they saw as unjust, outmoded commitments to states of affairs. And therefore, instability was much more of a—not simply negative state of affairs—

RH: —it was an accepted possibility—

DMS: —it was an accepted possibility, and it also promised change.

RH: But, again, the Boasians were interested in social reform.

DMS: Yes, but always, I thought, within a very narrow, highly constricted framework. We now know that Margaret Mead was, if anything, bisexual. But she was not proclaiming it from the rooftops.

RH: Right, but *Patterns of Culture,* for example, talks about the need for intelligent social change.

DMS: This is where I see the beginnings of it, because Mead and Benedict really came into their own during World War II or just after it. They were the beginnings. And now, of course, we regard Mead and Benedict as relatively conservative.

RH: I don't.

DMS: I do. I think Mead was extremely conservative. Mead was trying to tell us that we should all throw ourselves into supporting the Vietnam War. She was very definitely against all that antiwar agitation. And she was definitely very patriotic. Whereas I think patriotism is "the last refuge of the scoundrel."

RH: How does Lévi-Strauss fit in? My sense of it is that in the 1950s, British descent theory was unchallenged. You told me once that when you were in graduate school, you had to hew the party line. So Lévi-Strauss comes along and offers an alternative to British descent theory. In retrospect, his system looks as rigid as the system it replaced—

DMS: —absolutely—

RH: —but at the time, it gave people like you a kind of freedom, because if there were two ways to do it, then there were more than two ways to do it. Does that make sense?

DMS: That makes very good sense.

RH: Then that's another set of influences coming in from another intellectual world—the French academy. So are we talking about multiple influences here?

DMS: Yes, I left him out and I shouldn't have. There are a number of things to be said about Lévi-Strauss. In one respect, the Lévi-Strauss of the *Elementary Structures* was still of the old, well-established institutional category stuff.[3] It was definitely another way of seeing kinship, but it also saw kinship as where it's at. The mythology stuff was really the big break in structuralism, not the kinship stuff. His kinship work was a very brilliant and innovative opening of the field, but it opened it within what now, in retrospect, you can see was still the same framework. The mythology stuff is where it really took off.

It wasn't so much that if there were two different ways of doing it, then that really opened it up. It was that that was probably the last gasp of the old kinship study stuff.

RH: Yes, but didn't the fact that Lévi-Strauss created such a debate with these entrenched and, in the United States, highly esteemed British theorists give you a space—as they say these days—to operate?

DMS: I don't think that made a bit of difference. Well, once again, in retrospect, now, looking back, you can say that by emphasizing alliance, and by emphasizing the exchange aspects, he implicitly de-emphasized sex as the motor and sex as the danger. But, in fact, the opening of the *Elementary Structures* is the old business of the incest prohibition: that you've gotta have an incest prohibition to get started, and if you've gotta prohibit incest, why do you prohibit it? Not because you're gonna have two-headed babies, but because there might be trouble. But he passes over that lightly, so, in a way, yeah, it kind of de-emphasized sex and the family. It definitely de-emphasized the family. So, yeah, okay, it was a little bit of help. But that's about it. I don't think it had a major influence.

RH: I always thought that your "Muddles in the Models" paper came out of the opening that Lévi-Strauss's playing around with kinship models had given you.

DMS: Well, I saw the "Muddles in the Models" as the way of attacking both—to some extent, Lévi-Strauss's construction of kinship, and to some extent, also, the descent model. I thought I was trying to organize some good reasons to dump them both. Have I missed your point?

RH: No, it's just that it's always been my feeling that Lévi-Strauss's work created the chance to rethink all this stuff. But you were working on these problems in your own way, going back to the 1940s.

DMS: I was working on this stuff independently, in my own way, from the late 1940s, after I came back from Yap, and certainly by the time I went to England. But everybody else was secretly reading Lévi-Strauss, but I couldn't read French. Edmund Leach was reading it. Edmund had rented a room someplace, and when he didn't go home he would stay in his room and read Lévi-Strauss. And then he came out with his big cross-cousin marriage business.[4] And Needham was reading it, cause he could read French. But I couldn't read French, so I didn't really encounter Lévi-Strauss until after I came back, in the middle or late 1950s.

But that's neither here nor there. I was ready to break away from kinship certainly by the time I did the "Muddles in the Models" stuff. And the "Muddles in the Models" was for me, I think, a very good, convenient way of putting together all the problems I had. Not all the problems— but many of the problems I'd had with it. And also, many of the problems I'd had with what seemed to me to be—I don't know what you'd call it—the angels-dancing-on-the-head-of-a-pin aspect of kinship. You know: it was erudite, it was esoteric, it was angels on the head of a pin, something for only a highly specialized specialist who had no relationship to anything else. And I had certainly given up the notion—I was attacking at that time the notion of the kin-based society. So I couldn't see kinship as the be-all and end-all, the beginning and the end, the institution out of which every other institution grew. So it was a good chance for me to essentially say "Fuck off! I've had it with that stuff." And that was good.

The paper was first written in 1962, and I gave it at the center in 1962 or 1963. It wasn't published until later. But, you see, that was also the point at which I was beginning the American kinship stuff.

RH: How do these developments relate to another topic you mentioned at the beginning of our interviews—what was it, "the uselessness of data"?

DMS: No, on the peculiar position of data—on the strange case of data! I don't know what you'd call it. We'll figure out a good title.

The general supposition has been that data is important to prove or disprove or support or fail to support hypotheses or ideas. [Thomas]

Kuhn—wasn't it Kuhn?—didn't he argue that to some extent, data was not decisive in changing major ideas?[5] And, in that respect, I think he is right about anthropology.

To some extent, many of the problems were just not amenable to being changed by available data. To some extent, the data was just not available. There was no way to get it. There was no technology for it. Things like that.

But, even so, data never really, I don't think, seriously upset any major—or even minor—hypotheses. The shift from culture history as a subject didn't occur because the data did or didn't support any positions, or did or didn't prove to be decisive in any of the arguments. The shift from evolutionary to structural or structural-functional questions, again, didn't come about because there was no data—although, of course, many people said that, well, since there's no real data, we might as well look to something that we *can* deal with. But that was more in the way of a rationalization, I think.

All of this is leading up to two points of concern to me. One is that fame and fortune are not generally supported by ethnography. That is, you don't become a famous anthropologist by virtue of the magnificent fieldwork and the great ethnographies you write. You become famous because you have some idea which for some reason becomes popular and catches on.

People say that Malinowski invented serious, intensive, participant-observation fieldwork. I think Malinowski has become an icon for that idea, because, once again—I'm now doing what I say doesn't work—that is, if you look at the data, it doesn't support the idea that Malinowski inaugurated or initiated intense participant-observation fieldwork! But it doesn't matter. People say he did; he gets credit for it, and the fact that, you know, you read his diary and—he kept his distance from those natives.[6] He was furious with them half the time. But everybody gets furious with people they study. And if they don't, they're liars, or they're cuckoo.

But Malinowski was famous because he certainly was able to handle his public relations very well, because he wrote a fairly effective and efficient prose, and because at about the time that everybody was gradually, clearly getting disenchanted and discouraged and disinterested in culture history and evolution, and whether it was diffusion or independent invention—nobody cared much anymore—along came Malinowski and gave it a new shot in the arm, by shifting to a "functionalism" that was, I think, at that time beginning to become general in the social sciences and humanities.

Clifford Geertz—yes, he definitely did a lot of ethnography in Java and in Bali and in Morocco. And people even read some of his ethnography. But, basically, Geertz was not popular because of his ethnography.

RH: This brings up another one of your topics, "the apotheosis of ethnography." Can you elaborate on that?

DMS: I think that anthropology has always been in a state of flux. But at any particular point in its history, people are always saying, "Anthropology is in a state of flux." Anthropology has always had a problem defining itself. At any point in its history, that problem is evident. And at any point in its history, there is always a tendency to say, "Anthropology is really . . . !"

So, at one point, anthropology was really the study of primitive people in order to contribute something to our understanding of how "culture evolved," or how "culture developed," or how "culture was built." You know, *The Building of Culture* was the title of a book by Roland Dixon.[7]

Then anthropology moved away from culture history, evolution, and so forth and became "How do simple societies work?"—in order to gain some insight into how societies work. So, again, primitive societies became the object of anthropology. But, then it turned out that, well, maybe we haven't really learned very much about how societies work from studying "primitive" societies, and if you want to study how societies work, you've gotta study how societies work wherever you find society. Then some anthropologists began to argue that it was really culture, not society, that was the issue.

RH: And among those anthropologists were people like yourself.

DMS: Yes, I beat the culture drum. Geertz beat the culture drum. We both got it through Parsons from Kroeber and Kluckhohn, and Kroeber, in turn, was part of the whole American culture movement. Indeed, we were Boasians; if not directly from Boas, we were Boasians partly through Kroeber and Kluckhohn and Parsons, but partly also because that was the general climate of anthropology in America, in which we grew up and participated.

RH: So anthropology was then defined as the study of culture.

DMS: Yes. But now, once again, everybody is saying it's in flux—What is it all about? What is anthropology? What is anthropology's job? What's its domain? How does it identify itself?

So there's been a great tendency, I think, in certain quarters—Jim Clifford is one; I should mention a few others, but I can't think of them at the moment—to define anthropology as fieldwork and ethnography. Indeed, ethnography is so much a part of anthropology and so much a defining feature of anthropology that Bruno Latour has discovered that ethnography is what he does![8] He goes and studies laboratories, and he uses the ethnographic method, although I have no idea what he thinks the ethnographic method is.

Anyway, my complaint at this moment is that I don't know what anthropology really is, but I don't think that it is or should be defined by ethnography and fieldwork. Rather, I think it is and should be defined as the study of culture. Be that as it may for the moment, what I'm trying to indicate is that ethnography and fieldwork are not really exactly what it amounts to.

The argument about ethnography is that anthropologists who are "anybody"—that is, the rich and famous—no matter how far you go back, turn out not to depend on either ethnography or fieldwork. Frazer certainly never set foot in the field. Westermarck did set foot in the field, but it wasn't because he did that study of marriage in Morocco that he became famous. Malinowski's fame did not, really, rest on his Trobriand fieldwork, although everybody assumes that it did. It rested on the fact that he made a very strong case for functionalism, but functionalism of a very loose, almost sloppy sort—interrelations, everything was interrelated—yeah, sure!—and, of course, it served "human needs." That kind of functionalism became very popular and very widely accepted, and he was its greatest exponent.

Radcliffe-Brown's functionalism was much more of a Durkheimian functionalism in the way each part fitted into and contributed to the maintenance of a whole. But, again, Radcliffe-Brown certainly is not famous as a field-worker. He swiped most of the field data on the Australian stuff from other people. His Andaman Islands book was widely reprinted, but—you know, I mean, it's silly. It didn't amount to much. And again, the evidence on his fieldwork in the Andamans is that, very clearly, at that point many of the natives were under police control. So his fame doesn't rest on his ethnography.

The point I'm now in the process of making is that the theories that were really popular, the theories that made people famous, were not themselves a direct outcome of the ethnography they did or the field-work they did. Someplace along the line I should pick up fieldwork. But let me leave fieldwork for the moment, and stick to ethnography as the production of a book that, presumably, embodies a lot of data.

The point now is that all the "really famous" anthropologists are not famous because of their ethnography. Geertz, Lévi-Strauss—who is it you want to name? The people who are famous are famous for the ideas that they argued, and the ideas they argued were not simply, easily, me-chanically based on the fieldwork and ethnography that they produced.

Now the opposite side of the story is the really, really great field-workers, who really produced great ethnography, were never famous for that. Raymond Firth, of course, is my big case in point. He really was a fabulously good field-worker. He has been producing material on Tikopia to the present day—and he's ninety-six or ninety-seven. He continues to produce new material from the old fieldwork that had never been published before. And there is a larger corpus of ethnography on Tikopia than on—you know, it's three to four times the size of Malinowski's stuff. But, you know, nobody really regards Raymond Firth as a major intellectual figure.

Vic Turner certainly was a very good field-worker. He did produce some very good fieldwork, and very good ethnography. But he's not fa-mous as an ethnographer. He's famous because of his "liminal states" and his pilgrimage stuff and all those ideas.

Or, take Roy Wagner. Roy Wagner is a superb field-worker, and his ethnography is really some of the best. I think Roy Wagner is famous for his theoretical and innovative intellectual efforts as much as he is highly regarded for his ethnography.

The same thing applies to the critics of anthropology. I don't think Jim Clifford is famous for his monograph on Leenhardt.[9] I don't think that George Marcus has achieved some notoriety because he worked on Tonga. Indeed, I don't know anybody who's read the ethnography he wrote. In fact, I've often talked to people and asked them, "Hey, have you read George Marcus's ethnography?" "No!—but I read that other damn book."[10]

That's the way it goes! So where does ethnography get you? It gets you famous in a very small group of people, if you do it very well, who are interested in the particular geographic area, the particular kind of culture, and that's about it. But it doesn't make any major theoretical or major intellectual sense.

Insofar as ethnography is data, and insofar as data turns out, I think, to be rather unrelated to the ideas which the authors propagate—I don't know, it's at best a very loose connection, and it's a peculiar connection, because the image, the ideal, the presupposition is that it is a scientific endeavor, that we really try to see how things are and check our hypotheses, and so on. Basically, that doesn't seem to be what happens.

Now, going to me as an example, and very briefly, just touching a few high points: I was a graduate student at Yale in 1941. I was there only for about six months. I took a course in kinship from George Peter Murdock, and all I can remember is that it just did not make any sense to me, and that I found it intellectually kind of revolting. He was doing chi-square analyses that correlated kinship terms with kinship groupings, and that wasn't what I was into, and I didn't like it. I also didn't terribly like George Peter Murdock, and I don't think he liked me terribly much, either.

I quit anthropology, went to work, got into the army, went through the war and came back, went to Harvard, and went into the field in Yap. On Yap, I could only barely remember what the hell Murdock taught in that course, but for some reason I got involved in the goddamn kinship stuff. The reasons are not clear, but for some reason. So it turned out that on Yap, I did a lot of kinship work. But I had remembered enough about the kinship terminology stuff so that I was interested in pursuing kinship terms on Yap. And I did. And came back, and wrote my thesis, and then got a job at LSE.

By then, I was deeply involved with the kinship game. I read Murdock—meanwhile, his book *Social Structure* was published[11]—and I read Radcliffe-Brown, Rivers, all that stuff. And while I was in England, it occurred to me—"it occurred to me," you know?!—that they were absolutely all wrong about kinship terms. But I had known that on Yap, anyway. But now it seemed obvious that the simplest, most obvious way to demonstrate that they were all wrong was to use common American kinship terms as an example.

In formal kinship analysis, they always deal with "referential terminology." And they distinguish referential terminology from vocative. The presupposition involved there is that there are simply two systems which may indeed be one system. That is, sometimes the referential and vocative are identical. Or, if it isn't two systems that's one system, there will be a vocative system and a referential system where some terms will be both vocative and referential.

Well, it seemed self-evident, as a native speaker of English, or American English—we have to be careful of that. Anyway, American English, the kinship terms were just obvious: we called "father" father, dad, pop, poppa, a variety of terms—my old man; in some quarters he was called the governor. George Homans claimed they used to call their father the governor. I never encountered that, but Boston Brahmins may have done it.

Anyway, it was obvious: not only were there alternate terms, there were a large number of terms. Over and above that, the referential terms themselves—if you use reference in some way that was perhaps not technically exact—the referential terms themselves varied. If I talk to you, and you are a total stranger, and you ask me, "Who is that man?" I will say to you, "That is my father." But if you are my brother, I say, "Oh, you mean pop?" or "You mean dad?" So, how you use these things in reference varies with the circumstances and situation.

Now at that time, I didn't realize that I was talking pragmatics. It's the old Voltaire business about not realizing you talk prose. That's pragmatics, yes? I had discovered pragmatics without knowing it. It was pragmatics. So when I came back from England to Harvard, I spouted this idea around, and George Homans was very enthusiastic about it. "Good, good, good," he said. "Let's get some money from the Laboratory of Social Relations and do a study." And I said, "Good."

So I got some money from the Laboratory of Social Relations and I did a study. I interviewed graduate students and faculty in the Department of Social Relations. I got a brief genealogy from them, and I said, "What do you call this person and that person? And what else do you call them? And how do you call them in various circumstances?" and so on.

Sure enough, it came out exactly as I expected. I was able to say, "I have done a study, I have collected genealogies, I have talked to informants"—and not only that, but that paper became very famous, and I gained a lot of kudos.[12] I was absolutely bowled over when Melville Herskovits wrote me a polite note and said he had enjoyed the paper very much and would I please send him a reprint. Wow!—I was on the map.

But you know, it really wasn't necessary to collect all that stuff from the graduate students and faculty of Social Relations. In any case, what the hell kind of sample are they? At best they're a bunch of kooks and a bunch of nuts and a rather peculiar selection of odd people. I did get a few women in there. I got some of the secretaries. But that didn't matter.

But again, the presupposition was that the data supported the conclusions. Now whether I'm right, wrong, or indifferent about kinship terms is quite apart from that whole thing.

So I'm back from England, and Raymond Firth comes over to be at the Center for Advanced Study while I'm teaching at Berkeley. And they're desperate for research money. So Raymond proposes that he and I do a joint study comparing American and English kinship. I felt a deep obligation to Raymond. He had given me my very first job. He had been extremely kind, extremely generous, extremely supportive all the while I was in London. I felt I owed him, you know. Addy, on the other hand, felt very strongly that I was getting myself in over my head, that doing a big joint study was silly, that I had work I had to do, that I was prepared to write this book and was figuring on writing that book and that I wanted to start new research myself. I was going to start working in Mescalero, and she said, "Don't get yourself involved in it."

But, nevertheless, I felt very strongly that I owed Raymond, and so I went ahead. But I made a deal with Addy. The deal was that I would be the mastermind, and I would hire somebody to do the day-to-day running of the project. So before I even put in for the grant, I arranged for Hilly Geertz—by this time, Geertz, Fallers, and I had agreed to move to Chicago, we had agreed that we would start the study in Chicago if it got funded, etc. Since Hilly was coming to Chicago, and her kids were just about big enough so that she wanted to have a job, she was anxious at that point and willing to be the day-to-day supervisor of all the work.

So I satisfied Addy that I would not be bogged down in it. Hilly would do it, and I could still do my share to support Raymond.

Trouble, of course, immediately eventuated. Hilly decided for some reason that she couldn't do the job. I, then, had to find somebody else. I found Alice Rossi who, again, was trying to come back after having a couple of kids and wanted a job and wanted to get back into sociology. She was interested in family and kinship, so I hired her to do it. And all seemed to be fine and well at that point.

But then, once again, trouble arose. I discovered that Alice Rossi—the details of this aren't important now—anyway, in a fit of whatever it was, I fired Alice Rossi. So Alice Rossi goes and I continued the study. It was my study, so I ran it. There was only one fixed question in the whole interview, and that was something like "Give me a list of all of your relatives." It was an opening question to begin to collect genealogy, and then, presumably, the interviewer would do what "good anthropology field-workers" generally do, and that is, you know, any place the interview led, you followed. And if it had any bearing at all on kinship and family, you wrote it down. At that time, tape recorders were not readily available. Anyway, I felt strongly that these kids should learn how to do an interview and write it up afterward. It was good field technique.

So we piled up lots and lots and lots of interviews, and we had really nice genealogies. I had some small projects going at the same time. For example, I wanted to compare the genealogies of the husband and wife, and the genealogies of the parents and children, and brothers and brothers, and sisters and sisters, and brothers and sisters. That is to say, to take from the same presumptive genealogical pool, to compare who reported whom. For example, reported and not reported—Did they remember the name or not remember the name? Did they remember occupation? Did they remember specific details?—all of that. And all of that data is still available and I still have it, and I wish somebody'd work on it because I—anyway, the project went on.

Now, let me go to the main point of the whole episode. I read every single interview that came in, and I talked to every interviewer either about that interview or about how things were going, and we met weekly and discussed what was happening, etc. And I do not believe that anything more than minor alterations or emendations or ornamentations on my basic presuppositions arose either from the interview material or from the discussions from the interviewers that in some way changed my picture of what the hell was happening, what the schema was like.

So at the end of that period, I got a second visit to the Center for Advanced Study at Palo Alto, at Stanford. It was my task to write the monograph up.

RH: Is this about 1966?

DMS: Yes, '66. The field part of the study went from '63 to '66. Naturally, I carried all the interviews out with me, or sent them. They were all in boxes, and I never looked at 'em! However, Addy did. On the way out, she discovered a lump in her breast, and she had a mastectomy, and that upset all of her plans, it upset all of my plans, it upset the hell out of everything. She was at that point really beginning to open her life out. She was beginning to learn French. We were going to go to France. I had agreed only to stay at the center for six months because I knew I could write this monograph in six months with no problem at all. And she was going to go to San Francisco and learn French, and then she was going to get back into the job market. It was going to be the beginning of life again for her. However, in Coeur d'Alene, Idaho, she discovered a lump in her breast. We got to Palo Alto. It had to be removed, and that was it.

So, it took me a little more than six months, partly owing to the fact that she was sick. When she began to get back on her feet again, she came in and sat in the little study that I had there, and she read over interviews. And she selected out quotations that generally supported what I was saying. She got a million of them. She was trained as a historian and to her authorial statements had to be grounded in archival evidence. She had examined the archives and found the evidence, she said. I mention this in the book—it was at that point that I really faced the question of, do you use "and the informant said" as a way of giving evidence to support your hypothesis or support your statement? [13]

It seemed to me very clear by that time—I don't think I had formulated this before, but by that time it seemed to me very clear that this is a lot of baloney, you know. On the one hand, you could mostly make any goddamn informant say anything you wanted to. At worst, you could even pay him. At best, you so finagled the interview around to that— God, from my experience on Yap I knew perfectly well that if you keep pounding on the same kind of question long enough, they begin to get a damn good idea as to what you're looking for. And then, you know, they figure it's time to eat, they want to go out, they want to quit. They've had it. And they'll tell you—they don't care. It doesn't bother them. I mean, I've done the same thing when I've been interviewed.

So, I decided that I was not going to pad the monograph with a lot of quotations to support it. But Addy was furious. She said, "God, you mean you spent all this money, you spent all this time collecting all this information, and you're not using it?"

And I said, "Yes." I said, "I don't want to pretend that this is evidence to prove something."

So she said, "But you are saying in the beginning of it that you did do the study, that you did do the fieldwork, that you did collect so many pages."

And I said, "Yeah, but I know that that's—you know—it's not a lie. It's just—it's like—what would you call it? Flim-flam. Ornamentation. It's the sort of thing you have to put in a monograph. Anyway, it was important to tell NSF."

So she got absolutely livid, very angry. She accused me of really being dishonest, because on the one hand, I wouldn't use the quotations to support the statements I made, but on the other hand, I was allowing other people to think that what I had written had somehow arisen from all the interviews and all the study and all the time and all the fieldwork. When, as I was readily telling her, I knew exactly what it was going to come out to be before I started it!

So, I think, with some justice she did accuse me of being dishonest. And with some justice, I of course had to say, "Yeah—it was not quite honest." But, that was it.

RH: How did she respond to the fact that you dedicated the book to her?

DMS: By never mentioning it, never acknowledging it, and not caring one damn bit. She responded in another way. 'Cause we went back up to my study in the center, and it took her two days to literally destroy every single piece of paper on which she had written anything. All those quotations she had extracted and copied, etc., etc., by God, she tore them all up, and nobody was going to get them, and nobody could dip into them later or anything else. If I wasn't going to use them, to hell with it. So, at that point, we were having a pretty serious war with each other over that. So that was it.

Now, it is not simply that I knew everything that I was going to say in the monograph before I did the study. A lot of the actual thinking-through of what I was going to write came as I drove from Chicago—oh, we were driving to Portland, Oregon, to drop Jonathan off for his first year at Reed. And, you know, you sit and drive and you think. You can't sing "Green Bottles on the Wall" songs all the time. The kids were too big to be amused, and they were past the stage of counting up out-of-state license plates, and stuff like that. So a lot of the thinking I did, I know, as I drove from Chicago to Oregon. A lot of the thinking I also did when I was actually typing and writing. But the thinking was of the sort of—you know, How do you make this point? How do you formulate it?

Oh, you know, I put in a little squiggy gook about kinship terminology which I later much regretted. I shouldn't have messed it up with that. But it was another one of my gestures to orthodox, proper anthropology, and kinship and crap. And I made a nice little gesture to recognize Goodenough's kinship terms, stuff like that. But, basically, I have not looked at those interviews since.

RH: Okay, now, to make a counterargument against the position you've been elaborating upon—

DMS: Well, there's one obvious source of data that I have not mentioned, but it's self-evident.

RH: What's that?

DMS: I had myself.

RH: Right. But what I would say is that anthropology is the study of culture *and* it's based on an ethnographic method. My quarrel with cultural studies is that a lot of it is elite texts commenting on elite texts. One of the great virtues of anthropology is going out into the world and talking to people and looking at situations. It's not exactly that we go out to test hypotheses, but the field situation does offer a resistance to our preconceptions, and our theorizing comes out of our engagement with that situation.

DMS: Absolutely. You're completely and perfectly correct.

RH: Okay, one more thought: the American kinship stuff may be a very special case, because you were the informant.

DMS: There are two points to be made. First, when you go to a place like Quebec to study the Québécois—and you really didn't know anything about them, had not lived as one or anything else like that—and I had gone to Yap to study Yapese culture, and I didn't know a thing about it—it is in the process of talking to people, watching people, being with people, observing people, and interacting that you get your ideas about what you think may be going on.

Let me go back just a moment. I went to Yap, and I didn't know I was going to get interested in kinship, but for some reason it happened. I'm not even clearly sure why it happened, but it happened. So I began following that. That became one of my major problems. I began just doing it. And certainly in the course of all that interaction, yeah, I got ideas. And certainly in the course of all that interaction, I carried ideas in with me. But the process of fieldwork *does* give you new ideas, and this is where you learn, and what you learn is ideas, and all that—absolutely true.

And the fact that I had, by living in America, and having been around enough and having heard people and seen people—as I say, I didn't really learn much except perhaps a few ornaments and perhaps a thing was a little more widely distributed than I had expected, or something like that—so that I didn't have to do that here. Again, what I was doing was—and here you have to nod to Geertz—I was doing the interpretation as I was doing it.

RH: The interpretation of—?

DMS: You're doing—you are creating the interpretations as you presumably do the fieldwork.

RH: Are we talking about Yap now, or the United States?

DMS: It could be both. United States, a peculiar and special case because I knew the culture and I had lived it. And therefore, many of the interpretations had already emerged from both my interaction with the intellectual atmosphere of anthropology and just living in it. But in Yap, I didn't know the culture, and in Quebec you didn't know the culture. So the interpretations emerge as you're doing it.

And the evidence for this is in that other famous theme of field notes. There have been a few instances where field notes have yielded some kind of ethnography, pitifully poor as it may be. Bob Murphy got Buell Quain's field notes and whipped them into some kind of shape.[14] Somebody did something on I think it was Beatrice Blackwood's field notes—

there have been a few of those.[15] But mostly, field notes are really trash! They're absolute trash. They're your diary of "This is what happened to me today," or "This is what somebody said to me." Or they are recorded texts: you sit down with somebody and you say, "Tell me the story of the origin of the world." Or, text in another sense: "Tell me, how does the political system work; who is chief? How do they get to be chief?" etc.

All right, at the low level of what are the concrete, specific prerequisites to chieftainship in a village on Ramung in Yap, yeah, I would go back to my field notes. But you know, most ethnography is not really that. It includes that, but, you know, it has a long thing on chieftainship, and what chieftainship means, and who gets to be chief, and how they get to be chief, and so on. It isn't all that detailed crap. So that the interpretation comes out, and it is that interpretation that, presumably, yields the "ethnography."

RH: I agree with you that the interpretation comes right there as you're working along with the data, and that, therefore, there's no neat separation between interpretation and data. I agree with that—

DMS: —absolutely—

RH: —or hypothesis and data. But, we oughtn't to minimize the importance of that encounter with the world.

DMS: Oh no, I should not minimize that importance . . .

RH: Okay, so your argument really is against the notion of data as some kind of set of facts that are out there that one discovers.

DMS: Not only that, but that somehow are embodied in the field note. Again, this is one of the Jim Clifford problems. I don't know if he says this explicitly, but, you know, that stupid book by [Roger] Sanjek[16]— you can quote me—arose from Jim Clifford suggesting that field notes were important. I think Jim Clifford did think that field notes—you know, there's a real nasty positivist bias in a lot of the cultural studies stuff.

RH: On the part of whom?

DMS: A lot of the "text" stuff—things like that. In the end you ain't got nothing but the text. You have no idea what the authorial intention is, you have no idea about the social context in which it arose. All you've got is the text, and don't presuppose anything else. I think that that turns out to come from, and to be very closely related to, the old positivist notions—avoiding subjectivity at all costs and focusing on objectivity.

RH: But if we go back to your notion of who the great people in anthropology were, there are extreme examples of people who really weren't field-workers, like Lévi-Strauss. But I don't think you can say that about somebody like Geertz, or even Malinowski. I don't know that you would want to separate, in their work, the contribution that fieldwork made and the contribution that theory made.

DMS: But I do.

RH: Why?

DMS: 'Cause I don't think any of it arose out of the fieldwork. I don't think they learned a thing out of the fieldwork.

RH: Did you learn anything on Yap?

DMS: Do I have to answer that question?

RH: Yes!

DMS: I learned what it was like to be lonely, I learned what it was like not to belong—although I had had hints of that before. I learned that a lot of my illusions about being able to live alone on a South Seas island were not true. I learned that in some respects I was psychologically sterner, stouter, and tougher than I had thought I was. I learned that some of my condescending notions about being kind, open, warm, generous, friendly were very romantic.

RH: But did you learn anything about the Yapese?

DMS: Yeah, a little—oh yeah, I learned a lot about the Yapese in the sense that my guess that the way in which kinship was studied in England and America, and probably Germany, France, and Russia, too, was mostly bullshit.

RH: But then the contact with Yapese experience—

DMS: —it confirmed—

RH: —no!—

DMS: —it confirmed all the prejudices I had carried into the field.

RH: It helped you to think about it. It was part of your thinking about it.

DMS: Nope!

RH: But now you're separating the data from the theory.

DMS: I really am, that's the whole point of this. I don't think—you see, there are two senses in which the data don't make a damn bit of difference. To become a great, famous anthropologist does not depend on your fieldwork, does not depend on your field data, does not depend on your ethnography. It depends on a whole bunch of ideas that are relatively independent of that. That was true for Frazer, it was true for Lévi-Strauss, it was true for Clifford Geertz, it was true for Malinowski.

RH: Then, if anthropologists are students of culture, should anthropologists do fieldwork? What's the point of fieldwork, then?

DMS: That's the problem, isn't it.

RH: I have to repeat the question: Should we not be doing fieldwork at all?

DMS: Well, you see, I'm in a jam. I don't know. Logically, from what I've said, we shouldn't bother with it. And yet, I'm sure that I would be the first person to insist that we should continue to do fieldwork. Let me try to state reasonably clearly: I think that the stress on the significance of fieldwork should be minimized. It does not deserve the be-all, end-all place it has. I think that Lévi-Strauss had a lot of very important, and very influential and significant things to say. And to have made him actually go out and live with those Bororo would have been ridiculous. Same thing for Malinowski. So that fieldwork should not have that kind of fetishized place it has. But I'm not arguing that it should be prohibited. I wouldn't even argue that nobody can learn anything from fieldwork. My insistence that I didn't learn a helluva lot shouldn't be taken as a standard. It's not 'cause I was smarter, it's just 'cause I don't learn that well, that's all.

So that's the first point to make. And the second point is that a lot of people really do like to read ethnographies, like a lot of people like to read mystery stories or travel stories or political science. So, sure, ethnographies should be published. But again, I don't think that ethnography should be the sine qua non. It shouldn't have the fetishized position which I think Jim Clifford and various others have given it.

Jim Clifford is not the only one and the postmoderns are not the only ones. I think a lot of the "old-line" anthropologists do. I can remember when I was still a graduate student, people would say, "Oh, it's so wonderful to live in the field; oh, I'm so unhappy being here all the time, I just want to get back into the field." Well, one of the reasons for that is that they were nobodies here, and when they were in the field they were everybody because they had the whole colonial operation behind them, you know? They were the big chief. They could bring in all the goodies. They carried a lot of weight and they were highly regarded. They were just maladjusted and maladapted people. A lot of anthropologists are and were.

But my point only is that it isn't ethnography, it isn't fieldwork, that is the sine qua non. It is the study of culture, period. That's really all I'm saying.

Afterword

David M. Schneider

I had my seventy-sixth birthday last month and a stroke in June of 1993 which left my left leg lame and my left arm and hand lost its ability to type as it had before.

As I have frequently remarked, getting old has no future in it, and this means that older folks have to look back if we look anywhere.

Looking back now, I am moved to separate my personal life from my life as an anthropologist although any such separation is, of course, artificial. Personal life had its ups and downs, but on the whole I have no complaints and lots to be thankful for. As an anthropologist, I could have done much more, and done it far better.

But I did what I did, though it's not always clear that what happened is what I did. If anthropology is but one edifice in a house of social thought, I messed with but one of the smaller windows.

For reasons that are not clear at all, I got hooked on kinship at the outset. And the two books and the one with Smith and some papers are all I have to show for it. It is a great comfort to know that one is never really properly appreciated, for that shows that the problem is *them* and not *me*. Of course, Galileo was not fully appreciated at first, but after he was dead awhile . . . but I would gladly swap all the appreciation I might have coming for another few years of life, especially if I could keep a couple of people with me. But now I'm getting personal and I shouldn't.

As I indicated above, I had everything in place, mostly, when, driving to Oregon and then down to California during the very late summer of 1966, I began putting it together as I drove. I must have been lousy company at the time, but nobody complained that I remember. I had the Parsonian paradigm firmly in mind. The fascination of brilliant but sterile pyrotechnics with terminology had never really seized my imagination. I knew that if anything, working on American data could be both legitimate and productive. There was supposed to be a clear advantage to using emotionally neutral data from "other" societies sometimes, but not in this instance, especially since nothing much was really sacred to me. "The Family" was certainly sacred to a lot of people, but not to me. Nor did I have any vested interest in the religious or theoretical sanctity of marriage or parenthood. I was looking forward to six to eight months of intellectual bliss at the Center for Advanced Study. I did not say to myself in so many words "Now's my big chance," but I certainly acted that way. But Addy's breast cancer coming as it did just as we got to the Center was a bummer, to put it mildly, but her younger sister generously came out to help her through the mastectomy and convalescence, taking much weight from my shoulders.

So I had the formula; it was really just a matter of putting the right values in and the equation was solved. And I was able to put in what I thought were the right values and Voila! it just needed to be written. And that's how what the Dean called "that little pamphlet" was born out of Durkheim and Weber by Parsons and me.

Nor am I in any way ashamed of it, but really rather proud. Yes, the little bit on kinship terms was unnecessary and undesirable and I should have shown there and then how much race in America and Europe is part and parcel of kinship. But I did that in a separate paper shortly, and in another paper that followed the book very shortly I made my antigenealogical point most clearly.

So what's so special about American Kinship? First and foremost, it was a sustained and systematic demonstration of what I thought a *cultural* analysis should be and not either the functional analysis of social norms that so much of the sociological treatment of kinship and family is nor an analysis of the ways in which marriage, residence, and descent structure social groups and the bonds of solidarity, as so many anthropological monographs did it. And the bonds of solidarity are presupposed: "kinship" is in its nature necessarily a solidary bond, these anthropologists have always assumed. Lévi-Strauss, to put it in the simplest terms, showed that the functional interdependence which Durkheim and Mauss posited as the basis of social life could be brought about by exchanging women as if they were pigs, gongs, or vegetables, but that there were advantages to women which pigs, gongs, and vegetables did not share: women got pregnant and gave birth to people who entered into the network of interdependent relationships as kinsmen—something that pigs, gongs, and vegetables could not do. Again, kinship was just assumed to be a solidary relation. Of course, Lévi-Strauss showed lots more, but at rock bottom he took Durkheim's organic solidarity and Mauss's exchange a long way along what I think of as sociological or social-system lines using functional analysis; whereas *American Kinship,* I think, depends most heavily on establishing meaning, and showing the *meaningful* interrelations among a set of symbols.

It may well be that kinship as Euro-Americans understand and conceive of it is a very unusual (in the world or in a culture) set of symbols and meanings in that that set can be viewed as the unfolding and development of aspects of the image of sexual intercourse as culturally constituted, not as it is presumed actually or really to exist in nature. Once it became clear that that was the core symbol, it was easy to unpack it. Other domains may well not have a core symbol quite so easy to unpack if they have a core symbol at all.

Talcott Parsons was never lavish with praise but he made clear to me that he liked it pretty well, agreeing, too, that the anthropological task was to work with culture while his task as a sociologist was the sociological one, but that both tasks actually involved both social-system and cultural features. I didn't feel the least bit bad that Talcott liked it, but he was not, after all, a strategically placed anthropologist. Yet, as I have already said, he was crucial in saving me from unemployment at a critical time. It's nice to be nice to your mentors when they are nice to you and you like to be nice to them. Otherwise, it's a bore and another failure of capitalism but by no means its greatest failure.

The larger book, the *Critique,* was really the sum of my criticisms of the whole notion of kinship and the way it was conceptualized and studied from the 1800s till now. These criticisms started when I was a student for that one year at Yale and gradually got organized by the 1970s. The book was written under considerable pressure since I had to grab time from teaching and the fact that Addy's breast cancer had metastasized to her liver and she was rapidly getting sicker and sicker.

In fact, I just don't remember if it was published while she lived or only came out after she died.

But it was the sum of most of the thinking I had done about kinship since the late 1940s and it just took the effort to organize it and write it down. Nor did I notice till almost after it was all done how much the Euro-American notion of knowledge depended on the proposition that knowledge is *discovered,* not invented, and that knowledge comes when the "facts" of nature, which are hidden from us mostly, are finally revealed. Thus, for example, kinship was thought to be the social recognition of the actual facts of biological relatedness, give or take a few errors. This view is clearly embodied in Christian theology, but not being a Christian, I didn't know that. (Nor did I know any Jewish theology, having been saved from those superstitions by my militantly atheistic parents. I wish they had taught me Yiddish instead, but I got neither.) The idea that culture, and knowledge, is mostly a direct reflection of nature is still very much with us, however inadequate that view is.

Of course, when all was said and done, all I really did was to take the idea of sociocultural construction along the path toward its logical conclusion. Not all the way, of course, but far enough to annoy a lot of people. As I said, my friend from way, way back (Cornell), Ward Goodenough, took the trouble to fly to Chicago and convince me to make many changes in the manuscript, thus saving me from any number of stupidities, for which I remain grateful.

I'm still proud of having hit upon "pragmatics" long before it was named and became popular, having insisted early that the kinship terms that are actually employed in speech depend very heavily on the context of use, so that I may be respectful and say to my brother "What's on father's mind?" or less respectfully "What's bothering pop?"—although that last usage was normal and respectful in my family of orientation.

I had early noticed how academics, scientists one and all, took simple folk notions and elevated them to the stratospheric position of scientific theory. This was early made most vivid to me at Yale where the learning theory of Clark Hull held sway. With Geoffrey Gorer in the background pushing Freudian ideas, it didn't take me long to observe that learning theory's punishment and reward scheme was very much like my mother's, and she was certainly no highflown scientist, but she could give a good slap when she felt a reward was not indicated. So it didn't take long for me to notice how congruent scientific kinship theory was with Euro-American folk beliefs, even if Lewis H. Morgan should have known better. Of course, Murdock should have known better, too, but it made me very pleased with myself to think that I knew better than Murdock and the experts. There's a lesson in there for teachers and students alike if I could only figure it out. But as a strong try at debunking the experts, that book, the *Critique,* and *American Kinship* as well, are ones that I remain very pleased and proud of.

Just why I have hardly mentioned teaching and relations with students is hard to tell but it may readily be blamed on the interviewer. (How could it be my fault?) Whatever is wrong with this document must, of course, be the interviewer's fault. But without naming names, one of the really great rewards has been teaching and the very strong and warm friendships that I have had and continue to have with those who were at one time "students," many of whom are now colleagues. This is not entirely a consequence of the fact that I gave everybody an "A" unless there was something which prevented me from doing so. But it was a fact that students had to really try extraordinarily hard to get anything less than an "A" in my courses. From time to time I would be chided by various bureaucrats for this policy, but I was intransigent, even if contrition was required. Following my policy while exuding contrition was not hard. This did not mean that I lacked standards or suffered from poor judgment. At Chicago, at the end of every year there was what we sometimes called "the last roundup," a meeting of the whole department at which the standing of each student was reviewed. If I had doubts or problems with a student's performance, I voiced them there and they were discussed in the light of the student's performance as a whole. So if a student was having trouble generally, that fact emerged in discussion, but if the student was only having trouble with me (and that happened, though I can't imagine why), that, too, would become clear.

But the point is that I found friends among the students, many of whom remain my closest and most valued friends. But I have not had any clones. Whether I was so much a prima donna that when I found students imitating my kind of anthropology I couldn't stand the competition, or, for other reasons, clones got no encouragement from me. But at some student parties, I am told, one young woman gave such accurate renditions of my lecturing style, as convulsed the entire assemblage, but for some reason she refused to perform when I was present.

It is certainly true that when you have a captive audience and can stand before them, pontificating in the most shameful manner, one's sense of one's importance is enhanced pleasurably. I remember going into some of the more esoteric aspects of patrilateral cross-cousin marriage at dinner one evening when I was asked what my day had been like, only to find myself alone at the table. The two children had slunk off somewhere and my wife had fled. But usually I enjoyed teaching and usually students had to stay and listen even if they didn't want to and learned something by talking to each other when they didn't have to listen to me.

But I have been careful, here, not to dwell on some of my less laudatory qualities or less than great accomplishments. For example, in 1974 I was a visiting professor at the University of California, Santa Cruz. Richard Randolph, provost of Cowell College at the time, invited Addy and me to a dinner party. We arrived fashionably late, as was appropriate, and were introduced to Gregory Bateson. I reminded him that I had been introduced to him twenty years previously, in Margaret Mead's office. At the end of a very pleasant evening, Bateson was the first to leave, and he went round the room saying goodbye to each person. When he came to me he put out his hand to shake and said, "Perhaps in another twenty years we may meet again."

This event reminds me of another—1949, I think. When I first arrived in London to take up teaching duties at the London School of Economics, there was a meeting of the Association of Social Anthropologists at LSE during the first week or so that I was there. At a gathering in one of the larger classrooms, Raymond Firth, always kind and generous, took me round the room and introduced me to everyone who was anyone, then had to leave the room for some reason. I found myself standing next to a gentleman somewhat older than I whom I did not know and had not been introduced to. I stuck out my hand and said in my firmest friendly manner, "I'm David Schneider." He looked carefully at my hand and said "Indeed" and walked away. That's how I met Reo Fortune. . . .

Notes

Introduction: The Origin of the Dog

1   Richard Handler, "An Interview with Clifford Geertz," *Current Anthropology* 32 (1991): 603–613.
2   Bashkow's essay appears in George W. Stocking Jr., ed., *Colonial Situations: Essays on the Contextualization of Ethnographic Knowledge* [= *History of Anthropology* 7] (Madison, 1991), 170–242. When preparing the final version of this introduction in December 1994, I spoke to Bashkow about the interviews he conducted with Schneider in 1989. He told me that he had not tape-recorded those interviews, nor had he used much material from them in the published article, sticking instead to documentary sources. Thus, the reader is urged to make the comparison between Bashkow's account and Schneider's reminiscences, especially those recorded in Chapters 1 and 6.
3   The first two interviews took place in Chicago, in Schneider's hotel room, during the 1991 annual meeting of the American Anthropological Association (November 21 and 23). We completed three more interviews at his home in Santa Cruz on January 23, 24, and 26, 1992; and two more during the 1992 American Anthropological Association meeting in San Francisco (December 2 and 3). A fourth series of interviews occurred during a second visit to Schneider's home, October 7–10, 1993. The final three interviews were conducted by telephone, from Charlottesville, Virginia, to Santa Cruz, on May 28, 29, and 30, 1994.

One. The Work of the Gods in Tikopia,
or, A Career in Anthropology

1   New York, 1928; New York, 1926.
2   Geoffrey Gorer, "The Psychology of Great Russians," in Geoffrey Gorer and John Rickman, *The People of Great Russia* (London, 1949), 91–194; Ruth Benedict, "Thai Culture and Behavior: An Unpublished War-Time Study Dated September, 1943," Data Paper 4, Southeast Asia Program, Department of Far Eastern Studies, Cornell University, 1952.

3   David Schneider, "The Culture of the Army Clerk," *Psychiatry* 9 (1946): 123–
129; Schneider, "The Social Dynamics of Physical Disability in Army Basic
Training," *Psychiatry* 10 (1947): 323–333 [reprinted in Clyde Kluckhohn, Henry
Murray, and David Schneider, eds., *Personality in Nature, Society, and Culture,*
2nd ed. (New York, 1953), 386–397].

4   Allan Berube, *Coming Out under Fire: The History of Gay Men and Women in
World War Two* (New York, 1990).

5   Alfred Kroeber, "Classificatory Systems of Relationship," *Journal of the Royal
Anthropological Institute* 39 (1909): 77–84 [reprinted in Alfred Kroeber, *The
Nature of Culture* (Chicago, 1952), 175–181].

6   David Schneider and George Homans, "Kinship Terminology and the American
Kinship System," *American Anthropologist* 57 (1955): 1194–1208 [reprinted in
Norman Bell and Ezra Vogel, eds., *A Modern Introduction to the Family* (New
York, 1960), 465–481]; George Homans and David Schneider, *Marriage, Au-
thority and Final Causes* (New York, 1955) [reprinted in George Homans, *Senti-
ments and Activities: Essays in Social Science* (Glencoe, Ill., 1962), 202–256].

7   David Schneider and Kathleen Gough, eds., *Matrilineal Kinship* (Berkeley,
1961).

8   Schneider, "Double Descent on Yap," *Journal of the Polynesian Society* 71 (1962):
1–24; Schneider, *A Critique of the Study of Kinship* (Ann Arbor, 1984).

9   The allusion is to Raymond Firth, *The Work of the Gods in Tikopia* (London,
1940).

Two. Youth

1   Sinclair Lewis, *Babbitt* (New York, 1922).

Four. Surveying the Army

1   The first five paragraphs of this chapter are taken from a letter from Schneider
to Handler, June 18, 1988.

2   Samuel Stouffer et al., *The American Soldier: Adjustment during Army Life,*
Studies in Social Psychology in World War II, vol. I (Princeton, N.J., 1949).

Five. An Education in Anthropology

1   Talcott Parsons, "Illness and the Role of the Physician: A Sociological Perspec-
tive," *American Journal of Orthopsychiatry* 21 (1951): 452–460 [reprinted in
Clyde Kluckhohn, Henry Murray, and David Schneider, eds., *Personality in
Nature, Society, and Culture,* 2nd ed. (New York, 1953), 609–617].

2   Talcott Parsons and Edward Shils, "Values, Motives and Systems of Action,"
in T. Parsons, ed., *Toward a General Theory of Action* (Glencoe, Ill., 1951),
247–275.

3   Alfred Kroeber and Clyde Kluckhohn, *Culture: A Critical Review of Concepts and Definitions,* Papers of the Peabody Museum of American Archaeology and Ethnology, Harvard University, vol. 47, no. 1 (1952).

4   Alfred Kroeber and Talcott Parsons, "The Concepts of Culture and of Social System," *American Sociological Review* 23 (1958): 582–583.

5   Kluckhohn (1905–1960) received his B.A. at the University of Wisconsin in 1928, his M.A. at Oxford in 1932, and his Ph.D. at Harvard in 1936.

Six. Fieldwork on Yap

1   Wilhelm Muller, *Yap,* 2 vol. (Hamburg, 1917).

2   W. Robert Moore, "Pacific Wards of Uncle Sam," *National Geographic* 94 (1948): 73–104.

3   The *tabinau* is "a cultural unit on Yap . . . with its own name made up of a collection of plots of land that holds a more or less distinctive set of personal names for both men and women. These names are given to the children of women who marry men of the *tabinau.*" Schneider, *A Critique of the Study of Kinship* (Ann Arbor, 1984), 21; see also David Labby, *The Demystification of Yap: Dialectics of Culture on a Micronesian Island* (Chicago, 1976).

4   The actual duration of the fieldwork was nine months—from September 1947 to June 1948.

Seven. From Harvard to England

1   E. E. Evans-Pritchard, "Some Aspects of Marriage and the Family among the Nuer," *Rhodes-Livingstone Papers,* no. 11 (1945).

2   Chicago, 1969.

3   Robert Lowie, *Primitive Society* (New York, 1920), 441.

4   Rodney Needham, "A Structural Analysis of Purum Society," *American Anthropologist* 60 (1958): 75–101; Edmund Leach, "Jinghpaw Kinship Terminology," in Edmund Leach, *Rethinking Anthropology* (London, 1961), 28–53.

5   Richard Handler, "An Interview with Clifford Geertz," *Current Anthropology* 32 (1991): 608.

6   Schneider, "Some Muddles in the Models: Or, How the System Really Works," in *The Relevance of Models for Social Anthropology* (London, 1965), 25–85.

Eight. Mescalero Apache: The Romance and Politics of Fieldwork

1   On the implications of the Andrew Cheyne incident, see Richard Parmentier, *The Sacred Remains: Myth, History, and Polity in Belau* (Chicago, 1987).

2   Claire Farrer, *Living Life's Circle: Mescalero Apache Cosmovision* (Albuquerque, 1991).

3 Morris Opler, *An Apache Life-way: The Economic, Social, and Religious Institutions of the Chiricahua Indians* (Chicago, 1941).

4 Harry W. Basehart, *Mescalero Apache Subsistence Patterns and Socio-political Organization* (New York, 1974).

5 L. Bryce Boyer, *Childhood and Folklore: A Psychoanalytic Study of Apache Personality* (New York, 1979). Needless to say, Schneider's version of their falling-out may not agree with Boyer's account of the same dispute. Schneider withdrew from the research after the summer of 1958, but Boyer continued working among the Mescalero Apache for many years thereafter. Boyer's many publications on the Apache make it clear that notwithstanding Schneider's feeling that Boyer relied too heavily on one informant, Boyer worked with a great many informants, at least after Schneider left the field; see, for example, L. B. Boyer, "Remarks on the Personalities of Shamans, with Special Reference to the Apache of the Mescalero Indian Reservation," *The Psychoanalytic Study of Society* 2 (1962): 245–247, and "The Man Who Turned Into a Water Monster: A Psychoanalytic Contribution to Folklore," *The Psychoanalytic Study of Society* 6 (1975): 102.

Boyer's conference paper, to which Schneider refers, was first presented to the Asociacion Psicoanalitica Mexicana in Mexico City in July, 1958; it was published as "Notes on the Personality Structure of a North American Indian Shaman," *Journal of Hillside Hospital* 10 (1961): 14–33. In the published version, Boyer argued that his main informant, a shaman whom he called Black Eyes, "had intense feelings of inadequacy and strong dependency on the approval of others for maintenance of self-esteem. Although he was not obviously soft or effeminate, there were strong hints that he struggled with a problem of latent passive homosexuality" (p. 27). In later papers, Boyer wrote similarly about Apache personality in general; see "Remarks on the Personalities of Shamans, with Special Reference to the Apache of the Mescalero Indian Reservation," *The Psychoanalytic Study of Society* 2 (1962): 248–249 and "Psychological Problems of a Group of Apaches: Alcoholic Hallucinosis and Latent Homosexuality among Typical Men," *The Psychoanalytic Study of Society* 3 (1964): 267–271.

In the interview, Schneider's chronology is vague. Claire Farrer, to whom Schneider has entrusted his Apache fieldnotes, checked those notes and found that Schneider was working in New Mexico in the summers of 1955, 1957, and 1958, in November 1955, and in spring 1956. He was also engaged, with Boyer, in interviewing Apaches in San Francisco and Oakland throughout 1958. For the chronology of Boyer's research, see L. B. Boyer and R. M. Boyer, "Some Influences of Acculturation on the Personality Traits of the Old People of the Mescalero and Chiricahua Apaches," *The Psychoanalytic Study of Society* 4 (1967): 170, note 1.

6 This paragraph and the previous one were inserted by Schneider after he had read the transcript of the interview.

7   George W. Stocking Jr., ed., *Colonial Situations: Essays on the Contextualization of Ethnographic Knowledge* [= History of Anthropology 7] (Madison, 1991).
8   James Clifford, *The Predicament of Culture* (Cambridge, Mass., 1988), 24–29.

Nine. From Berkeley to Chicago

1   Washington, 1953.
2   Sol Tax, "Some Problems of Social Organization" and "From Lafitau to Radcliffe-Brown: A Short History of the Study of Social Organization," in Fred Eggan, ed., *Social Anthropology of North American Tribes* (Chicago, 1937), 3–32, 445–481.
3   Esther Newton, *Mother Camp: Female Impersonators in America* (Englewood Cliffs, N.J., 1972).
4   W. H. R. Rivers, *Kinship and Social Organization; together with The Genealogical Method of Anthropological Inquiry,* edited by David Schneider and Raymond Firth (London, 1968).

Ten. Studying Kinship

1   Marilyn Strathern, *After Nature: English Kinship in the Late Twentieth Century* (Cambridge, 1992); Kath Weston, *Families We Choose: Lesbians, Gays, Kinship* (New York, 1991); Ellen Lewin, *Lesbian Mothers: Accounts of Gender in American Culture* (Ithaca, N.Y., 1993); Sylvia Yanagisako and Jane Collier, eds., *Gender and Kinship: Essays toward a Unified Analysis* (Stanford, 1987).
2   Fustel de Coulanges, *The Ancient City: A Study on the Religion, Laws, and Institutions of Greece and Rome,* 4th ed. (Boston, [1864] 1882).
3   Claude Lévi-Strauss, *The Elementary Structures of Kinship* (Boston, [1949] 1969).
4   Edmund Leach, "The Structural Implications of Matrilateral Cross-Cousin Marriage," *Journal of the Royal Anthropological Institute* 81 (1951): 23–55.
5   Thomas Kuhn, *The Structure of Scientific Revolution* (New York, 1962).
6   Bronislaw Malinowski, *A Diary in the Strict Sense of the Term* (New York, 1967).
7   New York, 1928.
8   Bruno Latour and Steve Woolgar, *Laboratory Life: The Construction of Scientific Facts* (Princeton, N.J., [1979] 1986).
9   James Clifford, *Person and Myth: Maurice Leenhardt in the Melanesian World* (Berkeley, 1982).
10 George Marcus, *The Nobility and the Chiefly Tradition in the Modern Kingdom of Tonga* (Wellington, 1980); Marcus (with Michael M. J. Fischer), *Anthropology as Cultural Critique* (Chicago, 1986).
11 New York, 1949.
12 David Schneider and George Homans, "Kinship Terminology and the American Kinship System," *American Anthropologist* 57 (1955): 1194–1208.

13   David Schneider, "Twelve Years Later," in *American Kinship: A Cultural Account,* 2nd ed. (Chicago, 1980), 123–124.

14   Robert Murphy and Buell Quain, *The Truma I Indians of Central Brazil* (Locust Valley, N.Y., 1955).

15   Beatrice Blackwood and C. R. Hallpike, *The Kukukuku of the Upper Watut* (Oxford, 1978).

16   Roger Sanjek, ed., *Fieldnotes: The Makings of Anthropology* (Ithaca, N.Y., 1990).

Writings of David M. Schneider

[Editor's note: This bibliography is based on a curriculum vita that David Schneider sent to Richard Handler in December 1994; it is not exhaustive but includes all of Schneider's major works]

1946
"The Culture of the Army Clerk." *Psychiatry* 9: 123–129.

1947
"The Social Dynamics of Physical Disability in Army Basic Training." *Psychiatry* 10: 323–333. [Reprinted in Clyde Kluckhohn, Henry Murray, and David Schneider, eds., *Personality in Nature, Society, and Culture*, 2nd ed., 386–397. New York: Knopf, 1953.]

1949
"The Micronesians of Yap and Their Depopulation" (with William Stevens, Nathaniel Kidder, and Edward Hunt). Pacific Science Board, National Research Council, and Peabody Museum, Cambridge, Massachusetts. Mimeo.

1953
"Yap Kinship Terminology and Kin Groups." *American Anthropologist* 55: 215–236.
"A Note on Bridewealth and the Stability of Marriage." *Man* 53: 55–57.
Personality in Nature, Society, and Culture, edited by Clyde Kluckhohn, Henry Murray, and David M. Schneider, 2nd ed. New York: Knopf.

1954
"The Depopulation of Yap" (with Edward Hunt and Nathaniel Kidder). *Human Biology* 26: 21–51.

1955

Marriage, Authority and Final Causes (with George Homans). New York: Glencoe, Ill.: Free Press. [Reprinted in George Homans, *Sentiments and Activities: Essays in Social Science*, 202–256. Glencoe, Ill.: Free Press, 1962.]

"Abortion and Depopulation on a Pacific Island." In Benjamin Paul, ed., *Health, Culture and Community*, 211–235. New York: Russell Sage Foundation.

"Kinship Terminology and the American Kinship System" (with George Homans). *American Anthropologist* 57: 1194–1208. [Reprinted in Norman Bell and Ezra Vogel, eds., *A Modern Introduction to the Family*, 465–481. New York: Free Press, 1960.]

1956

"Zuni Kin Terms" (with John M. Roberts). Notebook No. 3, Monograph 1, Laboratory of Anthropology, University of Nebraska, Lincoln. [Reprinted in Human Relations Area Files Behavior Science Reprint Series, 1965.]

1957

"Political Organization, Supernatural Sanctions and the Punishment for Incest on Yap." *American Anthropologist* 59: 791–800.

1958

"Typhoons on Yap." *Human Organization* 16: 10–15.

1961

"Sibling Solidarity: A Property of American Kinship" (with Elaine Cumming). *American Anthropologist* 63: 498–507.

Matrilineal Kinship, edited by David M. Schneider and Kathleen Gough. Berkeley: University of California Press.

"The Distinctive Features of Matrilineal Descent Groups." In Schneider and Gough, *Matrilineal Kinship*, 1–29.

"Truk." In Schneider and Gough, *Matrilineal Kinship*, 202–233.

1962

"Mother's Brother in Wikmunkan Society (with George Homans). *Ethnology* 1: 529–532.

"Double Descent on Yap." *Journal of the Polynesian Society* 71: 1–24.

1963

"Kinship." *Encyclopedia Hebraica*, vol. 18.

1964

"Incest." In J. Gould and W. L. Kolb, eds., *A Dictionary of the Social Sciences,* 322–323. New York: Free Press.

"Residence." In Gould and Kolb, *Dictionary of the Social Sciences,* 596–597.

"The Nature of Kinship." *Man* 64: 180–181.

1965

"Some Muddles in the Models: Or, How the System Really Works." In *The Relevance of Models for Social Anthropology,* ASA Monographs no. 1, 25–85. London: Tavistock.

"Kinship and Biology." In A. J. Coale et al., eds., *Aspects of the Analysis of Family Structure,* 83–101. Princeton, N.J.: Princeton University Press.

"American Kin Terms and Terms of Kinsmen: A Critique of Goodenough's Componential Analysis of Yankee Kinship Terminology." In E. A. Hammel, ed., *Formal Semantic Analysis,* 288–308. *American Anthropologist* 67, 5, part 2.

"The Content of Kinship." *Man* 65: 122–123.

1967

"Descent and Filiation as Cultural Constructs." *Southwestern Journal of Anthropology* 23: 65–73.

"Foreword." In Roy Wagner, *The Curse of Souw,* vii–viii. Chicago: University of Chicago Press.

1968

American Kinship: A Cultural Account. Englewood Cliffs, N.J.: Prentice Hall. [Reprinted with a new chapter, "Twelve Years Later." Chicago: University of Chicago Press, 1980.]

"Rivers and Kroeber on the Study of Kinship." In W. H. R. Rivers, *Kinship and Social Organization; together with The Genealogical Method of Anthropological Inquiry,* edited by David Schneider and Raymond Firth, 7–16. London: Athlone Press.

"Virgin Birth." *Man* [n.s.] 3: 126–129.

1969

"Kinship, Nationality and Religion in American Culture: Toward a Definition of Kinship." In Robert F. Spencer, ed., *Forms of Symbolic Action,* 116–125. Proceedings of the 1969 Annual Spring Meeting of the American Ethnological Society. Seattle: University of Washington Press. [Reprinted in Janet Dolgin, David Kemnitzer and David Schneider, eds., *Symbolic Anthropology: A Reader in the Study of Symbols and Meanings,* 63–71. New York: Columbia University Press, 1977.]

"Foreword." In Martin Silverman, *Disconcerting Issue,* xiii–xiv. Chicago: University of Chicago Press.

"Componential Analysis: A State-of-the-Art Review." Paper presented at the Wenner-Gren Symposium on Cognitive Studies and Artificial Intelligence Research, March 2–8, Chicago.

"A Re-analysis of the Kinship System of Yap in the Light of Dumont's Statement." Paper presented at the Wenner-Gren Symposium on Kinship and Locality, August 23–September 1, Vurg Wartenstein, Austria.

1970

"American Kin Categories." In Pierre Maranda and Jean Pouillon, eds., *Echanges et communications: Mélanges offerts à Claude Lévi-Strauss*, 370–381. The Hague: Mouton.

"What Should Be Included in a Vocabulary of Kinship Terms?" In *Proceedings of the Eighth International Congress of Anthropological and Ethnological Sciences* [Tokyo: Science Council of Japan, 1968], vol. 2: 88–90.

"Middle Class and Lower Class American Kinship." American Kinship Project. Mimeo.

1972

"What Is Kinship All About?" In Priscilla Reining, ed., *Kinship Studies in the Morgan Centennial Year*, 32–63. Washington, D.C.: Anthropological Society of Washington.

1973

Class Differences and Sex Roles in American Kinship and Family Structure (with Raymond T. Smith). Englewood Cliffs, N.J.: Prentice-Hall. [Reprinted with a new introduction. Ann Arbor: University of Michigan Press, 1978.]

1974

"Depopulation and the Yap Tabinau." In Robert J. Smith, ed., *Social Organization and the Applications of Anthropology*, 94–113. Ithaca, N.Y.: Cornell University Press.

"Kinship vis-à-vis Myth: Contrasts in Lévi-Strauss's Approaches to Cross-Cultural Comparison" (with James A. Boon). *American Anthropologist* 76: 799–817.

"Reply to Ember." *American Anthropologist* 76: 573.

1975

The American Kin Universe: A Genealogical Study (with Calvert B. Cottrell). Chicago: University of Chicago Press.

"Foreword." In Gary Witherspoon, *Navajo Kinship and Marriage*, vii–viii. Chicago: University of Chicago Press.

1976

"Notes toward a Theory of Culture." In Keith Basso and Henry Selby, eds., *Meaning in Anthropology*, 197–220. Albuquerque: University of New Mexico Press.

"The Meaning of Incest." *Journal of the Polynesian Society* 85: 149–169.
"A Warning in Regard to *The Stone Money of Yap*." *American Anthropologist* 78: 893–894.

1977
Symbolic Anthropology: A Reader in the Study of Symbols and Meanings, edited by Janet Dolgin, David Kemnitzer, and David Schneider. New York: Columbia University Press.
"Introduction: As People Express Their Lives, So They Are . . ." In Dolgin, Kemnitzer, and Schneider, *Symbolic Anthropology*, 3–44.

1979
"Kinship, Community, and Locality in American Culture." In Allan J. Lichtman and Joan R. Challinor, eds., *Kin and Communities*, 155–174. Washington, D.C.: Smithsonian Institution Press.
"Letter [concerning H. W. Scheffler's review of David Labby, *The Demystification of Yap*]." *American Ethnologist* 6: 219–220.
"A Note on 'Excess Access and Incest,' by Busch and Gundlach." *American Anthropologist* 81: 120.

1980
American Kinship: A Cultural Account, 2nd ed. Chicago: University of Chicago Press.

1981
"Conclusions." In Mac Marshall, ed., *Siblingship in Oceania*, 389–404. Ann Arbor: University of Michigan Press.

1984
A Critique of the Study of Kinship. Ann Arbor: University of Michigan Press.
"When the Natives Manipulate Their Own Culture." *Rain* 64: 5–7.

1985
"A Reply to Keesing" (with Mac Marshall). *American Anthropologist* 87: 146–148.

1986
"The Study of Kinship." *Man* [n.s.] 21: 541.

1989
"Australian Aboriginal Kinship: Cultural Construction, Deconstruction and Misconstruction." *Man* [n.s.] 24: 165–166.

1992

"Comment on Bradd Shore, 'Virgin Births and Sterile Debates.'" *Current Anthropology* 33: 307–310.

"Ethnocentrism and the Notion of Kinship." *Man* [n.s.] 27: 629–631.

1994

"Comment on Eugene Cooper's 'Cousin Marriage in Rural China.'" *American Ethnologist* 21: 863–864.

Index

David Murray Schneider was born November 11, 1918 in Brooklyn, New York and spent his childhood in the Bronx. He received his B.A. (1940) and M.A. (1941) degrees from Cornell University, and his Ph.D. (1949) in anthropology from Harvard University. He taught at the London School of Economics (1949–1951), Harvard (1951–1955), the University of California, Berkeley (1956–1960), the University of Chicago (1960–1984), and the University of California, Santa Cruz (1984–1987), where he is currently Professor Emeritus of Anthropology. He is the author of *American Kinship: A Cultural Account* (1968; second edition, 1980), *A Critique of the Study of Kinship* (1984), and many essays on kinship and culture theory.

Richard Handler is Associate Professor of Anthropology at the University of Virginia. He is the author of *Jane Austen and the Fiction of Culture: An Essay on the Narration of Social Realities* (with Daniel Segal) and *Nationalism and the Politics of Culture in Quebec,* and the editor-designate of *History of Anthropology.*

Library of Congress Cataloging-in-Publication Data
Schneider, David Murray.
Schneider on Schneider: The conversion of the Jews and other anthropological stories / David M. Schneider as told to Richard Handler; edited, transcribed, and with an introduction by Richard Handler.
Includes bibliographical references.
ISBN 0-8223-1679-X. — ISBN 0-8223-1691-9 (pbk.)
1. Schneider, David Murray, 1918–   . 2. Anthropologists—United States—Biography.   3. Kinship—United States.
4. United States—Social life and customs.   I. Handler, Richard.
II. Title.
GN21.S29A3   1995
301'.092—dc20   95-10338 CIP